REVELATION OF CHRIST

A TEACHER'S GUIDE

A Thorough Interpretation and Commentary of the Book
of Revelation Complete with Symbol, Color, and Number
Definitions Reinforced with Biblical Scripture.

BY: JERRY N. UPTON

PRESS

Revelation of Christ
A Teacher's Guide
by Jerry N. Upton

Printed in the United States of America

ISBN 9781613794821

www.xulonpress.com

TABLE OF CONTENTS

INTRODUCTION

T he Book of Revelation is an excellent literary composition given by Jesus Christ through his angel unto his servant John. The use of symbolism is a superior method of providing many enlightening thoughts in each sentence. It is very easy to understand and comprehend the message being presented by following the guide that has been set forth. Understanding the various symbols, colors, and numbers will not only allow the comprehension of the message of this book as put forth by Jesus Christ but will also enable the reader to have a better understanding of many Scriptures throughout the Bible.

While there are differences of opinion as to the correct identity of the author of the Book of Revelation, the majority of Biblical scholars believe that John, the apostle of Jesus Christ, is the true author and this commentary is based on that assumption.

John was an apostle of Jesus Christ as was his brother, James. They were the sons of Zebedee and Salome. Zebedee was a fisherman who resided by the sea of Galilee with his family and there pursued his vocation. The apostle John wrote the book of Revelation while in exile on the isle of Patmos which is a small island in the Aegean Sea that in size is approximately 10 miles long and six miles wide. It is a volcanic, bare, and rocky island located about 60 miles south of Ephesus and about 26 miles from the coast of Turkey. It is in that body of water between the city of Corinth and the city of Ephesus. A Roman emperor banished John to Patmos in an attempt to exterminate Christianity.

There have been many theories and philosophies used to interpret the Book of Revelation. This is very important because we must determine the philosophy that we are going to use in our approach to understand the Book of Revelation. Some of these theories and philosophies with their various points of view overlap as it is difficult to make them agree with all of the Scripture in the Bible.

I am going to briefly outline some of the various methods of interpretation in order for you to become somewhat knowledgeable when discussing the Book of Revelation with others.

Some rely on the futurist method of interpretation which believes that chapters 4 through 22 of the book were written for the events to take place some time in the future. This approach maintains that these chapters deal with the end of time and they are not concerned with the date that the book was written, or with the historical events that surround that period. They say that it is concerned with last things such as the second coming of Christ, the millennial reign, the end of the age, the loosing of Satan, the second resurrection and the final judgment.

Some of those who accept this futurist method believe that at the end of time or near the end of the millennium that the actual temple spoken of in chapter eleven is going to be rebuilt in Jerusalem and the Jewish worship would then be renewed as it was previously under the Mosaic Law. The two witnesses mentioned in that book are taken to be two great prophets that will come forth in the last days and call men back to God. All the numbers in the book such as the thousand-year reign, the three and one half days, the 144,000 and all the other numerals are given an actual mathematical value. This viewpoint takes the writing as a literal interpretation and would be mostly prophetic. The futurist view puts the book of Revelation somewhere out in the future to be fulfilled in the last days. We can't accept this point of view because it is not consistent with the statements: "shortly come to pass" **and** "the time is at hand". Secondly, it has no message of comfort for the early Christians during John's day. They needed encouragement to hold fast to the faith as they were under tremendous persecution.

John the Baptist came preaching repentance as a forerunner for the Messiah proclaiming the kingdom of heaven is at hand.
Matthew 3:2; And saying, Repent ye: for the kingdom of heaven is at hand.
Matthew 4:17; From that time Jesus began to preach, and to say, *Repent: for the kingdom of heaven is at hand.*

This meant that within a short period of time the kingdom of God would be established here on earth.
Matthew 6:10; *Thy kingdom come. Thy will be done in earth, as it is in heaven.*

Notice what Jesus said when he was betrayed by Judas Iscariot:
Matthew 26:18; *My time is at hand;* also in verse 45; *behold, the hour is at hand, and the Son of man is betrayed into the hands of sinners.*

These events were just prior to the establishment of Christ's Kingdom (Church) here on earth. The teaching of God's word is the binding of Satan as related in Revelation chapter twenty, verses one through four.

Another viewpoint places the time period in the past with the events having being fulfilled during the time of the Roman Empire and that interpretation is called the preterit. This makes the book having value only in a literary sense. We also must reject this theory because it says that everything is in the past and the book of Revelation is for literary value only. This theory has no application for Christians of today and future Christians.

These theories do not agree with the message of Jesus Christ regarding his instructions to his servant, John, as reflected in chapter one, verse nineteen, that states that the events in this book will cover past, present, and future.
Revelation 1:19; Write the things which thou hast seen, and the things which are, and the things which shall be hereafter;

Many Biblical scholars or commentators are concerned with the period of time covered by The Book of Revelation which determines how they interpret the book. One of these methods of interpretation is the continuous historical viewpoint which places the starting time as the date that the book was written

by John and encompasses the history of the church from that period of time to the second coming of Christ. This viewpoint generally tries to relate the prophecies to specific events in history and must also be rejected for that very reason.

For example, just using military history, one might point to the conquests of Nebuchadnezzar, king of the Chaldean Empire, also called the Babylonian Empire, the Medo-Persian Empire of Cyrus and Darius, the Macedonian Empire of Alexander the Great, the Roman Empire, the conquests of Genghis Kahn, Napoleon, Hitler, and even the Islamists throughout the ages up to and including the present day such as Osama Bin Laden, Al Quaida, and the Taliban. Each of these periods of history involved military conflict usually with religious consequences. There will be others in the future, so it is useless to try to pinpoint or isolate specific events from the Book of Revelation.

I believe that the events in the Book of Revelation relate to conditions or principles of conduct that re-occur throughout the Christian dispensation rather than with specific individual events that have occurred throughout history. You probably have heard the old adage, "If we do not learn from history, we are condemned to repeat it." From my own observation I have noticed that mankind does not seem to learn from history and continually repeats errors of the past in regard to conditions or principles of conduct.

Persecutions to the followers of God throughout the Mosaic Law and the Christian Church dispensation periods have been continuous throughout history. Specific events have been different and the degree of persecution will vary, but the same general principles remain the same.

Ephesians 6:12; For we wrestle not against flesh and blood, but against principalities, against powers, against the rulers of the darkness of this world, against spiritual wickedness in high places.

A common fault among people attempting to interpret the Book of Revelation is that they form opinions on the symbolic language then read into the Scriptures attempting to justify their opinions. This generally leads them further astray. We need to read out of the Scriptures with an open mind, not read into the Scriptures endeavoring to confirm an opinion.

Many of these commentators and Biblical scholars tend to focus on what is termed the millennium and how it affects the people. The word millennium is derived from a Latin word meaning one thousand. Some theorists believe in post-millennium which applies a literal interpretation of Chapter 20 of the Book of Revelation with the belief that Christ will come at the end of the 1,000 years that Satan was bound. Others follow the theory of pre-millennium that believes that Christ will return to introduce the "thousand year reign". These theories are based on the misinterpretation of chapter twenty.

Also, there have been many books and viewpoints written about Revelation that do not agree with the Scriptures. I disagree with the premises put forth in these books as they do not agree with the Biblical Scriptures that we intend to study and reference in this book.

Anyone who has attended my classes on the Scriptures knows that I do not always agree with the commentaries of others. If I disagree with a commentator I will reinforce my opinion with Scripture or I will put forth opposing points of view for your own determination. My viewpoints regarding the interpretation of the Book of Revelation will be based upon these premises.

SCRIPTURES vs FALSE THEORIES

To help maintain focus on the correct interpretation of the Book of Revelation, I have prepared several Scriptures that tend to eliminate many of the prevalent false theories. By using these Scriptures as a guide and accepting them as true, this will help insure that this interpretation stays aligned and in agreement with the Scriptures.

II Timothy 3:12-17; Yea, and all that will live godly in Christ Jesus shall suffer persecution. But evil men and seducers shall wax worse and worse, deceiving, and being deceived. But continue thou in the things which thou hast learned and hast been assured of, knowing of whom thou hast learned them; And that from a child thou hast known the holy scriptures, which are able to make thee wise unto salvation through faith which is in Christ Jesus. All scripture is given by inspiration of God, and is profitable for doctrine, for reproof, for correction, for instruction in righteousness: That the man of God may be perfect, thoroughly furnished unto all good works.

By these verses, we know that we are able to use the Scriptures to help understand the study of the Book of Revelation. With these being true statements, then wherever you find two or more passages of Scripture that seem to conflict, the problem is not the Scripture, but the misinterpretation or an error in translation of one or more Scriptures. This reliance upon the Scriptures should greatly aid the interpretation of the symbolism along with the understanding of the Book of Revelation.

Isaiah 11:1-5,10; And there shall come forth a rod out of the stem of Jesse, and a Branch shall grow out of his roots: And the spirit of the LORD shall rest upon him, the spirit of wisdom and understanding, the spirit of counsel and might, the spirit of knowledge and of the fear of the LORD; And shall make him of quick understanding in the fear of the LORD: and he shall not judge after the sight of his eyes, neither reprove after the hearing of his ears: But with righteousness shall he judge the poor, and reprove with equity for the meek of the earth: and he shall smite the earth: with the rod of his mouth, and with the breath of his lips shall he slay the wicked. And righteousness shall be the girdle of his loins, and faithfulness the girdle of his reins. And in that day there shall be a root of Jesse, which shall stand for an ensign of the people; to it shall the Gentiles seek: and his rest shall be glorious.

Through this prophecy of Isaiah we learn that the coming of Christ as our salvation was to be made available to all people including the Gentiles and that the Word of God was to be the method used to combat Satan and his evil dominion that was upon earth.

Notice in verse four the phrase "with the rod of his mouth, and with the breath of his lips shall he slay the wicked." **This proves the spiritual manner in which the battle with Satan is being waged.** Hebrews 4:12; For the word of God is quick, and powerful, and sharper than any twoedged sword, piercing even to the dividing asunder of soul and spirit, and of the joints and marrow, and is a discerner of the thoughts and intents of the heart.

The ongoing battle of Christ versus Satan is being fought by the spreading of God's Word throughout the Christian Gospel Dispensation.
Romans 15:8-12; Now I say that Jesus Christ was a minister of the circumcision for the truth of God, to confirm the promises made unto the fathers: And that the Gentiles might glorify God for his mercy; as it is written, For this cause I will confess to thee among the Gentiles, and sing unto thy name. And again he saith, Rejoice, ye Gentiles, with his people. And again, Praise the Lord, all ye Gentiles; and laud him, all ye people. And again, Esaias saith, There shall be a

root of Jesse, and he that shall rise to reign over the Gentiles; in him shall the Gentiles trust.

In his letter to the Romans, the apostle Paul confirmed the prophecy of Isaiah that showed that Jesus Christ was sent by God to establish his kingdom upon earth.

I John 5:4; For whatsoever is born of God overcometh the world: and this is the victory that overcometh the world, even our faith.

This is the First Resurrection and reveals why God sent His Son to die on our behalf.

THE SECOND COMING
OF CHRIST

T here is a need to review the Scriptures as Jesus Christ used
many parables regarding his teachings of the kingdom
that he established on earth and his second coming in order to
gather his people unto God.

Parable of the tares of the field.

Matthew 13:24-30; Another parable put he forth unto them, saying,
*The kingdom of heaven is likened unto a man which sowed good
seed in his field: But while men slept, his enemy came and sowed
tares among the wheat, and went his way. But when the blade was
sprung up, and brought forth fruit, then appeared the tares also. So
the servants of the householder came and said unto him, Sir, didst
not thou sow good seed in thy field? from whence then hath it tares?
He said unto them, An enemy hath done this. The servants said unto
him, Wilt thou then that we go and gather them up? But he said,
Nay; lest while ye gather up the tares, ye root up also the wheat with
them. Let both grow together until the harvest: and in the time of
harvest I will say to the reapers, Gather ye together first the tares,
and bind them in bundles to burn them: but gather the wheat into
my barn.*

Matthew 13:36-43; Then Jesus sent the multitude away, and went
into the house: and his disciples came unto him, saying, Declare
unto us the parable of the tares of the field. He answered and said
unto them, *He that soweth the good seed is the Son of man; The field
is the world; the good seed are the children of the kingdom; but the*

tares are the children of the wicked one; The enemy that sowed them is the devil; the harvest is the end of the world; and the reapers are the angels. As therefore the tares are gathered and burned in the fire; so shall it be in the end of this world. The Son of man shall send forth his angels, and they shall gather out of his kingdom all things that offend, and them which do iniquity; And shall cast them into a furnace of fire: there shall be wailing and gnashing of teeth. Then shall the righteous shine forth as the sun in the kingdom of their Father. Who hath ears to hear, let him hear.

This parable of the tares in the field by Jesus Christ, *the Son of Man,* **shows the establishment of his kingdom on earth and when he returns the second time it will be with his angels to separate the righteous from the wicked with the righteous being taken to the** *Father* **in heaven and the wicked cast into a furnace of fire.**

Matthew 16:27; For the Son of man shall come in the glory of his Father with his angels; and then he shall reward every man according to his works.

Matthew 24:35-36; Heaven and earth shall pass away, but my words shall not pass away. But of that day and hour knoweth no man, no, not the angels of heaven, but my Father only.

Jesus Christ confirms that we do not know when judgment day will be, that only God knows. This disproves many of the false predictions that attempt to establish a date regarding the second coming of Christ.

Matthew 25:31-34,41,46; When the Son of man shall come in his glory, and all the holy angels with him, then shall he sit upon the throne of his glory: And before him shall be gathered all nations: and he shall separate them one from another, as a shepherd divideth his sheep from the goats: And he shall set the sheep on his right hand, but the goats on the left. Then shall the King say unto them on his right hand, Come, ye blessed of my Father, inherit the kingdom prepared for you from the foundation of the world: Then shall he say also unto them on the left hand, Depart from me, ye cursed, into everlasting fire, prepared for the devil and his angels: And these shall go away into everlasting punishment: but the righteous into life eternal.

Mark 8:38; Whosoever therefore shall be ashamed of me and of my words in this adulterous and sinful generation; of him also shall the Son of man be ashamed, when he cometh in the glory of his Father with the holy angels.

These verses reveal that judgment day will be pleasant for many, but unpleasant for others and that our preparation needs to made now.

John 5:28-29; Marvel not at this: for the hour is coming, in the which all that are in the graves shall hear his voice, And shall come forth; they that have done good, unto the resurrection of life; and they that have done evil, unto the resurrection of damnation.

These Scriptures indicate that when the Lord returns the second time, all people that are in the graves will be raised in the same hour to be judged, both good and evil. This indicates that the resurrection and the judgment will be on the last day.

John 6:38-40; For I came down from heaven, not to do mine own will, but the will of him that sent me. And this is the Father's will which hath sent me, that of all which he hath given me I should lose nothing, but should raise it up again at the last day. And this is the will of him that sent me, that every one which seeth the Son, and believeth on him, may have everlasting life: and I will raise him up at the last day.

Jesus Christ states that he came to do God's will and that only those who believe on him will be in his kingdom and will be raised up on the last day which will be when he comes the second time.

John 12:48; He that rejecteth me, and receiveth not my words, hath one that judgeth him: the word that I have spoken, the same shall judge him in the last day.

Christ warns to not reject him nor his words as judgment will be on the last day.

John 14:1-3; Let not your heart be troubled: ye believe in God, believe also in me. In my Father's house are many mansions: if it were not so, I would have told you. I go to prepare a place for you. And if I go and prepare a place for you, I will come again, and receive you unto myself; that where I am, there ye may be also.

Jesus Christ confirms that he left this world after his sacrifice on our behalf to prepare a place for us in heaven that when he returns it will be to take us there.

John 18:36-37; Jesus answered, *My kingdom is not of this world: if my kingdom were of this world, then would my servants fight, that I should not be delivered to the Jews: but now is my kingdom not from hence.* Pilate therefore said unto him, Art thou a king then? Jesus answered, *Thou sayest that I am a king. To this end was I born, and for this cause came I into the world, that I should bear witness unto the truth. Every one that is of the truth heareth my voice.*

This is confirmation from Christ that his kingdom is a spiritual kingdom, not a physical one, and was established with his first arrival upon earth which rules out his coming a second time to reestablish his kingdom upon earth.

I Corinthians 15:20-24; But now is Christ risen from the dead, and become the firstfruits of them that slept. For since by man came death, by man came also the resurrection of the dead. For as in Adam all die, even so in Christ shall all be made alive. But every man in his own order: Christ the firstfruits; afterward they that are Christ's at his coming. Then cometh the end, when he shall have delivered up the kingdom to God, even the Father; when he shall have put down all rule and all authority and power.

The Apostle Paul's letter to the Corinthians confirms that Christ is reigning now in his kingdom that he established on earth. When Christ comes again it will be to deliver his kingdom to God. This means that the "Thousand Year Reign" is ongoing now. These Scriptures are further proof that there will be no second reign on earth.

The following Scriptures in the Book of I Corinthians also confirm that Christ is reigning now and that his kingdom is spiritual, not physical. These Scriptures also confirm God's plan for mankind on earth.

I Corinthians 15:25-26,28,35-38,42-44,46,49-54,57; For he must reign, till he hath put all enemies under his feet. The last enemy that shall be destroyed is death. And when all things shall be subdued unto him, then shall the Son also himself be subject unto him that put all things under him, that God may be all in all. But some man will say, How are the dead raised up? and with what body do they come? Thou fool, that which thou sowest is not quickened, except it die: And that which thou sowest, thou sowest not that body that shall be, but bare grain, it may chance of wheat, or of some other grain: But God giveth it a body as it hath pleased him, and to every seed his own body. So also is the resurrection of the dead. It is sown in corruption; it is raised in incorruption: It is sown in dishonour; it is raised in glory: it is sown in weakness; it is raised in power: It is sown a natural body; it is raised a spiritual body. There is a natural body, and there is a spiritual body. Howbeit that was not first which is spiritual, but that which is natural; and afterward that which is spiritual. And as we have borne the image of the earthy, we shall also bear the image of the heavenly. Now this I say, brethren, that flesh and blood cannot inherit the kingdom of God; neither doth corruption inherit incorruption. Behold, I shew you a mystery; We shall not all sleep, but we shall all be changed, In a moment, in the twinkling of an eye, at the last trump: for the trumpet shall sound, and the dead shall be raised incorruptible, and we shall be changed. For this corruptible must put on incorruption, and this mortal must put on immortality. So when this corruptible shall have put on incorruption, and this mortal shall have put on immortality, then shall be brought to pass the saying that is written, Death is swallowed up in victory. But thanks be to God, which giveth us the victory through our Lord Jesus Christ.

Ephesians 6:17; And take the helmet of salvation, and the sword of the Spirit, which is the word of God:

These Scriptures confirm that the resurrection will be a change from our natural and physical body into a spiritual body and also confirms that the ongoing battle between Christ and Satan is being waged by the Word of God as symbolized in the phrase "and the sword of the Spirit, which is the word of God:".

Philippians 3:20-21; For our conversation is in heaven; from whence also we look for the Saviour, the Lord Jesus Christ: Who shall change our vile body, that it may be fashioned like unto his glorious body, according to the working whereby he is able even to subdue all things unto himself.

This description of change from a physical body unto a spiritual body also contradicts another physical kingdom upon earth. I Thessalonians 4:13-18; But I would not have you to be ignorant, brethren, concerning them which are asleep, that ye sorrow not, even as others which have no hope. For if we believe that Jesus died and rose again, even so them also which sleep in Jesus will God bring with him. For this we say unto you by the word of the Lord, that we which are alive and remain unto the coming of the Lord shall not prevent them which are asleep. For the Lord himself shall descend from heaven with a shout, with the voice of the archangel, and with the trump of God: and the dead in Christ shall rise first: Then we which are alive and remain shall be caught up together with them in the clouds, to meet the Lord in the air: and so shall we ever be with the Lord. Wherefore comfort one another with these words.

This letter by the Apostle Paul unto the church at Thessalonica informs us that Jesus Christ will not set foot on earth again, but rather, that we will meet him in the air. This is further confirmation that Christ is not coming back to reign on earth a second time, but instead, we shall meet the Lord in the air and so shall we ever be with the Lord.

I Thessalonians 5:1-3,9-10; But of the times and the seasons, brethren, ye have no need that I write unto you. For yourselves know perfectly that the day of the Lord so cometh as a thief in the night. For when they shall say, Peace and safety; then sudden destruction cometh upon them, as travail upon a woman with child; and they shall not escape. For God hath not appointed us to wrath, but to obtain salvation by our Lord Jesus Christ, Who died for us, that, whether we wake or sleep, we should live together with him.

These passages of Scripture warn us that we will not know when judgment day will come, therefore our preparation needs to be made now. This warning would not be necessary if there was a second chance, but the Scriptures prove that there will be no second chance to determine our salvation.

II Thessalonians 1:7-10; And to you who are troubled rest with us, when the Lord Jesus shall be revealed from heaven with his mighty angels, In flaming fire taking vengeance on them that know not God, and that obey not the gospel of our Lord Jesus Christ: Who shall be punished with everlasting destruction from the presence of the Lord, and from the glory of his power; When he shall come to be glorified in his saints, and to be admired in all them that believe (because our testimony among you was believed) in that day.

This letter by the Apostle Paul reveals that when Christ comes again the second time that the saints will receive rest with the Lord but the wicked will receive vengeance by flaming fire. This eliminates the theories of a second chance to join the kingdom of Christ.

II Thessalonians 2:1-4,7-10; Now we beseech you, brethren, by the coming of our Lord Jesus Christ, and by our gathering together unto him, That ye be not soon shaken in mind, or be troubled, neither by spirit, nor by word, nor by letter as from us, as that the day of Christ is at hand. Let no man deceive you by any means: for that day shall not come, except there come a falling away first, and that man of sin be revealed, the son of perdition; Who opposeth and exalteth himself above all that is called God, or that is worshipped; so that he as God sitteth in the temple of God, shewing himself that he is God. For the mystery of iniquity doth already work: only he who now letteth will let, until he be taken out of the way. **(This means that Satan is already promoting an evil doctrine which will lead to apostasy, but it is hidden and will remain a mystery until whatever is restraining it is removed, then the wicked one will be revealed.)** And then shall that Wicked be revealed, whom the Lord shall consume with the spirit of his mouth, and shall destroy with the brightness of his coming: Even him, whose coming is after the working of Satan with all power and signs and lying wonders, And with all deceivableness of unrighteousness in them that perish; because they received not the love of the truth, that they might be saved.

The "day of the Lord" simply means the day that the Lord comes back a second time to judge the righteous and the wicked which will be the last day of earth and mankind otherwise called final judgment day. It will be the day that the righteous will be rewarded with their place in heaven and the wicked will be cast into the everlasting fire with Satan and his angels. It is the day that Christ will deliver his kingdom unto God.

II Timothy 4:1; I charge thee therefore before God, and the Lord Jesus Christ, who shall judge the quick and the dead at his appearing and his kingdom;

This further confirms that the second coming of Christ is for judgment and to deliver his kingdom unto God.

Hebrews 9:26-28; For then must he often have suffered since the foundation of the world: but now once in the end of the world hath he appeared to put away sin by the sacrifice of himself. And as it is appointed unto men once to die, but after this the judgment: So Christ was once offered to bear the sins of many; and unto them that look for him shall he appear the second time without sin unto salvation.

These Scriptures prove that Christ has already established his kingdom upon earth and that his return a second time will be for judgment to disperse the wicked into eternal fire and to convey the saints unto salvation to God in heaven.

Hebrews 12:25-27; See that ye refuse not him that speaketh. For if they escaped not who refused him that spake on earth, much more shall not we escape, if we turn away from him that speaketh from heaven: Whose voice then shook the earth: but now he hath promised, saying, Yet once more I shake not the earth only, but also heaven. And this word, Yet once more, signifieth the removing of those things that are shaken, as of things that are made, that those things which cannot be shaken may remain.

These Scriptures are a warning to heed the Gospel that is being put forth for our salvation and to also confirm that the second coming of Christ is for judgment.

II Peter 3:7-8,10-13,16-17; But the heavens and the earth, which are now, by the same word are kept in store, reserved unto fire against the day of judgment and perdition of ungodly men. But, beloved, be not ignorant of this one thing, that one day is with the Lord as a thousand years, and a thousand years as one day. But the day of the Lord will come as a thief in the night; in the which the heavens shall pass away with a great noise, and the elements shall melt with fervent heat, the earth also and the works that are therein shall be burned up. Seeing then that all these things shall be dissolved, what manner of persons ought ye to be in all holy conversation and godliness,

Looking for and hasting unto the coming of the day of God, wherein the heavens being on fire shall be dissolved, and the elements shall melt with fervent heat? Nevertheless we, according to his promise, look for new heavens and a new earth, wherein dwelleth righteousness. As also in all his epistles, speaking in them of these things; in which are some things hard to be understood, which they that are unlearned and unstable wrest, as they do also the other scriptures, unto their own destruction. Ye therefore, beloved, seeing ye know these things before, beware lest ye also, being led away with the error of the wicked, fall from your own stedfastness.

The Apostle Peter confirms that the second coming of Christ will be without notice and will be for judgment with those found worthy going to a new heaven and a new earth as the old heavens and earth will be destroyed by fervent heat. The Apostle Peter also warns that we should use our knowledge of the Scriptures to keep from being led astray from the truth and to remain firm in our faith.

Revelation 1:7;Behold, he cometh with clouds; and every eye shall see him, and they also which pierced him: and all kindreds of the earth shall wail because of him. Even so, Amen.

Revelation 21:1,7;And I saw a new heaven and a new earth: for the first heaven and the first earth were passed away; and there was no more sea. He that overcometh shall inherit all things; and I will be his God, and he shall be my son.

These verses in Revelation confirm the teaching by the parables of Jesus Christ and also the writings of the Apostles Paul and Peter.

Revelation 22:12; And, behold, I come quickly; and my reward is with me, to give every man according as his work shall be.

This is confirmation by the direct Word of Christ that the second coming is for judgment and that we need to be prepared as there will be no second chance.

METHOD OF
INTERPRETATION

Now I will give my opinion on how we should focus our interpretation of the period of time covered by the Book of Revelation. Let us review what Jesus Christ told John to write regarding the Book of Revelation.

Revelation 1:19; Write the things which thou hast seen, and the things which are, and the things which shall be hereafter;

I read those instructions by Jesus Christ to the apostle John as past, present, and future. This means that the things that John was told to write in the Book of Revelation will cover events past, present, and future. With the aid of the Scriptures we will attempt to understand the intent of what was written.

Therefore, we need to realize that although this revelation was written primarily to comfort the heavily persecuted Christians during the time that it was revealed to John, it also applies to current and future Christians throughout all ages. Christians of today are also being persecuted. For example, the nation of Islam is in a religious war with us now and also our own nation's political leaders are removing references to God and Christianity from our public schools and our public places such as our courts of justice. What we learn from this is that the Book of Revelation may be applied to all people of every age. This revelation was not just for them, but it also has a benefit for current and future readers.

Why was John instructed by God through Jesus Christ to write the book of Revelation? The book was written to comfort the Christians during the time of John and also to comfort the church during the entire Christian Dispensation against all adversaries. It was written to give Christians courage and motivation to be faithful to the end, even unto death. The prophetical principle of this book is addressed to Christians of all ages and offers comfort to the faithful with the knowledge of Christ eventually triumphing over Satan.

Keeping in mind the phrases "must shortly come to pass" and "the time is at hand" we conclude that at least part of John's vision dealt with the people of that time period and was to be fulfilled shortly. While we know that the book was intended for the early Christians living during John's day, it is also applicable for Christians throughout all of these last days of the Christian dispensation.

At the time of this revelation to John, we know that the people at that time were under severe persecution and were subjected to many trials and tribulations. Many of the Jewish teachers were trying to convert the people back to the Mosaic Law or were trying to incorporate some of the Mosaic rites and ceremonies into the Christian worship. The Roman government was putting many Christians to death. They needed strong encouragement to continue in the faith and this vision gave them hope to endure by seeing that Jesus Christ would be victorious in the end. The things that were written were for the benefit of the people to whom it was addressed.

These were a people under severe tribulation and they needed some encouragement to continue. It may have appeared from their point of view brought about by their persecution that Satan was winning, so this Revelation of Jesus Christ was given to John to write this book to convince them that this was not going to happen. The book of Revelation repeatedly pictures the victory of our Lord Jesus Christ over the forces of evil with the eventual complete defeat of Satan and his angels. We will see this in some of the symbols in the book with the theme that

Christ will triumph and we also will triumph with him by being faithful to the end.

With the Jews and idolatry worshipers as an enemy pressing the Roman government for their persecution, many Christians were used for amusement as spectacles in the Roman arenas, murdered by gladiators and wild animals. Each and every person under Roman authority was required to offer incense and pledge allegiance to the emperor of Rome each year as their Lord. Many Christians were slain because they refused to do this as they felt that their allegiance should be to Christ as their Lord rather than an earthly emperor.

Another major problem for the Christians was poverty brought about by their refusal to worship false gods set in place by the trade guilds. Many of the trade guilds would hold feast days and require their members to participate by swearing allegiance to these false gods, eating meat dedicated to them, then participating in various abominations to God such as fornication rites or ceremonies. Refusal to do so could possibly have meant loss of employment thereby causing financial difficulties inducing famine or starvation as symbolized by the black horse in chapter six.

The benefit of this picture of Christ triumphing over Satan gave encouragement not only to the early Christians but also is encouraging to Christians of the present time and in the future that we will achieve victory if we remain faithful to the end. The purpose of this book of Revelation is to comfort the Christian Church in its fight against Satan and his evil forces. This message of encouragement was necessary for the past. It is necessary for the present and it will be necessary for the future until the second coming of Christ. Reassurance is continually repeated throughout this revelation given unto John for all persecuted Christians.

The main principle of this book is to provide encouragement that Christ will be victorious over Satan and his bottomless pit of evil thereby reassuring believers and also encouraging non-believers to join the kingdom of Christ. Throughout this revelation imparted to John by Christ is that his Kingdom will prevail over Satan and his angels because of the power of God, His Son, and The Holy Spirit who live forever and ever and will conquer Satan. All of these messages revealed to John were for the benefit of Christians with the intent for them to remain firm in their faith during their time of persecution. This encouragement and assurance were provided through many passages of Scripture such as:

Revelation 1:13; Christ is with us now in the midst of the seven candlesticks.

Revelation 1:17,18; And he laid his right hand upon me, saying unto me, *Fear not; I am the first and the last: I am he that liveth, and was dead; and, behold, I am alive for evermore, Amen; and have the keys of hell and of death.*

Revelation 2:10; Fear none of those things which thou shalt suffer: behold, the devil shall cast some of you into prison, that ye may be tried; and ye shall have tribulation ten days: be thou faithful unto death, and I will give thee a crown of life.

Revelation 6:9; And when he had opened the fifth seal, I saw under the altar the souls of them that were slain for the word of God, and for the testimony which they held:

Revelation 7:17, 21:4; God shall wipe away all tears from their eyes.

Revelation 8:3,4,5; Their prayers are heard in heaven by God upon the golden altar and their blood will be avenged.

Revelation 14:13; Their death is blessed and rest awaits them.

Revelation 15:2; Their victory is assured over the beast.

Revelation 20:4; Heaven awaits them which witness for Jesus.

Revelation 21: There would be a new heaven and a new earth.

While we know that the Book of Revelation gave immediate comfort to the Christians during the time of John amidst their heavy persecution, it also imparted comfort and warnings to Christians at later dates and will impart comfort and warnings to Christians of the present and future throughout the entire Christian dispensation. Reference the following Scriptures:

II Timothy 3:12,13; Yea, and all that will live godly in Christ Jesus shall suffer persecution. But evil men and seducers shall wax worse and worse, deceiving, and being deceived.

Matthew 24:24,29-31; For there shall arise false Christs, and false prophets, and shall shew great signs and wonders; insomuch that, if it were possible, they shall deceive the very elect. Immediately after the tribulation of those days shall the sun be darkened, and the moon shall not give her light, and the stars shall fall from heaven, and the powers of the heavens shall be shaken: And then shall appear the sign of the Son of man in heaven: and then shall all the tribes of the earth mourn, and they shall see the Son of man coming in the clouds of heaven with power and great glory. And he shall send his angels with a great sound of a trumpet, and they shall gather together his elect from the four winds, from one end of heaven to the other.

The revelations in this book relate to judgments by God in response to the persecutions by mankind of the disciples of Christ along with the principles of historical conduct and general events that continually reoccur throughout history so that they cannot be relegated to any single occurrence at any particular point in time, but rather are general in nature and will continually reoccur up to the second coming of Christ.

Ephesians 6:12; For we wrestle not against flesh and blood, but against principalities, against powers, against the rulers of the darkness of this world, against spiritual wickedness in high places.

For example, as we study chapters 2 and 3, regarding the letters that are addressed to the seven churches, we know that there were more than seven churches in the area such as Heriopolis, and Troas. Seven is the number that symbolizes perfection and completeness so as to cover all churches throughout all of the Christian Dispensation. These letters to each of the seven churches reveal that they were complimented for their virtues and condemned for their failures which shows that these principles are applicable for all churches throughout the various time periods, plus, we are told that all who read and study this book are called blessed which will cover any age or point in time.

Revelation 1:3; Blessed is he that readeth, and they that hear the words of this prophecy, and keep those things which are written therein: for the time is at hand.

Revelation 2:29; He that hath an ear, let him hear what the Spirit saith unto the churches.

Revelation 22:18; For I testify unto every man that heareth the words of the prophecy of this book, If any man shall add unto these things, God shall add unto him the plagues that are written in this book:

Brothers and Sisters in Christ,

I would like to present this commentary/teacher's guide on the Book of Revelation to your church. I believe that this commentary will be of great benefit to Christians interested in understanding the Book of Revelation. It is an excellent teaching and study guide developed through a tremendous amount of research and study. This study was concluded and prepared for use in teaching a Christian age group of thirteen to nineteen year old students for an LTC (Leadership Training for Christ) competition among seventy plus churches in the Midwest.

To the best of my knowledge, it is the most complete and detailed interpretation of the Book of Revelation available on the market with all commentary and Revelation verses reinforced with biblical scripture. It is written in a manner that it may also be taught to upper level elementary students.

The overall theme of this book is the Spiritual battle between Christ and Satan for the souls of mankind with the ultimate victory by Christ. This battle is being fought with the Word of God by God's disciples while under persecution by Satan's forces during the entire Gospel Dispensation time period. More information regarding this book is available online at http://jerryupton.wordpress.com.

The book is published by Xulon Press with the retail price being $9.50 for an e-book, $18.99 for a paperback, and $28.99 for a hardback copy. Xulon Press is the best place for Christians to purchase it as they will offer a 30% discount to churches and ministries by calling 866-381-2665 between the hours of 8:00 AM and 5:00 PM eastern time and referencing either my name or ISBN #9781613794821.

It is also available on line at www.xulonpress.com, www.lifewaystores.com,

...ible Availability through retail stores will depend upon ... policy from Xulon Press, all retail stores have a ...ial risk. Retail stores may order the book
... Arbor Book Distributors.

...ive comments on this commentary from many
...dentials as Biblical scholars are as follows: A
...for over forty years; "I have other commentaries
...ur book above all of the others." From a retired
...not know of anyone else who could have done
...e Book of Revelation." From a retired theology
...d needs to be on the market. I will show your
...urrent minister and previous college professor;
...ell done. Show it to the chairman of the bible
...ge." From another retired preacher; "People
...ng this book to the college where I received my

DAYTON CHURCH OF CHRIST

2230 East Highway 252
Huntington, Arkansas 72940
Phone: 479-996-2625
Minister: Larry Bridges

Web Site: www.daytoncofc.com   Phone: 479-928-4034

ELDERS

Brian Black
Joe Bridges
Larry Bridges
Larrie Owen

DEACONS

Jeff Brewer
Mike Brewer
Tom Dacus
Jodie Morgan
Cliff Wilson
Charlie Young
Chris Young

June 3, 2012

To Whom It May Concern:

This letter is written in recommendation of a Revelation titled *Revelation of Christ: A Teache* good friend and brother named Jerry Upton who the Dayton Church for many years. Over the ye this book which were written by capable and com read I have found Jerry's book to be the most pra ry spent years researching and writing regardin seek publication. His thoughts are clear and alw Old and New Testament. His book will make an or ~~sonal library.

~~nt the last forty plus years serving a ~~or the last several years servin ~~mendation for your co ~~ll as we seek to

PROGRESSIVE PARALLELISM

I am using a guide put forth by previous scholars called Progressive Parallelism that divides the Book of Revelation into seven sections. These seven sections are parallel to each other in the sense that each section follows the same general pattern of describing the events of the Christian Gospel Dispensation time period beginning with Satan being cast out of heaven or Christ being sent to earth until the final judgment day with the kingdom(church) of Christ being delivered to the Lord God in heaven. This kingdom of Christ is symbolized as the Bride of Christ, the Holy City, and New Jerusalem in the last section.

In order to aid in the understanding of the correct interpretation I am preparing a brief synopsis to use as a guide through the Book of Revelation. To enhance the divisions I will reference the events of Satan being cast out or falling from heaven, the sending of Christ to earth, and the events of the final judgment day. The seven sections are not only divided but they progress in the following manner:

The first section covers chapters one through three with Christ revealing to John the "things which must shortly come to pass" and also dictating to John the letters to the seven churches establishing parameters of conduct with praises of commendation coupled with words of condemnation. This section reveals that Christ is always with them in their midst and offers the reward of heaven in a separate manner to each individual church such as:

Revelation 2:7,10,11,17,26; To him that overcometh will I give to eat of the tree of life, which is in the midst of the paradise of God. Be thou faithful unto death, and I will give thee a crown of life. He that overcometh shall not be hurt of the second death. To him that overcometh will I give to eat of the hidden manna, and will give him a white stone. And he that overcometh, and keepeth my works unto the end, to him will I give power over the nations.
Revelation 3:5,12,21; He that overcometh, the same shall be clothed in white raiment; and I will not blot out his name out of the book of life, but I will confess his name before my Father, and before his angels. Him that overcometh will I make a pillar in the temple of my God, and he shall go no more out: and I will write upon him the name of my God, and the name of the city of my God, which is new Jerusalem, which cometh down out of heaven from my God: and I will write upon him my new name. To him that overcometh will I grant to sit with me in my throne, even as I also overcame, and am set down with my Father in his throne.

The second section covers chapters four through seven with John having a vision through an open door to heaven revealing the various disciples praising the Lord God and a throne from which determinations by God are made regarding the appropriate response to prayers being made by the saints on earth. These prayers were for relief of their tribulations and persecution on earth and are reflected in chapter five, verse eight. The response to these prayers are judgments made by God as symbolized by the seven seals. This progression continues with the book of seven seals being opened by Christ revealing his mission from God regarding these judgments. This mission is symbolized in chapter six as a rider on a white horse, a red horse, a black horse, and a pale horse. The final judgment day is recorded in chapter six, verse seventeen and is delayed until those that have earned salvation have been sealed in their foreheads as the servants of God reflected in chapter seven, verse three.

The third section covers chapters eight through eleven and is symbolized by angels being given trumpets to warn of the judgments to be implemented as contained in the book of seven seals. The judgments being dispensed are reflected in chapter eight, verse five as fire from the altar being cast into the earth by Christ with a golden censer. Satan falling from heaven is reflected in chapter eight, verse ten identified as Wormwood and chapter nine, verse one, as a star falling from heaven. Christ is portrayed as a mighty angel who sets his right foot upon the sea and his left foot upon the earth showing that he is in control of all of earth. The battle versus Satan being fought on earth is reflected in chapter eleven, verse three as power, which is God's Word, being given unto the two witnesses of God which are the Mosaic Law and Christ. The designated period of time for this battle with Satan is given in chapter eleven, verses two and three as forty-two months and a thousand two hundred and three-score days. Chapter eleven, verse eighteen indicates the final judgment day.

The fourth section covers chapters twelve through fourteen revealing God sending Christ to earth to establish his kingdom(church) as opposition to Satan and his evil forces. Chapter twelve opens with a vision of the birth or beginning of this church portrayed as the image of a "woman clothed with the sun, and the moon under her feet, and upon her head a crown of twelve stars: And she being with child cried, travailing in birth, and pained to be delivered" of the man-child which is Christ. This section deals with the persecution of Christ and of his church by Satan portrayed as the great red dragon in chapter twelve, verse three, along with his evil dominion represented as a sea beast in chapter thirteen, verse one, and an earth beast, verse eleven. Satan being cast out of heaven is reflected in chapter twelve, verse nine. The final judgment day is represented in chapter fourteen, verse eight as Babylon, that great city, being fallen.

The fifth section covers chapters fifteen through sixteen depicting the judgments of God being dispensed upon earth by seven angels with seven golden vials full of the wrath of God which results in the death of Satan and the destruction of his evil empire. The final judgment day is revealed as taking place at Armageddon, chapter sixteen, verse sixteen and reflected as victory by Christ with a great voice out of the temple of heaven, from the throne, saying in verse seventeen, "It is done".

The sixth section covers chapters seventeen through nineteen with an angel showing John the vision of a woman upon a scarlet colored beast which indicates its evil intent and also reveals its allegiance to Satan as "And upon her forehead was a name written, MYSTERY, BABYLON THE GREAT, THE MOTHER OF HARLOTS AND ABOMINATIONS OF THE EARTH." which is reflected in chapter seventeen, verses three and five. The origin of this beast indicates that it came from the bottomless pit which is Satan's place of abode and is recorded in chapter seventeen, verse eight. The demise of Satan's evil dominion is symbolized by Christ being shown as an angel from heaven having great power in chapter eighteen, verse one and as Babylon the great is fallen, verse two. The final judgment day is reflected in chapter nineteen, verse twenty as the beast and false prophet "were cast alive into a lake of fire burning with brimstone."

The seventh section covers chapters twenty through twenty-two beginning with Christ coming down from heaven with a great chain in his hand which is the Word of God in chapter twenty, verse one. The binding of Satan by Christ with this great chain is for a "thousand years" in chapter twenty, verse two and is accomplished by the preaching and teaching of God's Word. Satan is then loosed from his prison for a short period of time leading up to him being cast into the lake of fire as reflected in chapter twenty, verses seven and ten which depicts this as the final judgment day. The period of time from Satan being loosed until the final judgment day is also reflected in chapter eleven as "three days and an half" as shown in verse nine. The book of life is opened with judgment passed according to their works, chapter twenty, verse twelve, with those not found in the book of life being cast into the lake of fire, chapter twenty, verse fifteen. The reward of heaven being given to the saints is shown as a new heaven and a new earth in chapter twenty-one, verse one and also as the bride of Christ, the holy city, and new Jerusalem in verse two.

The seven sections, with some variations, indicate that they are parallel and progressive as they each cover the same period of time with many of the same events duplicated in different sections as reflected by the various symbols. In section one this period of time is very briefly reflected in chapter one, verses five, six, and seven. In other sections the period of time being covered by the book of Revelation is represented as forty-two months in chapter eleven, verse two and as a thousand two hundred and threescore days in verse three. This same period of time is next shown as a thousand two hundred and threescore days in chapter twelve, verse six and as a time, and times, and half a time in verse fourteen. This is the same period of time as revealed in chapter twenty, verses two through six as a thousand years. This period of time is the time designated by God for His Word to be spread throughout earth.

SYMBOLISM INTERPRETATION

To interpret and understand the Book of Revelation as presented by Jesus Christ through his angel to his servant, John, we need to not only know the meanings of the various symbols, colors, and numbers used in this book but we also need to remember that it was a common practice among the various teachers of the Scriptures to use parables and analogies of nature in order to convey a better understanding of the viewpoint being presented. While the lessons and viewpoints being conveyed in this book use physical terminology, we need to always keep in mind that in actuality they represent spiritual endeavors and occurrences.

The language in this book is mainly symbolic. While there are sections of this book, especially chapters two and three, that contain speech that is to be literally understood, we need to remember that for the most part this is symbolic language. The rule for interpreting literal language is that the wording is to be taken in its literal meaning unless the context demands otherwise. The rule for interpreting symbolic language is just the opposite of the rule for interpreting literal language. The wording is to be taken symbolically unless there is a reason to take it in a literal sense. Most of the symbolic language in the Book of Revelation can and will be interpreted by referencing Scripture in the Bible.

Symbolic language tends to reinforce our thoughts by painting pictures with symbols, colors, and numbers that enable us to better understand and remember the idea that the writer is trying to convey. It is easier to remember symbols such as living creatures full of eyes before and behind like unto a lion, a calf, the face of a man, and a flying eagle. You see riders on white and red horses armed for battle. You picture a rider on a black horse holding a pair of balance scales with still another rider named death upon a pale horse with Hell following him. You see smoke rising out of the bottomless pit, locusts appearing out of the smoke shaped like horses with heads of lions, a woman clothed with the sun, the moon under her feet, wearing a crown with twelve stars, the great red dragon with seven heads and ten horns and with its long tail casts a third of the stars of heaven to the earth while waiting to devour her child as soon as it is born. You see a mighty angel come down from heaven putting his right foot upon the sea and his left foot upon the earth. You remember seven angels with seven vials full of the wrath of God. Symbolic language with colors, numbers, and various beasts with evil intent paint a picture that makes it much easier to remember the message being conveyed to you.

The understanding of the symbolism in the Old and New Testaments greatly aids in the interpretation of the symbolism in the Book of Revelation just as the Mosaic Law was symbolic of the New Covenant by Christ.

GALATIONS 3:24; Wherefore the law was our schoolmaster to bring us unto Christ, that we might be justified by faith.

ABADDON: Destruction or place of the dead.

Revelation 9:11; And they had a king over them, which is the angel of the bottomless pit, whose name in the Hebrew tongue is Abaddon, but in the Greek tongue hath his name Apollyon.

AMEN: I agree, it is so, so be it.

Revelation 5:14; And the four beasts said, Amen. And the four and twenty elders fell down and worshipped him that liveth for ever and ever.

Revelation 22:21; The grace of our Lord Jesus Christ be with you all. Amen.

ARK of HIS TESTAMENT: New Covenant-Christianity. God's plan for the salvation of mankind.

Revelation 11:19; And the temple of God was opened in heaven, and there was seen in his temple the ark of his testament: and there were lightnings, and voices, and thunderings, and an earthquake, and great hail.

ARMAGEDDON: Symbolizes a great battle, usually in reference to the last great battle between Christ and Satan which will be the final judgment day.

Revelation 16:16; And he gathered them together into a place called in the Hebrew tongue Armageddon.

APOLLYON: Destroyer.

Revelation 9:11; And they had a king over them, which is the angel of the bottomless pit, whose name in the Hebrew tongue is Abaddon, but in the Greek tongue hath his name Apollyon.

BABYLON: The word "Babylon" is an all-encompassing term used to describe the source of all evil that is opposed to God and is also used to symbolize the various types of false religion or worship such as spiritual fornication, worship of false idols, and worship of emperors. It represents an evil city or empire from which false doctrine, idolatry, and enemies of Christ originate and is considered as the seat or throne of Satan. Under Nebuchadnezzar, Babylon forced citizens to bow to statute of an idol (Idolatry Worship). Under Roman rule, citizens were forced to declare the Roman emperor as lord.

Jeremiah 51:24; And I will render unto Babylon and to all the inhabitants of Chaldea all their evil that they have done in Zion in your sight, saith the LORD.

Jeremiah 51:44;And I will punish Bel in Babylon, and I will bring forth out of his mouth that which he hath swallowed up: and the nations shall not flow together any more unto him: yea, the wall of Babylon shall fall.

Jeremiah 51:47; Therefore, behold, the days come, that I will do judgment upon the graven images of Babylon: and her whole land shall be confounded, and all her slain shall fall in the midst of her. (Jeremiah 51:29,37.)

Revelation 14:8; And there followed another angel, saying, Babylon is fallen, is fallen, that great city, because she made all nations drink of the wine of the wrath of her fornication.

Revelation 17:5; And upon her forehead was a name written, MYSTERY, BABYLON THE GREAT, THE MOTHER OF HARLOTS AND ABOMINATIONS OF THE EARTH. (Revelation 16:19; 18:10,21.)

BEAST: All encompassing term used to symbolize all types of evil Anti-Christian doctrine through false prophets, governments, nations, or rulers of same. Also represents all types of abominations to God.

Jude 1:10; But these speak evil of those things which they know not: but what they know naturally, as brute beasts, in those things they corrupt themselves.

Revelation 13:1; And I stood upon the sand of the sea, and saw a beast rise up out of the sea, having seven heads and ten horns, and upon his horns ten crowns, and upon his heads the name of blasphemy.

Revelation 13:11; And I beheld another beast coming up out of the earth; and he had two horns like a lamb, and he spake as a dragon. (Revelation 13:2,4,12,14,15,17,18; 16:13; 19:19-20.)

BLACK: Opposite of white (which represents purity), represents darkness, despair, doom, famine or starvation (opposite of light which represents truth and God's word).

Isaiah 5:30; And in that day they shall roar against them like the roaring of the sea: and if one look unto the land, behold, darkness and sorrow, and the light is darkened in the heavens thereof. (Jeremiah 4:28, Job 30:30, I John 2:9-11.)

Revelation 6:5; And when he had opened the third seal, I heard the third beast say, Come and see. And I beheld, and lo a black horse; and he that sat on him had a pair of balances in his hand.

BLOOD: Loss of life. Spiritual death.

Genesis 4:10; And he said, What hast thou done? The voice of thy brother's blood crieth unto me from the ground.

Revelation 6:10; And they cried with a loud voice, saying, How long, O Lord, holy and true, dost thou not judge and avenge our blood on them that dwell on the earth?(Revelation 7:14.)

BOOK OF LIFE: Signifies those disciples of God and Christ that are found worthy of salvation in heaven.

Philippians 4:3; And I intreat thee also, true yokefellow, help those women which laboured with me in the gospel, with Clement also, and with other my fellowlabourers, whose names are in the book of life.

Revelation 3:5; He that overcometh, the same shall be clothed in white raiment; and I will not blot out his name out of the book of life, but I will confess his name before my Father, and before his angels. (Revelation 13:8; 17:8; 20:12,15; 21:27; 22:19.)

BOTTOMLESS PIT: Represents Satan's abode of never-ending evil.

Revelation 9:1; And the fifth angel sounded, and I saw a star fall from heaven unto the earth: and to him was given the key of the bottomless pit. (Revelation 9:2; 17:8; 20:1.)

BOW: short version of the word "Rainbow".

Genesis 9:13; I do set my bow in the cloud, and it shall be for a token of a covenant between me and the earth.

Revelation 4:3; And he that sat was to look upon like a jasper and a sardine stone: and there was a rainbow round about the throne, in sight like unto an emerald.

BOW: Instrument of warfare used to propel arrows. Symbolizes armed for battle.

Genesis 48:22; Moreover I have given to thee one portion above thy brethren, which I took out of the hand of the Amorite with my sword and with my Bow.

Revelation 6:2; And I saw, and behold a white horse: and he that sat on him had a bow; and a crown was given unto him: and he went forth conquering, and to conquer.

BOW: To pay respect or to honor by bending or kneeling.

Genesis 27:29; Let people serve thee, and nations bow down to thee: be lord over thy brethren, and let thy mother's sons bow down to thee: cursed be every one that curseth thee, and blessed be he that blesseth thee.

BRASS: Symbolizes a product made better by the process from which it was made. It also indicates beauty, stability, durability, and permanence. Brass was made from a composite of other metals by being treated and purified through a furnace of fire which signified a better product by this process and was

highly valued for beauty and durability. **Brass used as an adjective to describe the feet of Christ reveals His ability to proceed forward and accomplish the mission entrusted to Him by God.**

Revelation 1:15; And his feet like unto fine brass, as if they burned in a furnace; and his voice as the sound of many waters. (Revelation 2:18.)

BREASTPLATE: Signifies armor as protection and also preparation for battle.

Revelation 9:9; And they had breastplates, as it were breastplates of iron; and the sound of their wings was as the sound of chariots of many horses running to battle.

BRIMSTONE: Sulphur, Symbolizes punishment by God.

Genesis 19:24; Then the Lord rained upon Sodom and upon Gomorrah brimstone and fire from the Lord out of heaven.

Revelation 20:10; And the devil that deceived them was cast into the lake of fire and brimstone, where the beast and the false prophet are, and shall be tormented day and night for ever and ever. (Revelation 21:8.)

BURNING: Ever active or continuous activity.

Leviticus 6:13; The fire shall ever be burning upon the altar; it shall never go out.

Revelation 4:5; And out of the throne proceeded lightnings and thunderings and voices: and there were seven lamps of fire burning before the throne, which are the seven Spirits of God.

CALF: Animal used for sin offering.

Leviticus 9:8; Aaron therefore went unto the altar, and slew the calf of the sin offering, which was for himself.

CALF: Object used for false idolatry worship.

Acts 7:41; And they made a calf in those days, and offered sacrifice unto the idol, and rejoiced in the works of their own hands.

CALF OR OX: Symbol of the tribe of Ephraim.

Revelation 4:7; And the first beast was like a lion, and the second beast like a calf, and the third beast had a face as a man, and the fourth beast was like a flying eagle.

CANDLESTICKS: Brings the light (knowledge) of God's word unto the inhabitants of earth.

Matthew 5:15; Neither do men light a candle, and put it under a bushel, but on a candlestick; and it giveth light unto all that are in the house.

Revelation 1:12; And I turned to see the voice that spake with me. And being turned, I saw seven golden candlesticks; (Revelation 1:13.)

CENSER: A vessel used to contain coals of fire which is generally used in ceremonies about the altar.

Leviticus 16:12; And he shall take a censer full of burning coals of fire from off the altar before the Lord, and his hands full of sweet incense beaten small, and bring it within the veil:

Revelation 8:3; And another angel came and stood at the altar, having a golden censer; and there was given unto him much incense, that he should offer it with the prayers of all saints upon the golden altar which was before the throne.

CHERUBIM: Attendants, Servants, and Guards of Deity.

Ezekiel 10:7; And one cherub stretched forth his hand from between the cherubims unto the fire that was between the cherubims, and took thereof, and put it into the hands of him that was clothed with linen: who took it, and went out.

Revelation 15:7; And one of the four beasts gave unto the seven angels seven golden vials full of the wrath of God, who liveth for ever and ever.

CHILDREN OF ISRAEL: God's people, twelve tribes, descendants of Jacob, Isaac's son.

Exodus 2:25; And God looked upon the children of Israel, and God had respect unto them.

Exodus 3:10; Come now therefore, and I will send thee unto Pharaoh, that thou mayest bring forth my people the children of Israel out of Egypt.

CHURCH OF CHRIST: Kingdom of Christ, the Beloved City, the Holy City, New Jerusalem, Bride of Christ, the Lamb's Wife, and New Heaven and New Earth.

Revelation 21:1; And I saw a new heaven and a new earth: for the first heaven and the first earth were passed away; and there was no more sea.

Revelation 21:2; And I John saw the holy city, new Jerusalem, coming down from God out of heaven, prepared as a bride adorned for her husband. (Revelation 20:9; 21:9.)

CLOUD or CLOUDS: Signifies change with judgment coming. God and Christ always appear with, in, or on a cloud which signifies that a judgment or a change is to be made.

Exodus 16:10; And it came to pass, as Aaron spake unto the whole congregation of the children of Israel, that they looked toward the wilderness, and, behold, the glory of the LORD appeared in the cloud.

Exodus 40:34; Then a cloud covered the tent of the congregation, and the glory of the Lord filled the tabernacle.

Jeremiah 4:13; Behold, he shall come up as clouds, and his chariots shall be as a whirlwind: his horses are swifter than eagles. Woe unto us! for we are spoiled.

Ezekiel 1:28; As the appearance of the bow that is in the cloud in the day of rain, so was the appearance of the brightness round about. This was the appearance of the likeness of the glory of the LORD. And when I saw it, I fell upon my face, and I heard a voice of one that spake.

Matthew 17:5; While he yet spake, behold, a bright cloud overshadowed them: and behold a voice out of the cloud, which said, This is my beloved Son, in whom I am well pleased; hear ye him.

Matthew 24:30; And then shall appear the sign of the Son of man in heaven: and then shall all the tribes of the earth mourn, and they shall see the Son of man coming in the clouds of heaven with power and great glory.

I Thessalonians 4:17; Then we which are alive and remain shall be caught up together with them in the clouds, to meet the Lord in the air: and so shall we ever be with the Lord.

Revelation 1:7; Behold, he cometh with clouds; and every eye shall see him, and they also which pierced him: and all kindreds of the earth shall wail because of him. Even so, Amen. (Revelation 14:14.)

CROWN: Symbolizes royalty, a king or person with authority.

Revelation 2:10; Revelation 14:14; And I looked, and behold a white cloud, and upon the cloud one sat like unto the Son of man, having on his head a golden crown, and in his hand a sharp sickle.

CRYSTAL SEA: Represents purity, calmness, peace, safety, tranquility and transparency.

CRYSTAL SEA AS PURITY: Revelation 4:6; And before the throne there was a sea of glass like unto crystal: and in the midst of the throne, and round about the throne, were four beasts full of eyes before and behind.

Revelation 21:11; Having the glory of God: and her light was like unto a stone most precious, even like a jasper stone, clear as crystal;

Revelation 22:1; And he shewed me a pure river of water of life, clear as crystal, proceeding out of the throne of God and of the Lamb.

Philippians 4:7; And the peace of God, which passeth all understanding, shall keep your hearts and minds through Christ Jesus.

DARKNESS: Without knowledge of God's Word or God's Word being obscured.

I John 2:9; He that saith he is in the light, and hateth his brother, is in darkness even until now.

I John 2:10; He that loveth his brother abideth in the light, and there is none occasion of stumbling in him.

I John 2:11; But he that hateth his brother is in darkness, and walketh in darkness, and knoweth not whither he goeth, because that darkness hath blinded his eyes.

DARKENED: God's Word (Light) being removed or obscured. The air being darkened also implies the earth being tainted with Satan's evil doctrine.

Revelation 8:12; And the fourth angel sounded, and the third part of the sun was smitten, and the third part of the moon, and the third part of the stars; so as the third part of them was darkened, and the day shone not for a third part of it, and the night likewise.

Revelation 9:2; And he opened the bottomless pit; and there arose a smoke out of the pit, as the smoke of a great furnace; and the sun and the air were darkened by reason of the smoke of the pit.

DEFILED WITH WOMEN: Refers to Idolatry Worship or Spiritual Fornication.

Revelation 14:4; These are they which were not defiled with women; for they are virgins. These are they which follow the Lamb whithersoever he goeth. These were redeemed from among men, being the firstfruits unto God and to the Lamb

DIADEM: Signifies Royalty, Worn by Satan signifying him as ruler over evil.

DOOR (Open Door): Ability to enter, achieve or obtain something.

Revelation 3:8; I know thy works: behold, I have set before thee an open door, and no man can shut it: for thou hast a little strength, and hast kept my word, and hast not denied my name. (Revelation 4:1.)

DRAGON: Symbol of Satan (Serpent or Devil).

Revelation 12:4; And his tail drew the third part of the stars of heaven, and did cast them to the earth: and the dragon stood before the woman which was ready to be delivered, for to devour her child as soon as it was born. (Revelation 12:9.)

EAGLE: Signifies swiftness or speed and certainty of judgment.

Jeremiah 4:13; Behold, he shall come up as clouds, and his chariots shall be as a whirlwind: his horses are swifter than eagles. Woe unto us! for we are spoiled.

Jeremiah 49:22; Behold, he shall come up and fly as the eagle, and spread his wings over Bozrah: and at that day shall the heart of the mighty men of Edom be as the heart of a woman in her pangs.

Hosea 8:1. Set the trumpet to thy mouth. He shall come as an eagle against the house of the LORD, because they have transgressed my covenant, and trespassed against my law.

Also symbolizes protection by the Lord for His disciples.

Revelation 12:14; And to the woman were given two wings of a great eagle, that she might fly into the wilderness, into her place, where she is nourished for a time, and times, and half a time, from the face of the serpent.

Exodus 19:4; Ye have seen what I did unto the Egyptians, and how I bare you on eagles' wings, and brought you unto myself.

Deuteronomy 32:11; As an eagle stirreth up her nest, fluttereth over her young, spreadeth abroad her wings, taketh them, beareth them on her wings:

Isaiah 31:5; As birds flying, so will the LORD of hosts defend Jerusalem; defending also he will deliver it; and passing over he will preserve it.

EARTH: Symbolizes wilderness as Earth is unconquered spiritual territory and the battleground for the ongoing spiritual warfare between Christ and Satan.

Revelation 12:14; And to the woman were given two wings of a great eagle, that she might fly into the wilderness, into her place, where she is nourished for a time, and times, and half a time, from the face of the serpent.

Revelation 12:16; And the earth helped the woman, and the earth opened her mouth, and swallowed up the flood which the dragon cast out of his mouth.

EARTH BEAST: False Prophet that deceives many with Anti-Christian values.

Matthew 7:15; Beware of false prophets, which come to you in sheep's clothing, but inwardly they are ravening wolves.

Deuteronomy 13:1-5; If there arise among you a prophet, or a dreamer of dreams, and giveth thee a sign or a wonder, And the sign or the wonder come to pass, whereof he spake unto thee, saying, Let us go after other gods, which thou hast not known, and let us serve them; Thou shalt not hearken unto the words of that prophet, or that dreamer of dreams: for the LORD your God proveth you, to know whether ye love the LORD your God with all your heart and with all your soul. Ye shall walk after the LORD your God, and fear him, and keep his commandments, and obey his voice, and ye shall serve him, and cleave unto him. And that prophet, or that dreamer of dreams, shall be put to death; because he hath spoken to turn you away from the LORD your God, which brought you out of the land of Egypt, and redeemed you out of the house of bondage, to thrust thee out of the way which the LORD thy God commanded thee to walk in. So shalt thou put the evil away from the midst of thee.

Deuteronomy 18:20; But the prophet, which shall presume to speak a word in my name, which I have not commanded him to speak, or that shall speak in the name of other gods, even that prophet shall die.

Revelation 13:11; And I beheld another beast coming up out of the earth; and he had two horns like a lamb, and he spake as a dragon.

EARTHQUAKE: Judgment of God.

Isaiah 29:6; Thou shalt be visited of the Lord of hosts with thunder, and with earthquake, and great noise, with storm and tempest, and the flame of devouring fire.

Joel 3:16; The Lord also shall roar out of Zion, and utter his voice from Jerusalem; and the heavens and the earth shall shake:

Revelation 6:12; And I beheld when he had opened the sixth seal, and, lo, there was a great earthquake; and the sun became black as sackcloth of hair, and the moon became as blood; (Revelation 8:5; 11:13.)

EAST: The direction from which both the Lord God and Christ approach.

Ezekiel 43:2; And, behold, the glory of the God of Israel came from the way of the east: and his voice was like a noise of many waters: and the earth shined with his glory.

EUPHRATES: River designated as border of land given to descendants of Abraham by the Lord. Also, the great river Euphrates is used symbolically to depict the vast amount of false religion flowing from Babylon.

Genesis 15:18; In the same day the Lord made a covenant with Abram, saying, Unto thy seed have I given this land, from the river of Egypt unto the great river, the river Euphrates. (Deuteronomy 1:7; 11:24; Joshua 1:4; I Chronicles 5:9;)

Revelation 9:14; Saying to the sixth angel which had the trumpet, Loose the four angels which are bound in the great river Euphrates.

Revelation 16:12; And the sixth angel poured out his vial upon the great river Euphrates; and the water thereof was dried up, that the way of the kings of the east might be prepared.

EYES as a FLAME of FIRE: This refers to the ability to penetrate and discern a person's innermost thoughts.

Hebrews 4:13: Neither is there any creature that is not manifest in his sight: but all things are naked and opened unto the eyes of him with whom we have to do.

Revelation 1:14; His head and his hairs were white like wool, as white as snow; and his eyes were as a flame of fire;

FACE OF A MAN: Denotes Intelligence and also represents the tribe of Reuben.

Revelation 4:7; And the first beast was like a lion, and the second beast like a calf, and the third beast had a face as a man, and the fourth beast was like a flying eagle.

FALSE PROPHET: Teachers of evil or false doctrine.

Matthew 24:24; For there shall arise false Christs, and false prophets, and shall shew great signs and wonders; insomuch that, if it were possible, they shall deceive the very elect.

Jude 1:4,8,13,15-16; For there are certain men crept in unawares, who were before of old ordained to this condemnation, ungodly men, turning the grace of our God into lasciviousness, and denying the only Lord God, and our Lord Jesus Christ. Likewise also these filthy dreamers defile the flesh, despise dominion, and speak evil of dignities. Raging waves of the sea, foaming out their own shame; wandering stars, to whom is reserved the blackness of darkness for ever. To execute judgment upon all, and to convince all that are ungodly among them of all their ungodly deeds which they have ungodly committed, and of all their hard speeches which ungodly sinners have spoken against him. These are murmurers, complainers, walking after their own lusts; and their mouth speaketh great swelling words, having men's persons in admiration because of advantage.

Revelation 13:11; And I beheld another beast coming up out of the earth; and he had two horns like a lamb, and he spake as a dragon.

FAMINE: Method of Judgment by the Lord that denotes lacking the necessities of life.

Jeremiah 21:5; And I myself will fight against you with an outstretched hand and with a strong arm, even in anger, and in fury, and in great wrath. (Jeremiah 21:6-8)

Jeremiah 21:9-10; He that abideth in this city shall die by the sword, and by the famine, and by the pestilence: but he that goeth out, and falleth to the Chaldeans that besiege you, he shall live, and his life shall be unto him for a prey. For I have set my face against this city for evil, and not for good, saith the Lord: it shall be given into the hand of the king of Babylon, and he shall burn it with fire.

Revelation 6:8; And I looked, and behold a pale horse: and his name that sat on him was Death, and Hell followed with him. And power was given unto them over the fourth part of the earth, to kill with sword, and with hunger, and with death, and with the beasts of the earth. (Revelation 6:6.)

FAN: Instrument used to winnow grain.
Matthew 3:12; Whose fan is in his hand, and he will throughly purge his floor, and gather his wheat into the garner; but he will burn up the chaff with unquenchable fire.

FINE LINEN: Clothing made of this material signifies righteousness of saints.
Revelation 19:8; And to her was granted that she should be arrayed in fine linen, clean and white: for the fine linen is the righteousness of saints.

FIRE: Purification Process, Zechariah 13:9: **Fire to refine. (Burnt sacrifices used incense),** (Genesis 15:17; Exodus 3:2; 13:21; 19:18: indicates Divine Presence.)**
Revelation 4:5; And out of the throne proceeded lightnings and thunderings and voices: and there were seven lamps of fire burning before the throne, which are the seven Spirits of God. (**Represents ever-active omnipresence.)**

FIRE: Symbolizes Punishment by God.
Genesis 19:24; Then the Lord rained upon Sodom and upon Gomorrah brimstone and fire from the Lord out of heaven.
Exodus 9:23; And Moses stretched forth his rod toward heaven: and the Lord sent thunder and hail, and the fire ran along upon the ground; and the Lord rained hail upon the land of Egypt.
Isaiah 66:15; For, behold, the Lord will come with fire, and with his chariots like a whirlwind, to render his anger with fury, and his rebuke with flames of fire.
Jeremiah 5:14; Wherefore thus saith the Lord God of hosts, Because ye speak this word, behold, I will make my words in thy mouth fire, and this people wood, and it shall devour them. (**This verse also shows that Christ's battle against evil is being waged with the Word of God.)**
Revelation 8:5; And the angel took the censer, and filled it with fire of the altar, and cast it into the earth: and there were voices, and

thunderings, and lightnings, and an earthquake. (Revelation 8:7,8; 9:17,18; 20:9,10,14; 21:8.)

FIRE: Symbolizes Spiritual Destruction by Wickedness.

Isaiah 9:18; For wickedness burneth as the fire: it shall devour the briers and thorns, and shall kindle in the thickets of the forest, and they shall mount up like the lifting up of smoke.

FIRE BURNING: Represents ever-active omnipresence.

Revelation 4:5; And out of the throne proceeded lightnings and thunderings and voices: and there were seven lamps of fire burning before the throne, which are the seven Spirits of God.

FLYING EAGLE: Symbol of the tribe of Dan.

Revelation 4:7; And the first beast was like a lion, and the second beast like a calf, and the third beast had a face as a man, and the fourth beast was like a flying eagle.

FORNICATION: The act of worshiping any type of false religion as opposed to worshiping God.

FOUNTAIN OF WATERS: Represents the Source of Knowledge, Both Good and Evil.

REVELATION 8:10; And the third angel sounded, and there fell a great star from heaven, burning as it were a lamp, and it fell upon the third part of the rivers, and upon the fountains of waters; (Revelation 16:4.)

FROG: Unclean Spirits. Unclean/Abomination;

Leviticus 11:9-11; These shall ye eat of all that are in the waters: whatsoever hath fins and scales in the waters, in the seas, and in the rivers, them shall ye eat. And all that have not fins and scales in the seas, and in the rivers, of all that move in the waters, and of any living thing which is in the waters, they shall be an abomination unto you: They shall be even an abomination unto you; ye shall not eat of their flesh, but ye shall have their carcases in abomination.

Revelation 16:13; And I saw three unclean spirits like frogs come out of the mouth of the dragon, and out of the mouth of the beast, and out of the mouth of the false prophet.

GOG & MAGOG: Ezekiel 38; Evil Enemies of the Lord. In Ezekiel chapters 38 and 39 the Lord instructed Ezekiel to prophesy against Gog and Magog that when they came up against His people of Israel in the latter days that He would be

sanctified in them and His fury would come up in His face and in the fire of His wrath that all upon the earth would know that He was the Lord.

Revelation 20:8; And shall go out to deceive the nations which are in the four quarters of the earth, Gog, and Magog, to gather them together to battle: the number of whom is as the sand of the sea.

GOLDEN; Means Great Value. II Chronicles 4:19; And Solomon made all the vessels that were for the house of God, the golden altar also, and the tables whereon the shewbread was set; (II Chronicles 4:20-25.)

Revelation 1:12; And I turned to see the voice that spake with me. And being turned, I saw seven golden candlesticks; (Revelation 1:13; 8:3; 14:14.)

GRASS: Common People.

Isaiah 40:7; The grass withereth, the flower fadeth: because the spirit of the LORD bloweth upon it: surely the people is grass.

Revelation 8:7; The first angel sounded, and there followed hail and fire mingled with blood, and they were cast upon the earth: and the third part of trees was burnt up, and all green grass was burnt up.

Revelation 9:4; And it was commanded them that they should not hurt the grass of the earth, neither any green thing, neither any tree; but only those men which have not the seal of God in their foreheads.

GREAT VOICE: Identifies God as the speaker.

Revelation 16:17; And the seventh angel poured out his vial into the air; and there came a great voice out of the temple of heaven, from the throne, saying, It is done.

GREEN: Symbolizes a birth or renewing of Spiritual Life.

Revelation 9:4; And it was commanded them that they should not hurt the grass of the earth, neither any green thing, neither any tree; but only those men which have not the seal of God in their foreheads.

HAIL: Indicates one method of punishment by God.

Revelation 8:7; The first angel sounded, and there followed hail and fire mingled with blood, and they were cast upon the earth: and the third part of trees was burnt up, and all green grass was burnt up.

HALF AN HOUR; Very short period of time.

Habakkuk 2:20; But the LORD is in his holy temple: let all the earth keep silence before him.

Revelation 8:1; And when he had opened the seventh seal, there was silence in heaven about the space of half an hour.

HARLOT: Symbolizes the worship of false religion or idolatry worship as opposed to the worship of God.

Revelation 17:5; And upon her forehead was a name written, MYSTERY, BABYLON THE GREAT, THE MOTHER OF HARLOTS AND ABOMINATIONS OF THE EARTH.

HARP: Used to recognize and honor royalty and those in power with authority.

Revelation 5:8; And when he had taken the book, the four beasts and four and twenty elders fell down before the Lamb, having every one of them harps, and golden vials full of odours, which are the prayers of saints.

HEAT: Persecution from False Religion. Travails of sin.

Isaiah 4:6; And there shall be a tabernacle for a shadow in the day time from the heat, and for a place of refuge, and for a covert from storm and from rain.

Isaiah 25:4; For thou hast been a strength to the poor, a strength to the needy in his distress, a refuge from the storm, a shadow from the heat, when the blast of the terrible ones is as a storm against the wall.

Revelation 7:16; They shall hunger no more, neither thirst any more; neither shall the sun light on them, nor any heat.

HORN: Symbol of Power. (Daniel 8:7; Zechariah 1:18-21); **Denotes Power.** (Habakkuk 3:4); **God's Power.** (Daniel 7:7-24, 8:3,9,20,21.)

Revelation 12;3; And there appeared another wonder in heaven; and behold a great red dragon, having seven heads and ten horns, and seven crowns upon his heads.

(Revelation 13:1; 17:3,7,12,16): **Same Beast with many horns symbolize power through successive nations or rulers.**

Revelation 5:6; And I beheld, and, lo, in the midst of the throne and of the four beasts, and in the midst of the elders, stood a Lamb as it had been slain, having seven horns and seven eyes, which are the seven Spirits of God sent forth into all the earth. **Seven horns denote complete Power of Christ.**

Revelation 13:11; And I beheld another beast coming up out of the earth; and he had two horns like a lamb, and he spake as a dragon. **Earthly, lesser power than Satan.**

HORSE: Represents strength usually in war or battle.

Psalms 20:7;Some trust in chariots, and some in horses: but we will remember the name of the LORD our God.

Psalms 33:17; An horse is a vain thing for safety: neither shall he deliver any by his great strength. (II Kings 2:11; Job 39:19-25; Psalms 76:6.)

Proverbs 21:31; The horse is prepared against the day of battle: but safety is of the LORD.

Ezekiel 26:10-11; By reason of the abundance of his horses their dust shall cover thee: thy walls shall shake at the noise of the horsemen, and of the wheels, and of the chariots, when he shall enter into thy gates, as men enter into a city wherein is made a breach. With the hoofs of his horses shall he tread down all thy streets: he shall slay thy people by the sword, and thy strong garrisons shall go down to the ground.

Revelation 6:2; And I saw, and behold a white horse: and he that sat on him had a bow; and a crown was given unto him: and he went forth conquering, and to conquer.

Revelation 6:4; And there went out another horse that was red: and power was given to him that sat thereon to take peace from the earth, and that they should kill one another: and there was given unto him a great sword. (Revelation 6:5,8; 19:11.)

HOUR: Denotes short period of time.

Revelation 18:10; Standing afar off for the fear of her torment, saying, Alas, alas that great city Babylon, that mighty city! for in one hour is thy judgment come.

Revelation 18:17; For in one hour so great riches is come to nought. And every shipmaster, and all the company in ships, and sailors, and as many as trade by sea, stood afar off, *(Revelation 3:10.)*

INCENSE: Makes aroma more palatable and acceptable unto God. Smoke from burning incense raises prayers to heaven.

Luke 1:9-11; According to the custom of the priest's office, his lot was to burn incense when he went into the temple of the Lord. And the whole multitude of the people were praying without at the time of incense. And there appeared unto him an angel of the Lord standing on the right side of the altar of incense.

Revelation 8:3; And another angel came and stood at the altar, having a golden censer; and there was given unto him much incense, that he should offer it with the prayers of all saints upon the golden altar which was before the throne.

Revelation 8:4; And the smoke of the incense, which came with the prayers of the saints, ascended up before God out of the angel's hand. (Revelation 5:8.)

ISLES or ISLANDS: Far away distances.

Jeremiah 31:10; Hear the word of the LORD, O ye nations, and declare it in the isles afar off, and say, He that scattered Israel will gather him, and keep him, as a shepherd doth his flock.

Ezekiel 26:15,18; Thus saith the Lord GOD to Tyrus; Shall not the isles shake at the sound of thy fall, when the wounded cry, when the slaughter is made in the midst of thee?

Now shall the isles tremble in the day of thy fall; yea, the isles that are in the sea shall be troubled at thy departure.

Revelation 16:20. And every island fled away, and the mountains were not found.

JASPER STONE: A precious stone that is very hard reflecting durability and longevity. It usually comes in various shades of green indicating a rebirth or new beginning although some stones are a reddish brown or earth-tone color.

Ezekiel 28:13; Thou hast been in Eden the garden of God; every precious stone was thy covering, the sardius, topaz, and the diamond, the beryl, the onyx, and the jasper, the sapphire, the emerald, and the carbuncle, and gold: the workmanship of thy tabrets and of thy pipes was prepared in thee in the day that thou wast created. (Exodus 28:20; 39:13.)

Revelation 4:3; And he that sat was to look upon like a jasper and a sardine stone: and there was a rainbow round about the throne, in sight like unto an emerald.

Revelation 21:11; Having the glory of God: and her light was like unto a stone most precious, even like a jasper stone, clear as crystal; (Revelation 21:18,19.)

JERUSALEM: Symbolically deemed the abode of saints upon earth called "the camp of the saints", "the beloved city" and "the holy city".

Nehemiah 11:1; And the rulers of the people dwelt at Jerusalem: the rest of the people also cast lots, to bring one of ten to dwell in Jerusalem the holy city, and nine parts to dwell in other cities.

Isaiah 52:1; Awake, awake; put on thy strength, O Zion; put on thy beautiful garments, O Jerusalem, the holy city: for henceforth there shall no more come into thee the uncircumcised and the unclean.

Jeremiah 3:17; At that time they shall call Jerusalem the throne of the LORD; and all the nations shall be gathered unto it, to the name of the LORD, to Jerusalem: neither shall they walk any more after the imagination of their evil heart.

Revelation 20:9; And they went up on the breadth of the earth, and compassed the camp of the saints about, and the beloved city: and fire came down from God out of heaven, and devoured them.

KEY/KEYS: Indicates Authority, Control, or Power.

Isaiah 22:22; And the key of the house of David will I lay upon his shoulder; so he shall open, and none shall shut; and he shall shut, and none shall open.

Matthew 16:19; And I will give unto thee the keys of the kingdom of heaven: and whatsoever thou shalt bind on earth shall be bound in heaven: and whatsoever thou shalt loose on earth shall be loosed in heaven.

Revelation 1:18; I am he that liveth, and was dead; and, behold, I am alive for evermore, Amen; and have the keys of hell and of death.

Revelation 20:1; And I saw an angel come down from heaven, having the key of the bottomless pit and a great chain in his hand. (Revelation 9:1.)

LAKE of FIRE and BRIMSTONE: Place of eternal torment.

Genesis 19:24; Then the LORD rained upon Sodom and upon Gomorrah brimstone and fire from the LORD out of heaven;

Revelation 19:20; And the beast was taken, and with him the false prophet that wrought miracles before him, with which he deceived them that had received the mark of the beast, and them that worshipped his image. These both were cast alive into a lake of fire burning with brimstone.

Revelation 20:10; And the devil that deceived them was cast into the lake of fire and brimstone, where the beast and the false prophet are, and shall be tormented day and night for ever and ever. (Revelation 20:14.)

LAMB: Religious Symbol denoting Purity, Meekness, and without Sin.

Because the Lamb does not physically fight, even in self-defense, it is the perfect symbol of the ongoing battle between Christ and Satan as it indicates that this is not a physical battle but, rather, a spiritual one.

Isaiah 53:7; He was oppressed, and he was afflicted, yet he opened not his mouth: he is brought as a lamb to the slaughter, and as a sheep before her shearers is dumb, so he openeth not his mouth.

Acts 8:32; The place of the scripture which he read was this, He was led as a sheep to the slaughter; and like a lamb dumb before his shearer, so opened he not his mouth:

Revelation 5:6; And I beheld, and, lo, in the midst of the throne and of the four beasts, and in the midst of the elders, stood a Lamb as it had been slain, having seven horns and seven eyes, which are the seven Spirits of God sent forth into all the earth. (Revelation 5:12,13; 6:16; 7:17; 14:1,10; 21:14 22:1,3.)

LAMB of GOD: Jesus Christ. Indicates subjectivity to God.

John 1:29; The next day John seeth Jesus coming unto him, and saith, Behold the Lamb of God, which taketh away the sin of the world. (John 1:36;)

Revelation 7:10; And cried with a loud voice, saying, Salvation to our God which sitteth upon the throne, and unto the Lamb. (Revelation 7:14; 12:10; 14:4; 15:3: 19:9; 21:22-23: 22:1,3.)

LIGHT: Imparting of knowledge, both good and evil. Also, knowledge of God's Word.

Job 33:30; To bring back his soul from the pit, to be enlightened with the light of the living.

Revelation 22:5; And there shall be no night there; and they need no candle, neither light of the sun; for the Lord God giveth them light: and they shall reign for ever and ever.

LIGHTNINGS, VOICES, THUNDERINGS, EARTHQUAKE, and GREAT HAIL: Represents God's Power and Judgments.

Isaiah 29:6: Thou shalt be visited of the Lord of hosts with thunder, and with earthquake, and great noise, with storm and tempest, and the flame of devouring fire.

(Exodus 19:16; Job 26:14, 37:4; Psalms 29:3; John 12:29.)

Revelation 11:19; And the temple of God was opened in heaven, and there was seen in his temple the ark of his testament: and there were lightnings, and voices, and thunderings, and an earthquake, and great hail.

LIVING CREATURES: Cherubims: (Also called beasts in KJV)

Ezekiel 1:5; Also out of the midst thereof came the likeness of four living creatures. And this was their appearance; they had the likeness of a man.

Ezekiel 11:22; Then did the cherubims lift up their wings, and the wheels beside them; and the glory of the God of Israel was over them above.

Revelation 4:6; And before the throne there was a sea of glass like unto crystal: and in the midst of the throne, and round about the throne, were four beasts full of eyes before and behind. (Revelation 4:7-9; 5:6,8,11,14; 6:1,6-7.)

LION: Signifies great strength, bravery, cunning, stealth, and ferocity in battle. Also, represents the symbol of the tribe of Judah.

Judges 14:18; And the men of the city said unto him on the seventh day before the sun went down, What is sweeter than honey? And what is stronger than a lion? and he said unto them, If ye had not plowed with my heifer, ye had not found out my riddle.

(II Samuel 17:10; I Chronicles 12:8; Psalms 7:2.)

Psalms 10:9; He lieth in wait secretly as a lion in his den: he lieth in wait to catch the poor: he doth catch the poor, when he draweth him into his net. (Psalms 17:12; Proverbs 19:12; Lamentations 3:10; Hosea 5:14.)

I Peter 5:8; Be sober, be vigilant; because your adversary the devil, as a roaring lion, walketh about, seeking whom he may devour:

Revelation 4:7; And the first beast was like a lion, and the second beast like a calf, and the third beast had a face as a man, and the fourth beast was like a flying eagle. (Revelation 5:5; 13:2.)

LOCUSTS: Devastation, to devour. Symbolizes destruction of green herbs which are symbols of spiritual life.

Exodus 10:4,14; Else, if thou refuse to let my people go, behold, tomorrow will I bring the locusts into thy coast. And the locusts went up over all the land of Egypt, and rested in all the coasts of Egypt: very grievous were they: before them there were no such locusts as they, neither after them shall be such.

II Chronicles 7:13; If I shut up heaven that there be no rain, or if I command the locusts to devour the land, or if I send pestilence among my people;

Revelation 9:3; And there came out of the smoke locusts upon the earth: and unto them was given power, as the scorpions of the earth have power.

LOUD VOICE/GREAT VOICE: Announcements of change or warnings of judgments. The adjectives loud and great signify enough volume as insurance that all will hear the message.

Revelation 8:13; And I beheld, and heard an angel flying through the midst of heaven, saying with a loud voice, Woe, woe, woe, to the inhabiters of the earth by reason of the other voices of the trumpet of the three angels, which are yet to sound!

Revelation 10:3; And cried with a loud voice, as when a lion roareth: and when he had cried, seven thunders uttered their voices. (Revelation 10:4.)

Revelation 11:15; And the seventh angel sounded; and there were great voices in heaven, saying, The kingdoms of this world are become the kingdoms of our Lord, and of his Christ; and he shall reign for ever and ever.

Revelation 16:17; And the seventh angel poured out his vial into the air; and there came a great voice out of the temple of heaven, from the throne, saying, It is done.

MADE DRUNK: Enticed, lured, or led away spiritually unto damnation.

Isaiah 51:17; Awake, awake, stand up, O Jerusalem, which hast drunk at the hand of the LORD the cup of his fury; thou hast drunken the dregs of the cup of trembling, and wrung them out.

Revelation 18:3; For all nations have drunk of the wine of the wrath of her fornication, and the kings of the earth have committed fornication with her, and the merchants of the earth are waxed rich through the abundance of her delicacies.

MAN-CHILD: Jesus Christ.

Revelation 12:5; And she brought forth a man child, who was to rule all nations with a rod of iron: and her child was caught up unto God, and to his throne.

MILLSTONE: Symbolizes severe punishment.

Judges 9:53; And a certain woman cast a piece of a millstone upon Abimelech's head, and all to brake his skull. (II Samuel 11:21.)

Matthew 18:6; But whoso shall offend one of these little ones which believe in me, it were better for him that a millstone were hanged about his neck, and that he were drowned in the depth of the sea. (Mark 9:42; Luke 17:2.)

Revelation 18:21; And a mighty angel took up a stone like a great millstone, and cast it into the sea, saying, Thus with violence shall that great city Babylon be thrown down, and shall be found no more at all.

MOON: Symbol of the light of God's Word through the Mosaic Law. It is also reflective of their civil government as their government ruled their society based upon the Mosaic Law.

Genesis 1:15-17; And let them be for lights in the firmament of the heaven to give light upon the earth: and it was so. And God made two great lights; the greater light to rule the day, and the lesser light to rule the night: he made the stars also. And God set them in the firmament of the heaven to give light upon the earth,

The moon is the lesser light of God's Word with this light being reflective of the true light of the sun disappearing and being replaced by the coming light of the sun. This is reflective of the system of worship under the Mosaic Law being replaced by the establishment of the Kingdom of Christ.

Galatians 3:23-24; But before faith came, we were kept under the law, shut up unto the faith which should afterwards be revealed.

Wherefore the law was our schoolmaster to bring us unto Christ, that we might be justified by faith.

Isaiah 13:9-11; Behold, the day of the LORD cometh, cruel both with wrath and fierce anger, to lay the land desolate: and he shall destroy the sinners thereof out of it. For the stars of heaven and the constellations thereof shall not give their light: the sun shall be darkened in his going forth, and the moon shall not cause her light to shine. And I will punish the world for their evil, and the wicked for their iniquity; and I will cause the arrogancy of the proud to cease, and will lay low the haughtiness of the terrible.

Isaiah 24:21; And it shall come to pass in that day, that the Lord shall punish the host of the high ones that are on high, and the kings of the earth upon the earth.

Isaiah 60:19-20; The sun shall be no more thy light by day; neither for brightness shall the moon give light unto thee: but the LORD shall be unto thee an everlasting light, and thy God thy glory. Thy sun shall no more go down; neither shall thy moon withdraw itself: for the LORD shall be thine everlasting light, and the days of thy mourning shall be ended.

Ezekiel 32:7; And when I shall put thee out, I will cover the heaven, and make the stars thereof dark; I will cover the sun with a cloud, and the moon shall not give her light.

Joel 2:10,31; The earth shall quake before them; the heavens shall tremble: the sun and the moon shall be dark, and the stars shall withdraw their shining. The sun shall be turned into darkness, and the moon into blood, before the great and the terrible day of the Lord come.

Revelation 12:1; And there appeared a great wonder in heaven; a woman clothed with the sun, and the moon under her feet, and upon her head a crown of twelve stars: (Revelation 6:12;)

MORNING STAR: Jesus Christ.

Matthew 2:2; Saying, Where is he that is born King of the Jews? for we have seen his star in the east, and are come to worship him. (II Peter 1:19)

Revelation 2:28; And I will give him the morning star.

MOUNTAINS: In Hebrew literature, mountains are sometimes used to indicate kingdoms. Also is symbolic of everlasting.

Jeremiah 51:24-25; And I will render unto Babylon and to all the inhabitants of Chaldea all their evil that they have done in Zion in your sight, saith the Lord. Behold, I am against thee, O destroying mountain, saith the Lord, which destroyest all the earth: and I will stretch out mine hand upon thee, and roll thee down from the rocks, and will make thee a burnt mountain.

Revelation 6:14; And the heaven departed as a scroll when it is rolled together; and every mountain and island were moved out of their places.

Revelation 8:8; And the second angel sounded, and as it were a great mountain burning with fire was cast into the sea: and the third part of the sea became blood;

Revelation 16:20; And every island fled away, and the mountains were not found.

Also, representative of the strong foundation of Earth: (Genesis 49:26; Deuteronomy 33:15; Job 15:7; Habakkuk 3:6.) **Mountains are creation of God and show God's power:** (Psalms 18:7; 97:5; Isaiah 40:12; 41:15; 54:10; Jeremiah 4:24; Nahum 1:5; Habakkuk 3:6.) **Holy Mountain:** (Daniel 9;20.)

NEW JERUSALEM: The Church of Christ or Kingdom of Christ. The new place of abode in heaven for the saints also called "the holy city".

Revelation 21:2; And I John saw the holy city, new Jerusalem, coming down from God out of heaven, prepared as a bride adorned for her husband.

NEW SONG: Means to honor and recognize achievement.

Isaiah 42:10; Sing unto the Lord a new song, and his praise from the end of the earth, ye that go down to the sea, and all that is therein; the isles, and the inhabitants thereof.

Revelation 5:9; And they sung a new song, saying, Thou art worthy to take the book, and to open the seals thereof: for thou wast slain, and hast redeemed us to God by thy blood out of every kindred, and tongue, and people, and nation;

Revelation 14:3; And they sung as it were a new song before the throne, and before the four beasts, and the elders: and no man could learn that song but the hundred and forty and four thousand, which were redeemed from the earth.

ONE HOUR: Denotes short period of time.

Daniel 3:6; And whoso falleth not down and worshippeth shall the same hour be cast into the midst of a burning fiery furnace. (Daniel 3:15; 4:19,33; 5:5.)

Matthew 8:13; And Jesus said unto the centurion, *Go thy way; and as thou hast believed, so be it done unto thee*. And his servant was healed in the selfsame hour. (Matthew 9:22; 10:19; 15:28; 17:18; 26:40.)

Revelation 17:12; And the ten horns which thou sawest are ten kings, which have received no kingdom as yet; but receive power as kings one hour with the beast.

Revelation 18:10; Standing afar off for the fear of her torment, saying, Alas, alas that great city Babylon, that mighty city! for in one hour is thy judgment come.

Revelation 18:17; For in one hour so great riches is come to nought. And every shipmaster, and all the company in ships, and sailors, and as many as trade by sea, stood afar off,

OX: Beast of burden, work; Also, is the ensign of the tribe of Ephraim. (Ox or Calf)

Exodus 23:12; Six days thou shalt do thy work, and on the seventh day thou shalt rest: that thine ox and thine ass may rest, and the son of thy handmaid, and the stranger, may be refreshed.

Revelation 4:7; And the first beast was like a lion, and the second beast like a calf, and the third beast had a face as a man, and the fourth beast was like a flying eagle.

PALE HORSE: Symbol of Death.

Revelation 6:8; And I looked, and behold a pale horse: and his name that sat on him was Death, and Hell followed with him. And power was given unto them over the fourth part of the earth, to kill with sword, and with hunger, and with death, and with the beasts of the earth.

PALM LEAF/PALM BRANCH: Symbol used to recognize and honor royalty.

Leviticus 23:40; And ye shall take you on the first day the boughs of goodly trees, branches of palm trees, and the boughs of thick trees, and willows of the brook; and ye shall rejoice before the Lord your God seven days.

Ezekiel 41:18; And it was made with cherubims and palm trees, so that a palm tree was between a cherub and a cherub; and every cherub had two faces.

John 12:13; Took branches of palm trees, and went forth to meet him, and cried, Hosanna: Blessed is the King of Israel that cometh in the name of the Lord.

Revelation 7:9; After this I beheld, and, lo, a great multitude, which no man could number, of all nations, and kindreds, and people, and tongues, stood before the throne, and before the Lamb, clothed with white robes, and palms in their hands;

PEARL: Symbol of great spiritual value worth more than all material wealth.

Matthew 13:45-46; Again, the kingdom of heaven is like unto a merchant man, seeking goodly pearls: Who, when he had found one pearl of great price, went and sold all that he had, and bought it.

Revelation 21:21; And the twelve gates were twelve pearls: every several gate was of one pearl: and the street of the city was pure gold, as it were transparent glass. (Revelation 18:12.)

PERDITION: Eternal Spiritual Damnation and Destruction.

II Peter 3:7; But the heavens and the earth, which are now, by the same word are kept in store, reserved unto fire against the day of judgment and perdition of ungodly men. (John 17:12; Philippians 1:28; II Thessalonians 2:3; I Timothy 6:9; Hebrews 10:39.)

Revelation 17:8; The beast that thou sawest was, and is not; and shall ascend out of the bottomless pit, and go into perdition: and they that dwell on the earth shall wonder, whose names were not written in the book of life from the foundation of the world, when they behold the beast that was, and is not, and yet is. (Revelation 17:11.)

PESTILENCE: Method of Judgment by the Lord.

Jeremiah 21:5-10. Jeremiah 21:6; And I will smite the inhabitants of this city, both man and beast: they shall die of a great pestilence.

PRINCE OF PEACE: Christ.

Isaiah 9:6; For unto us a child is born, unto us a son is given: and the government shall be upon his shoulder: and his name shall be called Wonderful, Counsellor, The mighty God, The everlasting Father, The Prince of Peace.

PRINCE OF THE AIR: Satan.

Ephesians 2:2;Wherein in time past ye walked according to the course of this world, according to the prince of the power of the air, the spirit that now worketh in the children of disobedience:

PRINCE OF THIS WORLD: Satan.

John 12:31; Now is the judgment of this world: now shall the prince of this world be cast out.

John 16:11; Of judgment, because the prince of this world is judged.

PURPLE: Represents royalty such as a king or leader.

Mark 15:17-18; And they clothed him with purple, and platted a crown of thorns, and put it about his head, And began to salute him, Hail, King of the Jews!

Revelation 17:4; And the woman was arrayed in purple and scarlet colour, and decked with gold and precious stones and pearls, having a golden cup in her hand full of abominations and filthiness of her fornication: (Revelation 18:12,16.)

RAINBOW: Represents God's covenant with all living creatures and God's promise of hope and mercy. A rainbow has seven colors in the spectrum.

Genesis 9:12-13. And God said, This is the token of the covenant which I make between me and you and every living creature that is with you, for perpetual generations; I do set my bow in the cloud, and it shall be for a token of a covenant between me and the earth.

Revelation 4:3; And he that sat was to look upon like a jasper and a sardine stone: and there was a rainbow round about the throne, in sight like unto an emerald. (Genesis 9:14-17.)

RED: Color that represents spiritual bloodshed, death, sins, and warfare. Also used to identify sins.

Isaiah 1:18; Come now, and let us reason together, saith the Lord: though your sins be as scarlet, they shall be as white as snow; though they be red like crimson, they shall be as wool.

Revelation 6:4; And there went out another horse that was red: and power was given to him that sat thereon to take peace from the earth, and that they should kill one another: and there was given unto him a great sword.

Revelation 12:3; And there appeared another wonder in heaven; and behold a great red dragon, having seven heads and ten horns, and seven crowns upon his heads.

REED: Instrument used for measurement. Symbolically used to determine the capability of the temple of God to withstand persecution from the Gentiles.

Ezekiel 40:3; And he brought me thither, and, behold, there was a man, whose appearance was like the appearance of brass, with a line of flax in his hand, and a measuring reed; and he stood in the gate.

Habakkuk 3:6; He stood, and measured the earth: he beheld, and drove asunder the nations; and the everlasting mountains were scattered, the perpetual hills did bow: his ways are everlasting.

Revelation 11:1; And there was given me a reed like unto a rod: and the angel stood, saying, Rise, and measure the temple of God, and the altar, and them that worship therein. (Revelation 21:15,16.)

RIGHT HAND: Place or position of prominence.

Psalms 110:1; The Lord said unto my Lord, Sit thou at my right hand, until I make thine enemies thy footstool.

Matthew 22:44; The Lord said unto my Lord, Sit thou on my right hand, till I make thine enemies thy footstool?

Acts 2:33; Therefore being by the right hand of God exalted, and having received of the Father the promise of the Holy Ghost, he hath shed forth this, which ye now see and hear.

Revelation 1:16; And he had in his right hand seven stars: and out of his mouth went a sharp twoedged sword: and his countenance was as the sun shineth in his strength.

RIVER: Represents the flowing of knowledge, either good or evil knowledge.

Isaiah 8:5-8; The LORD spake also unto me again, saying, Forasmuch as this people refuseth the waters of Shiloah that go softly, and rejoice in Rezin and Remaliah's son; Now therefore, behold, the Lord bringeth up upon them the waters of the river, strong and many, even the king of Assyria, and all his glory: and he shall come up over all his channels, and go over all his banks: And he shall pass through Judah; he shall overflow and go over, he shall reach even to the neck; and the stretching out of his wings shall fill the breadth of thy land, O Immanuel.

Revelation 16:12; And the sixth angel poured out his vial upon the great river Euphrates; and the water thereof was dried up, that the way of the kings of the east might be prepared. (Revelation 16:4.)

ROD OF IRON: To maintain strict control and firmly govern people or nations with God's Word. A rod was used by shepherds when attending their flocks to control the animals and to defend them from wild beasts. A rod or sceptre was also used by a ruler or king to symbolize authority.

Psalms 2:9; Thou shalt break them with a rod of iron; thou shalt dash them in pieces like a potter's vessel.

Hebrews 1:8; But unto the Son he saith, Thy throne, O God, is for ever and ever: a sceptre of righteousness is the sceptre of thy kingdom.

Revelation 2:27; And he shall rule them with a rod of iron; as the vessels of a potter shall they be broken to shivers: even as I received of my Father. (Revelation 12:5; 19:15.)

SCARLET: Represents Evil Ruler or Prestige. The word scarlet is also used to describe the multitude and severity of sins as it is symbolic for the word "double". This refers to the process of dying clothes scarlet as it required the clothing to be dyed twice.

Isaiah 1:18; Come now, and let us reason together, saith the Lord: though your sins be as scarlet, they shall be as white as snow; though they be red like crimson, they shall be as wool. (Lamentations 4:5.)

Revelation 17:3; So he carried me away in the spirit into the wilderness: and I saw a woman sit upon a scarlet coloured beast, full of names of blasphemy, having seven heads and ten horns. (Revelation 17:4; 18:12,16.)

SCORPION: Reflects Spiritual pain and torment.

Deuteronomy 8:15; Who led thee through that great and terrible wilderness, wherein were fiery serpents, and scorpions, and drought, where there was no water; who brought thee forth water out of the rock of flint;

I Kings 12:11; And now whereas my father did lade you with a heavy yoke, I will add to your yoke: my father hath chastised you with whips, but I will chastise you with scorpions.

Revelation 9:5; And to them it was given that they should not kill them, but that they should be tormented five months: and their torment was as the torment of a scorpion, when he striketh a man. (Revelation 9:3,10.)

SEA: Represents a great number of people, a multitude of nations, or the immense volume of evil power of the beast that is adverse to Christ's kingdom.

Isaiah 17:12-13; Woe to the multitude of many people, which make a noise like the noise of the seas; and to the rushing of nations, that make a rushing like the rushing of mighty waters! The nations shall rush like the rushing of many waters: but God shall rebuke them, and they shall flee far off, and shall be chased as the chaff of the mountains before the wind, and like a rolling thing before the whirlwind.

Isaiah 57:20; But the wicked are like the troubled sea, when it cannot rest, whose waters cast up mire and dirt.

Ezekiel 26:16; Then all the princes of the sea shall come down from their thrones, and lay away their robes, and put off their broidered garments: they shall clothe themselves with trembling; they shall sit upon the ground, and shall tremble at every moment, and be astonished at thee.

Revelation 13:1; And I stood upon the sand of the sea, and saw a beast rise up out of the sea, having seven heads and ten horns, and upon his horns ten crowns, and upon his heads the name of blasphemy. (Revelation 16:3.)

SEA BEAST: Relates to a succession and multitude of Anti-Christian empires or nations affecting an immense number of people with false worship such as idolatry or emperor worship.

Isaiah 17:12-13; Woe to the multitude of many people, which make a noise like the noise of the seas; and to the rushing of nations, that make a rushing like the rushing of mighty waters! The nations shall rush like the rushing of many waters: but God shall rebuke them, and they shall flee far off, and shall be chased as the chaff of the mountains before the wind, and like a rolling thing before the whirlwind.

Isaiah 57:20; But the wicked are like the troubled sea, when it cannot rest, whose waters cast up mire and dirt.

Revelation 13:1; And I stood upon the sand of the sea, and saw a beast rise up out of the sea, having seven heads and ten horns, and upon his horns ten crowns, and upon his heads the name of blasphemy.

SEA OF GLASS: Represents transparency. Upon the death of Jesus Christ the veil of the temple was rent symbolizing that Levitical priests were no longer needed to offer sacrifices for us as we are now able to approach God directly in prayer through Christ. We are now no longer blinded by the veil of separation.
II Corinthians 3:16,18; Nevertheless when it shall turn to the Lord, the vail shall be taken away. But we all, with open face beholding as in a glass the glory of the Lord, are changed into the same image from glory to glory, even as by the Spirit of the Lord.
Revelation 4:6; And before the throne there was a sea of glass like unto crystal: and in the midst of the throne, and round about the throne, were four beasts full of eyes before and behind.
Revelation 15:2; And I saw as it were a sea of glass mingled with fire: and them that had gotten the victory over the beast, and over his image, and over his mark, and over the number of his name, stand on the sea of glass, having the harps of God.

SEAL: To close tightly and/or to restrict.
Revelation 20:3; And cast him into the bottomless pit, and shut him up, and set a seal upon him, that he should deceive the nations no more, till the thousand years should be fulfilled: and after that he must be loosed a little season.
Revelation 22:10; And he saith unto me, Seal not the sayings of the prophecy of this book: for the time is at hand.

SEAL or SEALED OF GOD: Reflects ownership of whatever is sealed.
Revelation 7:3; Saying, Hurt not the earth, neither the sea, nor the trees, till we have sealed the servants of our God in their foreheads. (Revelation 7:4-8.)
Revelation 9:4; And it was commanded them that they should not hurt the grass of the earth, neither any green thing, neither any tree; but only those men which have not the seal of God in their foreheads.

SEAL/SEALS: To keep hidden whatever is manifested and under the control of the person who keeps it hidden. The following verses using the word "seals" reflects determinations by God of the judgments to be given to Christ to implement upon earth.

Daniel 12:4; But thou, O Daniel, shut up the words, and seal the book, even to the time of the end: many shall run to and fro, and knowledge shall be increased.

Revelation 5:1; And I saw in the right hand of him that sat on the throne a book written within and on the backside, sealed with seven seals. (Revelation 5:2,9; 6:1,3,5,7,9,12; 7:2; 8:1; 10:4.)

SECOND DEATH: Spiritual death, loss of salvation in heaven. The first death is loss of physical life.

Revelation 2:11; He that hath an ear, let him hear what the Spirit saith unto the churches; He that overcometh shall not be hurt of the second death.

Revelation 20:6; Blessed and holy is he that hath part in the first resurrection: on such the second death hath no power, but they shall be priests of God and of Christ, and shall reign with him a thousand years. (Revelation 20:14; 21:8.)

SERAPHIM: Angel of High Rank and Servant of Deity.

Isaiah 6:2, 6; Above it stood the seraphims: each one had six wings; with twain he covered his face, and with twain he covered his feet, and with twain he did fly.

SHARP TWO-EDGED SWORD: God's Word used both for salvation and judgment (Two-Edged).

Hebrews 4:12; For the word of God is quick, and powerful, and sharper than any two-edged sword, piercing even to the dividing asunder of soul and spirit, and of the joints and marrow, and is a discerner of the thoughts and intents of the heart. (Psalms 149:6-9. Ephesians 6:17.)

Revelation 1:16; And he had in his right hand seven stars: and out of his mouth went a sharp twoedged sword: and his countenance was as the sun shineth in his strength.

SICKLE: Symbol for the time of judgment. To reap or harvest the Christians on judgment day.

Joel 3:13; Put ye in the sickle, for the harvest is ripe: come, get you down; for the press is full, the vats overflow; for their wickedness is great.

Mark 4:29; But when the fruit is brought forth, immediately he putteth in the sickle, because the harvest is come.

Revelation 14:14; And I looked, and behold a white cloud, and upon the cloud one sat like unto the Son of man, having on his head a golden crown, and in his hand a sharp sickle. (Revelation 14:15,16,17,18,19.)

SMOKE: Reflects prayers ascending to heaven.

Revelation 8:4; And the smoke of the incense, which came with the prayers of the saints, ascended up before God out of the angel's hand.

SMOKE: Indicates the starting or rising up of an entity to begin an agenda. As an evil entity obscures the true doctrine of God usually by deceit.

Revelation 9:2; And he opened the bottomless pit; and there arose a smoke out of the pit, as the smoke of a great furnace; and the sun and the air were darkened by reason of the smoke of the pit. (Revelation 9:3.)

Revelation 9:18; By these three was the third part of men killed, by the fire, and by the smoke, and by the brimstone, which issued out of their mouths. (Revelation 9:2, 17.)

SORCERY: Witchcraft.

Acts 8:9; But there was a certain man, called Simon, which beforetime in the same city used sorcery, and bewitched the people of Samaria, giving out that himself was some great one.

Revelation 18:23; And the light of a candle shall shine no more at all in thee; and the voice of the bridegroom and of the bride shall be heard no more at all in thee: for thy merchants were the great men of the earth; for by thy sorceries were all nations deceived. (Revelation 21:8.)

STAR or STARS: Represents rulers, leaders, or those in authority, either Ecclesiastical or Civil Government.

Numbers 24:17; I shall see him, but not now: I shall behold him, but not nigh: there shall come a Star out of Jacob, and a Sceptre shall rise out of Israel, and shall smite the corners of Moab, and destroy all the children of Sheth.

Ezekiel 32:7; And when I shall put thee out, I will cover the heaven, and make the stars thereof dark; I will cover the sun with a cloud, and the moon shall not give her light.

Matthew 24:29; Immediately after the tribulation of those days shall the sun be darkened, and the moon shall not give her light, and the stars shall fall from heaven, and the powers of the heavens shall be shaken:

Jude 1:13; Raging waves of the sea, foaming out their own shame; wandering stars, to whom is reserved the blackness of darkness for ever.

Revelation 6:13; And the stars of heaven fell unto the earth, even as a fig tree casteth her untimely figs, when she is shaken of a mighty wind. (Revelation 12:1.)

SUN: Represents religion through the Word of God. The Word of God is represented as light and as the sun is the greatest physical purveyor of light unto the world, it became representative of the Word of God and His Religion.

Psalms 84:11; For the LORD God is a sun and shield: the LORD will give grace and glory: no good thing will he withhold from them that walk uprightly.

Ezekiel 32:7-8; And when I shall put thee out, I will cover the heaven, and make the stars thereof dark; I will cover the sun with a cloud, and the moon shall not give her light. All the bright lights of heaven will I make dark over thee, and set darkness upon thy land, saith the Lord GOD.

Isaiah 59:19; So shall they fear the name of the LORD from the west, and his glory from the rising of the sun. When the enemy shall come in like a flood, the Spirit of the LORD shall lift up a standard against him.

Isaiah 60:19-20; The sun shall be no more thy light by day; neither for brightness shall the moon give light unto thee: but the LORD shall be unto thee an everlasting light, and thy God thy glory. Thy sun shall no more go down; neither shall thy moon withdraw itself: for the LORD shall be thine everlasting light, and the days of thy mourning shall be ended.

Jeremiah 31:35-36; Thus saith the LORD, which giveth the sun for a light by day, and the ordinances of the moon and of the stars for a light by night, which divideth the sea when the waves thereof roar; The LORD of hosts is his name: If those ordinances depart from before me, saith the LORD, then the seed of Israel also shall cease from being a nation before me for ever.

Malachi 4:2; But unto you that fear my name shall the Sun of righteousness arise with healing in his wings; and ye shall go forth, and grow up as calves of the stall.

Matthew 17:2; And was transfigured before them: and his face did shine as the sun, and his raiment was white as the light.

Matthew 24:29; Immediately after the tribulation of those days shall the sun be darkened, and the moon shall not give her light, and the stars shall fall from heaven, and the powers of the heavens shall be shaken:

John 8:12; Then spake Jesus again unto them, saying, *I am the light of the world: he that followeth me shall not walk in darkness, but shall have the light of life.*

II Corinthians 4:6; For God, who commanded the light to shine out of darkness, hath shined in our hearts, to give the light of the knowledge of the glory of God in the face of Jesus Christ.

Revelation 1:16; And he had in his right hand seven stars: and out of his mouth went a sharp twoedged sword: and his countenance was as the sun shineth in his strength.

Revelation 12:1; And there appeared a great wonder in heaven; a woman clothed with the sun, and the moon under her feet, and upon her head a crown of twelve stars: (Revelation 6:12; 16:8.)

THIRD PART: Hebrew terminology that simply means a large quantity and is symbolic of what is to be lost on Judgment Day.

Ezekiel 5:2; Thou shalt burn with fire a third part in the midst of the city, when the days of the siege are fulfilled: and thou shalt take a third part, and smite about it with a knife: and a third part thou shalt scatter in the wind; and I will draw out a sword after them.

Zechariah 13:8; And it shall come to pass, that in all the land, saith the LORD, two parts therein shall be cut off and die; but the third shall be left therein.

Revelation 8:12; And the fourth angel sounded, and the third part of the sun was smitten, and the third part of the moon, and the third part of the stars; so as the third part of them was darkened, and the day shone not for a third part of it, and the night likewise. (Revelation 8:7,8,9,10,11; 9:15,18; 12:4.)

THRONE: Seat of power or authority.

Isaiah 6:1; 66:1; Thus saith the Lord, The heaven is my throne, and the earth is my footstool: (Genesis 41:40; I Kings 2:19; 22:19; I Chronicles 29:23; Job 36:7; Psalms 11:4; Ezekiel 1:26; Zechariah 6:13.)

Matthew 5:34; But I say unto you, Swear not at all; neither by heaven; for it is God's throne.

Revelation 4:2; And immediately I was in the spirit: and, behold, a throne was set in heaven, and one sat on the throne. (Revelation 4:3,4,5,6,9,10; 5:1,6,7,11,13; 7:15,17; 14:3,5; 20:4; 21:5; 22:3.)

THUNDER: Implies loud volume which denotes power and authority. Sound is louder and stronger than other sounds.

Job 26:14; Lo, these are parts of his ways: but how little a portion is heard of him? But the thunder of his power who can understand? (Job 40:9.)

Revelation 6:1; And I saw when the Lamb opened one of the seals, and I heard, as it were the noise of thunder, one of the four beasts saying, Come and see.

Revelation 14:2; And I heard a voice from heaven, as the voice of many waters, and as the voice of a great thunder: and I heard the voice of harpers harping with their harps:

THUNDERINGS: God's Judgments.

Exodus 9:28; Intreat the LORD (for it is enough) that there be no more mighty thunderings and hail; and I will let you go, and ye shall stay no longer.

Revelation 8:5; And the angel took the censer, and filled it with fire of the altar, and cast it into the earth: and there were voices, and thunderings, and lightnings, and an earthquake. (Revelation 4:5; 11:19.)

TREES: Leaders. Those in authority.

Daniel 4:20,22; The tree that thou sawest, which grew, and was strong, whose height reached unto the heaven, and the sight thereof to all the earth; It is thou, O king, that art grown and become strong: for thy greatness is grown, and reacheth unto heaven, and thy dominion to the end of the earth.

Revelation 8:7; The first angel sounded, and there followed hail and fire mingled with blood, and they were cast upon the earth: and the third part of trees was burnt up, and all green grass was burnt up.

Revelation 9:4; And it was commanded them that they should not hurt the grass of the earth, neither any green thing, neither any tree; but only those men which have not the seal of God in their foreheads.

TRUMPET: To sound an alarm, alert or notify people of an immediate upcoming event or message by one with authority.

Leviticus 25:9; Then shalt thou cause the trumpet of the jubilee to sound on the tenth day of the seventh month, in the day of atonement shall ye make the trumpet sound throughout all your land.

Numbers 10:4-5; And if they blow but with one trumpet, then the princes, which are heads of the thousands of Israel, shall gather themselves unto thee. When ye blow an alarm, then the camps that lie on the east parts shall go forward.

II Samuel 6:15; So David and all the house of Israel brought up the ark of the Lord with shouting, and with the sound of the trumpet.

Revelation 8:2; And I saw the seven angels which stood before God; and to them were given seven trumpets. (Revelation 8:6,13; 9:14.)

TWO WITNESSES: Mosaic Law and Christ.

Revelation 11:3; And I will give power unto my two witnesses, and they shall prophesy a thousand two hundred and threescore days, clothed in sackcloth.

Revelation 11:10; And they that dwell upon the earth shall rejoice over them, and make merry, and shall send gifts one to another; because these two prophets tormented them that dwelt on the earth.

VIALS OF WRATH: Symbolic containers of God's Judgments.

Revelation 16:1; And I heard a great voice out of the temple saying to the seven angels, Go your ways, and pour out the vials of the wrath of God upon the earth. (Revelation 16.)

Revelation 21:9; And there came unto me one of the seven angels which had the seven vials full of the seven last plagues, and talked with me, saying, Come hither, I will shew thee the bride, the Lamb's wife.

VOICE AS THE SOUND OF MANY WATERS: Denotes Power, Authority, and commands Obeisance from all nations. Also indicates knowledge being imparted by God.

Ezekiel 43:2; And, behold, the glory of the God of Israel came from the way of the east: and his voice was like a noise of many waters: and the earth shined with his glory.

Revelation 1:15; And his feet like unto fine brass, as if they burned in a furnace; and his voice as the sound of many waters.

Revelation 14:2; And I heard a voice from heaven, as the voice of many waters, and as the voice of a great thunder: and I heard the voice of harpers harping with their harps:

VOICES: Prayers of the saints such as pleas for action, praise and/or mercy. Also, edicts from God usually coupled with the symbols of judgments such as earthquakes, lightnings, thunderings, fire, and hail.

Judges 21:2; And the people came to the house of God, and abode there till even before God, and lifted up their voices, and wept sore; (I Samuel 11:4.)

Isaiah 66:6; A voice of noise from the city, a voice from the temple, a voice of the LORD that rendereth recompence to his enemies.

Luke 17:13; And they lifted up their voices, and said, Jesus, Master, have mercy on us. (Luke 23:23; Acts 13:27; 14:11; 22:22;)

I Corinthians 14:10; There are, it may be, so many kinds of voices in the world, and none of them is without signification.

Revelation 4:5; And out of the throne proceeded lightnings and thunderings and voices: and there were seven lamps of fire burning before the throne, which are the seven Spirits of God.

Revelation 8:5; And the angel took the censer, and filled it with fire of the altar, and cast it into the earth: and there were voices, and thunderings, and lightnings, and an earthquake.

Revelation 11:19; And the temple of God was opened in heaven, and there was seen in his temple the ark of his testament: and there were lightnings, and voices, and thunderings, and an earthquake, and great hail.

Revelation 16:18; And there were voices, and thunders, and lightnings; and there was a great earthquake, such as was not since men were upon the earth, so mighty an earthquake, and so great.

WALL: Signifies protection, safety and peace.

Exodus 14:22,29; But the children of Israel walked upon dry land in the midst of the sea; and the waters were a wall unto them on their right hand, and on their left. (Joshua 2:15; 6:5,20; II Samuel 11:24; Nehemiah 3:8.)

Revelation 21:12; And had a wall great and high, and had twelve gates, and at the gates twelve angels, and names written thereon, which are the names of the twelve tribes of the children of Israel: (Revelation 21:14,15,17,18,19.)

Revelation 21:27; And there shall in no wise enter into it anything that defileth, neither whatsoever worketh abomination, or maketh a lie: but they which are written in the Lamb's book of life.

WATER: Represents the religious knowledge that directs and controls a person's spiritual destiny, either eternal salvation with Christ or forever lost in Satan's evil dominion. (Fountain of waters represents that source of knowledge, both good and evil.)

John 4:14; But whosoever drinketh of the water that I shall give him shall never thirst; but the water that I shall give him shall be in him a well of water springing up into everlasting life.

Revelation 16:12; And the sixth angel poured out his vial upon the great river Euphrates; and the water thereof was dried up, that the way of the kings of the east might be prepared.

WATERS: (Many Waters) Multitude of peoples, nations, and languages.

Isaiah 8:7-8; Now therefore, behold, the Lord bringeth up upon them the waters of the river, strong and many, even the king of Assyria, and all his glory: and he shall come up over all his channels, and go over all his banks: And he shall pass through Judah; he shall overflow and go over, he shall reach even to the neck; and the stretching out of his wings shall fill the breadth of thy land, O Immanuel.

Isaiah 17:12-13; Woe to the multitude of many people, which make a noise like the noise of the seas; and to the rushing of nations, that make a rushing like the rushing of mighty waters! The nations shall rush like the rushing of many waters: but God shall rebuke them, and they shall flee far off, and shall be chased as the chaff of the mountains before the wind, and like a rolling thing before the whirlwind.

Jeremiah 51:13; O thou that dwellest upon many waters, abundant in treasures, thine end is come, and the measure of thy covetousness. Revelation 17:1;And there came one of the seven angels which had the seven vials, and talked with me, saying unto me, Come hither; I will shew unto thee the judgment of the great whore that sitteth upon many waters:

Revelation 17:15; And he saith unto me, The waters which thou sawest, where the whore sitteth, are peoples, and multitudes, and nations, and tongues.

WHIRLWIND: Symbolizes the mode of transportation to and from heaven and is also used to signify the Lord coming in Judgment.

II Kings 2:1; And it came to pass, when the LORD would take up Elijah into heaven by a whirlwind, that Elijah went with Elisha from Gilgal. (II Kings 2:11. Job 38:1; 40:6; Proverbs 10:25; Isaiah 17:13.) Isaiah 66:15; For, behold, the Lord will come with fire, and with his chariots like a whirlwind, to render his anger with fury, and his rebuke with flames of fire.

Jeremiah 4:13; Behold, he shall come up as clouds, and his chariots shall be as a whirlwind: his horses are swifter than eagles. Woe unto us! For we are spoiled. (Jeremiah 23:19; 30:23; Amos 1:14; Nahum 1:3.)

WHITE: Purity and holiness as in free from sin. Also signifies being worthy of the reward of heaven.

Isaiah 1:18; Come now, and let us reason together, saith the Lord: though your sins be as scarlet, they shall be as white as snow; though they be red like crimson, they shall be as wool.

Mark 9:3; And his raiment became shining, exceeding white as snow; so as no fuller on earth can white them.

Revelation 1:14; His head and his hairs were white like wool, as white as snow; and his eyes were as a flame of fire;

Revelation 3:4; Thou hast a few names even in Sardis which have not defiled their garments; and they shall walk with me in white: for they are worthy. (Revelation 3:18; 4:4; 6:2; 7:9,13,14.)

WHORE: Represents that person that worships any type of false religion as opposed to worshipping God.

Isaiah 57:3; But draw near hither, ye sons of the sorceress, the seed of the adulterer and the whore. (Jeremiah 3:3;)

Ezekiel 16:28; Thou hast played the whore also with the Assyrians, because thou wast unsatiable; yea, thou hast played the harlot with them, and yet couldest not be satisfied.

Revelation 17:1; And there came one of the seven angels which had the seven vials, and talked with me, saying unto me, Come hither; I will shew unto thee the judgment of the great whore that sitteth upon many waters: (Revelation 17:15-16; 19:2.)

WIFE: Christ's Kingdom (Church) Christians that are found worthy.

Matthew 22:2; The kingdom of heaven is like unto a certain king, which made a marriage for his son.

Matthew 25:10; And while they went to buy, the bridegroom came; and they that were ready went in with him to the marriage: and the door was shut.

Revelation 19:7; Let us be glad and rejoice, and give honour to him: for the marriage of the Lamb is come, and his wife hath made herself ready.

WILDERNESS: Unconquered spiritual territory and battleground where spiritual warfare between Christ and Satan is being waged with earth being this unconquered territory and battleground. The worship of the one true Lord God began with Abraham and through his descendants organized religion became established in the wilderness with commandments given by God unto Moses establishing parameters for the proper conduct of this worship. Organized religion later became established again under Christ, the second witness of God, with earth still unconquered territory symbolized as wilderness. (Exodus 3:18; 7:16; 8:27.)

Deuteronomy 1:31; And in the wilderness, where thou hast seen how that the LORD thy God bare thee, as a man doth bear his son, in all the way that ye went, until ye came into this place.

Deuteronomy 2:7; For the LORD thy God hath blessed thee in all the works of thy hand: he knoweth thy walking through this great wilderness: these forty years the LORD thy God hath been with thee; thou hast lacked nothing.

Deuteronomy 8:2; And thou shalt remember all the way which the LORD thy God led thee these forty years in the wilderness, to humble thee, and to prove thee, to know what was in thine heart, whether thou wouldest keep his commandments, or no.

II Chronicles 1:3; So Solomon, and all the congregation with him, went to the high place that was at Gibeon; for there was the tabernacle of the congregation of God, which Moses the servant of the LORD had made in the wilderness.

Psalms 78:52; But made his own people to go forth like sheep, and guided them in the wilderness like a flock.

Psalms 136:16; To him which led his people through the wilderness: for his mercy endureth for ever.

Isaiah 43:19-20; Behold, I will do a new thing; now it shall spring forth; shall ye not know it? I will even make a way in the wilderness, and rivers in the desert. The beast of the field shall honour me, the dragons and the owls: because I give waters in the wilderness, and rivers in the desert, to give drink to my people, my chosen.

Isaiah 51:3; For the LORD shall comfort Zion: he will comfort all her waste places; and he will make her wilderness like Eden, and her desert like the garden of the LORD; joy and gladness shall be found therein, thanksgiving, and the voice of melody.

I John 5:19; And we know that we are of God, and the whole world lieth in wickedness.

Revelation 12:6; And the woman fled into the wilderness, where she hath a place prepared of God, that they should feed her there a thousand two hundred and threescore days. (Revelation 12:14.)

Revelation 12:16; And the earth helped the woman, and the earth opened her mouth, and swallowed up the flood which the dragon cast out of his mouth.

Revelation 17:3. So he carried me away in the spirit into the wilderness: and I saw a woman sit upon a scarlet coloured beast, full of names of blasphemy, having seven heads and ten horns.

WIND/WINDS: Brings judgment and punishment from the Lord God:

Exodus 10:13; And Moses stretched forth his rod over the land of Egypt, and the LORD brought an east wind upon the land all that day, and all that night; and when it was morning, the east wind brought the locusts.

Jeremiah 4:11-12; At that time shall it be said to this people and to Jerusalem, A dry wind of the high places in the wilderness toward the daughter of my people, not to fan, nor to cleanse, Even a full wind from those places shall come unto me: now also will I give sentence against them.

Jeremiah 18:17; I will scatter them as with an east wind before the enemy; I will shew them the back, and not the face, in the day of their calamity.

Jeremiah 49:32,36; And their camels shall be a booty, and the multitude of their cattle a spoil: and I will scatter into all winds them that are in the utmost corners; and I will bring their calamity from all sides thereof, saith the LORD. And upon Elam will I bring the four winds from the four quarters of heaven, and will scatter them toward all those winds; and there shall be no nation whither the outcasts of Elam shall not come.

Ezekiel 5:2; Thou shalt burn with fire a third part in the midst of the city, when the days of the siege are fulfilled: and thou shalt take a third part, and smite about it with a knife: and a third part thou shalt scatter in the wind; and I will draw out a sword after them.

Also represents power of retribution through the Lord's control of nature:

Exodus 14:21; And Moses stretched out his hand over the sea; and the LORD caused the sea to go back by a strong east wind all that night, and made the sea dry land, and the waters were divided.

Exodus 15:10; Thou didst blow with thy wind, the sea covered them: they sank as lead in the mighty waters.

Job 38:24; By what way is the light parted, which scattereth the east wind upon the earth?

Isaiah 41:16; Thou shalt fan them, and the wind shall carry them away, and the whirlwind shall scatter them: and thou shalt rejoice in the LORD, and shalt glory in the Holy One of Israel.

Revelation 7:1; And after these things I saw four angels standing on the four corners of the earth, holding the four winds of the earth, that the wind should not blow on the earth, nor on the sea, nor on any tree.

WINEPRESS: Symbol of severity and certainty of punishment:
Isaiah 63:3. I have trodden the winepress alone; and of the people there was none with me: for I will tread them in mine anger, and trample them in my fury; and their blood shall be sprinkled upon my garments, and I will stain all my raiment.
Revelation 14:19; And the angel thrust in his sickle into the earth, and gathered the vine of the earth, and cast it into the great winepress of the wrath of God.
Revelation 14:20; And the winepress was trodden without the city, and blood came out of the winepress, even unto the horse bridles, by the space of a thousand and six hundred furlongs.

WITNESSES, TWO: Mosaic Law and Christ. Through these two witnesses God's Word is being spread throughout earth combating the evil doctrines of Satan.
Revelation 11:3; And I will give power unto my two witnesses, and they shall prophesy a thousand two hundred and threescore days, clothed in sackcloth.
Revelation 11:10: And they that dwell upon the earth shall rejoice over them, and make merry, and shall send gifts one to another; because these two prophets tormented them that dwelt on the earth.

WOMAN: Symbolizes that an entity is to be brought forth. A beginning or a birth of an entity. The analogy is of a mother giving birth to an offspring. This analogy reflects the Christian Church in chapter twelve and Satan's dominion of evil in chapter seventeen.
Revelation 12:1; And there appeared a great wonder in heaven; a woman clothed with the sun, and the moon under her feet, and upon her head a crown of twelve stars:
Revelation 17:3; So he carried me away in the spirit into the wilderness: and I saw a woman sit upon a scarlet coloured beast, full of names of blasphemy, having seven heads and ten horns. (Revelation 17:4.)

WOOL: When used to describe hair as white as wool, the reference is ancient all-knowing wisdom with the white symbolizing purity in judgment.

Daniel 7:9; I beheld till the thrones were cast down, and the Ancient of days did sit, whose garment was white as snow, and the hair of his head like the pure wool: his throne was like the fiery flame, and his wheels as burning fire.

Revelation 1:14; His head and his hairs were white like wool, as white as snow; and his eyes were as a flame of fire;

WORKS: Means your deeds reflecting your chosen spiritual path in life, good or bad.

James 2:14,17,26; What doth it profit, my brethren, though a man say he hath faith, and have not works? can faith save him? Even so faith, if it hath not works, is dead, being alone. For as the body without the spirit is dead, so faith without works is dead also. (James 2:18, 20-22,25-26.)

Revelation 20:12; And I saw the dead, small and great, stand before God; and the books were opened: and another book was opened, which is the book of life: and the dead were judged out of those things which were written in the books, according to their works. (Revelation 20:13.)

WORMWOOD: Represents Satan and his evil doctrine being described as poison or bitters to Spiritual health.

Deuteronomy 29:18; Lest there should be among you man, or woman, or family, or tribe, whose heart turneth away this day from the LORD our God, to go and serve the gods of these nations; lest there should be among you a root that beareth gall and wormwood; (Proverbs 5:4; Jeremiah 23:15; Lamentations 3:15,19; Amos 5:7.)

Jeremiah 9:15: Therefore thus saith the Lord of hosts, the God of Israel; Behold, I will feed them, even this people, with wormwood, and give them water of gall to drink.

Revelation 8:11; And the name of the star is called Wormwood: and the third part of the waters became wormwood; and many men died of the waters, because they were made bitter.

NUMBERS INTERPRETATION

Also, to aid in the interpretation of the Scripture, remember that numbers were used as symbols by the writer John and were also significant for conveying meaning.

As the understanding of numerology is very important when studying the Scriptures, I want to briefly state how numbers are used and what they considered them to mean.

When there was a need to convey diversity of meanings, men also used numbers to impart an idea or thought. Numbers were the symbols of spiritual or moral value and a certain number would suggest to them a definite concept. When reading numbers in the book of Revelation, a certain mathematical value may not be intended, therefore, caution needs to be used when applying a mathematical value to numbers found in this book.

We use numbers in that same way today, such as we're number one or unlucky thirteen. Today, we use the number one to signify that we believe that we are the best at a particular event or feat of accomplishment. While we consider the number thirteen as an unlucky number, we also might say that we wish that we had a million dollars because a million dollars to us is symbolical of being wealthy. The people of John's day used numbers in that same sense.

Number one meant unity and when you see number one being used, it signifies unity, being of one mind such as the Godhead. I John 5:7; For there are three that bear record in heaven, the Father, the Word, and the Holy Ghost: and these three are one.

The number two represents confirmation of the truth. Under the Mosaic Law two witnesses were required for confirmation of testimony.

Deuteronomy 19:15; One witness shall not rise up against a man for any iniquity, or for any sin, in any sin that he sinneth: at the mouth of two witnesses, or at the mouth of three witnesses, shall the matter be established.

When Jesus appointed the seventy disciples as a prelude for His visitation into several cities, they were dispatched two by two as verification or proof of the message being sent in advance of his travel to these various places or cities during his ministry.

Luke 10:1; After these things the Lord appointed other seventy also, and sent them two and two before his face into every city and place, whither he himself would come.

The Apostle Paul also confirmed this fact in:

I Corinthians 13:1; In the mouth of two or three witnesses shall every word be established.

The Lord God also sent His Word unto earth by two witnesses, the Mosaic Law and Christ, which reflects confirmation of the truth.

Revelation 11:3; And I will give power unto my two witnesses, and they shall prophesy a thousand two hundred and threescore days, clothed in sackcloth.

The number three is a divine number indicating perfection like unto The Father, The Son, and The Holy Spirit.

The number three and one-half expressed in years indicates a time period relegated to mankind as it is one-half of the number seven, which is considered a complete or perfect number of God. This number three and one-half years is also equivalent to the time, times, and half a time along with the forty-two months and the twelve hundred sixty days as reflected in various parts of Scripture and it refers to the period of time given for mankind to preach and teach God's Word throughout earth as God has designated man to spread His Word.

Matthew 24:14; And this gospel of the kingdom shall be preached in all the world for a witness unto all nations; and then shall the end come.

This period of time portrayed as three and one-half years; time, times, and half a time; forty-two months; and twelve hundred sixty days plus the time period symbolized as three and one-half days reflects the period of time that mankind will be persecuted by the evil forces of Satan and is symbolic of the period of time as reflected by the prayer of Elijah when he prayed that it might not rain in retaliation for the persecution of God's disciples by King Ahab as Ahab had promoted the worship of false idols as detailed in I Kings.

James 5:17; Elias was a man subject to like passions as we are, and he prayed earnestly that it might not rain: and it rained not on the earth by the space of three years and six months. (I Kings 17:1)

There is also the number three and one-half expressed in days as reflected in Revelation chapter eleven, verse nine, which is a much shorter period of time designated by God that represents the time period beginning with the ceasing of God's Word being preached and taught upon earth until the final judgment day of God.

Matthew 24:21-22; For then shall be great tribulation, such as was not since the beginning of the world to this time, no, nor ever shall be. And except those days should be shortened, there should no flesh be saved: but for the elect's sake those days shall be shortened.

Revelation 11:9; And they of the people and kindreds and tongues and nations shall see their dead bodies three days and an half, and shall not suffer their dead bodies to be put in graves.

The number four is used to refer to the entire earth and heaven, such as four boundaries, four winds, four walls, four corners, and four quarters of heaven.

Isaiah 11:12; and gather together the dispersed of Judah from the four corners of the earth.

Jeremiah 49:36; And upon Elam will I bring the four winds from the four quarters of heaven, and will scatter them toward all those winds; and there shall be no nation whither the outcasts of Elam shall not come.

Ezekiel 37:9; Thus saith the Lord God; Come from the four winds, O breath, and breathe upon these slain, that they may live.

Daniel 7:2; Daniel spake and said, I saw in my vision by night, and, behold, the four winds of the heaven strove upon the great sea.

Daniel 8:8; Therefore the he goat waxed very great: and when he was strong, the great horn was broken; and for it came up four notable ones toward the four winds of heaven.

Daniel 11:4; And when he shall stand up, his kingdom shall be broken, and shall be divided toward the four winds of heaven; and not to his posterity, nor according to his dominion which he ruled: for his kingdom shall be plucked up, even for others beside those.

Zechariah 2:6; For I have spread you abroad as the four winds of the heaven, saith the Lord.

Another example is Jesus Christ speaking in reference to the second coming in:

Matthew 24:31; And he shall send his angels with a great sound of a trumpet, and they shall gather together his elect from the four winds, from one end of heaven to the other.

Also, there are many depictions of the numbers three and four in the Book of Revelation being revealed as three events coupled four activities or with four events coupled with three activities. The addition of the numbers three plus four totals seven revealing that these Scriptures indicate that the Trinity (Father, Son, and The Holy Spirit) are in control of all earth. In Proverbs chapter thirty, verses fourteen through thirty-three, Solomon repeatedly references three and four entities and/or actions totaling seven. This combination of entities and actions is repeated many times in the Book of Revelation.

The number five or multiples thereof usually indicate deeds or accomplishments by man reflecting human incompleteness with limited power.

The number six falls short of perfection and reflects mankind as man was created by God on the sixth day. The numeral six as used in the book of Revelation usually reflects sinister deeds by mankind.. The number "666" reflected in Revelation chapter thirteen, verse eighteen, expresses evil compounded leading many people astray with various evil acts such as, but not limited to, false prophecy and/or false idolatry worship.

The number seven reflects completeness with God's authority or complete power signifying perfection. Also the rainbow, which is a token of God's covenant with mankind, consists of seven colors.

Psalms 12:6; The words of the LORD are pure words: as silver tried in a furnace of earth, purified seven times.

Now being aware of the significance of the number seven and that it is used in a symbolic way, let us preview the Book of Revelation. We find the numeral seven occurring many times in this book. For example, we find letters to seven churches, seven golden candlesticks, seven stars, seven Spirits of God, seven lamps of fire, seven seals, a lamb with seven horns and seven eyes, seven angels, seven trumpets, earthquake were slain of men seven thousand, red dragon with seven heads and seven crowns, sea beast with seven heads, seven angels with seven plagues, seven golden vials full of wrath of God, a woman upon a scarlet coloured beast having seven heads which are seven mountains, and seven kings.

The number ten is a multiple of five and also conveys the idea of those things accomplished by mankind.

The next number of prominence is the number twelve. Spiritual Israel was composed of twelve tribes while Jesus had twelve apostles. The persecuted woman in Revelation chapter 12 is crowned with twelve stars. The heavenly city has twelve gates and is built on twelve foundations with twelve names in them. Then there are references to multiples of twelve such as twenty-four elders or the one hundred forty-four thousand. The number twelve or multiples thereof reflect organized religion.

The number thousand is the number ten multiplied by itself three times (ten to the third power) and indicates divine completeness or the time sufficient to complete God's will.

Psalms 50:10; For every beast of the forest is mine, and the cattle upon a thousand hills.

This verse relates that God owns the cattle on a thousand hills. As there are more than one thousand hills the meaning implied when used in the Scriptures is the complete period of time necessary to accomplish a particular act or deed or to indicate a complete number.

With the number ten indicating deeds by man and the number three reflecting the Holy Trinity, then ten to the third power, which equals one thousand, would be the period of time established by Divine will for mankind to preach and teach Christianity throughout the world. (The Christian or Gospel Dispensation Period.)

Chapter twenty relates the thousand years as the period of time that Satan was bound and also the period of time of those disciples that were beheaded as reigning with Christ.

The number twelve thousand used in Revelation chapter seven refers to each of the twelve tribes of Israel and reflecting the number twelve which stands for organized religion and the number thousand which is divine completeness. The number 144,000 is a composite of these twelve patriarchs and is used to signify all of the elect or disciples of God.

The numeral seven is very prominent, not only in the Book of Revelation, but also, throughout the Scriptures and is symbolical of completeness or is considered a perfect number. Each of the seven sections in the Book of Revelation covers the time period of the Christian Dispensation beginning with Christ being sent to earth or the ejection of Satan from heaven unto the second coming of Christ with judgment.

CHAPTER 1

Even though John's letters were directed to seven real churches in Asia depicting the conditions in each of the various churches, each individual church reflected no particular instance in history, but rather a condition or principle of conduct that is constantly repeated throughout history in the actual life of the various individual churches that cover the entire Christian Dispensation. Therefore, this first section, Revelation chapters 1-3, describes the virtues of Christ as the ruler over the churches, his qualifications reflecting his power and ability, his continual presence in their midst, his ever awareness of their works, the principles of conduct to be followed within the seven churches in regard to their duties as Christians, the proper conduct of members with words of commendation for their satisfactory behavior, words of condemnation in regard to unsatisfactory behavior followed by threats of punishment if those actions remain uncorrected and the violators remain unrepentant, a statement to hear and heed what the Spirit said unto the churches, and words of caution of always remaining steadfast in their faith followed by promises of salvation in heaven unto those that comply.

Revelation 1:1; The Revelation of Jesus Christ, which God gave unto him, to shew unto his servants things which must shortly come to pass; and he sent and signified it by his angel unto his servant John.

The word "Revelation" means unveiling or uncovering. Jesus Christ is revealing to John events that are to happen within a short period of time. **This revealing to John came from God to Jesus Christ, then through his angel unto his servant John.**

Revelation 1:2; Who bare record of the word of God, and of the testimony of Jesus Christ, and of all things that he saw.

At the instruction of Christ, John recorded the word of God, and the testimony of Jesus Christ, and of all the visions that were presented unto him.

Revelation 1:3; Blessed is he that readeth, and they that hear the words of this prophecy, and keep those things which are written therein: for the time is at hand.

John recorded that those people who read or heard the words of this prophecy and kept them would be blessed. This blessing not only applied to those of John's day, but also to past, present, and future readers or hearers of this prophecy who kept or will keep those things written therein. The phrase's "which must shortly come to pass" and "for the time is at hand" meant that these events were to take place in the near future from the time of this writing.

Luke 11:28; But he said, *Yea rather, blessed are they that hear the word of God, and keep it.*

II Peter 3:8; But, beloved, be not ignorant of this one thing, that one day is with the Lord as a thousand years, and a thousand years as one day.

Revelation 1:4; John to the seven churches which are in Asia: Grace be unto you, and peace, from him which is, and which was, and which is to come; and from the seven Spirits which are before his throne;

John addressed the seven churches in Asia with the greeting of grace and peace from God and the seven Spirits before His throne. Grace is God's benevolence of forgiving our sins and bestowing eternal salvation upon all who accept Him through Jesus Christ who died for our sins. John also described Him as eternal by existing throughout all ages past, present, and future. The phrase "which is, and which was, and which is to come" reveals that God is eternal. The phrase "and from the seven Spirits which are before his throne" refers to God's ability to

**see everything throughout the whole earth because the number
seven reflects completeness of God's authority and power.**

Zechariah 3:9; For behold the stone that I have laid before Joshua;
upon one stone shall be seven eyes: behold, I will engrave the
graving thereof, saith the Lord of hosts, and I will remove the iniquity of that land in one day.

Zechariah 4:10; For who hath despised the day of small things?
For they shall rejoice, and shall see the plummet in the hand of
Zerubbabel with those seven; they are the eyes of the Lord, which
run to and fro through the whole earth.

Revelation 1:5; And from Jesus Christ, who is the faithful witness,
and the first begotten of the dead, and the prince of the kings of the
earth. Unto him that loved us, and washed us from our sins in his
own blood,

**Verse five describes Jesus Christ in three ways; (Remember,
the number three is a divine number.) First as 'the faithful witness' which means one with honor who can be fully trusted to
teach and fulfill God's will. Secondly, as "the first begotten of the
dead" which refers to Jesus as being the first to be raised from
the dead and establishing proof of our promised salvation for all
others who are worthy. The firstborn of the dead also indicates
power over life and death. Thirdly, as a "prince of the kings of
the earth" shows Christ as having authority and as the ruler
over all kings of the earth which indicates Christ's victory in the
end. This is what Satan promised him in Matthew, chapter 4,
verses 8 and 9 if Jesus would fall down and worship him.**

**The phrase "Unto him that loved us, and washed us from
our sins in his own blood" refers to our spiritual redemption
through Christ's love and sacrifice on our behalf.**

**Notice in verses five and six the threefold relationship of
the giver and those who receive these blessings. Number one,
He loved us. This message in the original Greek version is in
the present tense which means continuous action. Number two,
he washed us from our sins in his own blood which indicates
that we are made pure by his sacrifice. This purity is absolutely
necessary as nothing unclean will be allowed to enter heaven.
His sacrifice was God's plan from the foundation of the world.**

Reference what Jesus said when he took the cup and gave thanks, then instructed his disciples to drink all of it in:

Matthew 26:28; For this is my blood of the new testament, which is shed for many for the remission of sins.

Hebrews 9:14; How much more shall the blood of Christ, who through the eternal Spirit offered himself without spot to God, purge your conscience from dead works to serve the living God?

Revelation 1:6; And hath made us kings and priests unto God and his Father: to him be glory and dominion for ever and ever. Amen.

This verse refers to the saints as a spiritual house, a royal priesthood unto Jesus Christ. Being a priest is the highest honor that can be achieved by man. Reference:

Isaiah 61:6; But ye shall be named the Priests of the LORD: men shall call you the Ministers of our God: ye shall eat the riches of the Gentiles, and in their glory shall ye boast yourselves.

Ephesians 2:20-22; And are built upon the foundation of the apostles and prophets, Jesus Christ himself being the chief corner stone; In whom all the building fitly framed together groweth unto an holy temple in the Lord: In whom ye also are builded together for an habitation of God through the Spirit.

I Peter 2:5,9; Ye also, as lively stones, are built up a spiritual house, an holy priesthood, to offer up spiritual sacrifices, acceptable to God by Jesus Christ. But ye are a chosen generation, a royal priesthood, an holy nation, a peculiar people; that ye should shew forth the praises of him who hath called you out of darkness into his marvellous light:

Verse six refers to the third part of the relationship, that of Christ making us priests in His Kingdom unto God and his Father. Under the Mosaic Law priests were the only ones allowed to enter the holy place and to petition God for atonement on the people's behalf. Christ has now made it possible for us to petition God directly in prayer through him. The phrase "to him be glory and dominion for ever and ever" is our recognition of these blessings and the regal status of Christ through all eternity.

Revelation 1:7; Behold, he cometh with clouds; and every eye shall see him, and they also which pierced him: and all kindreds of the earth shall wail because of him. Even so, Amen.

Verse seven reveals the goal of Christians regarding the book of Revelation. "Behold, he cometh with clouds", relates to Christ coming the second time to execute judgment upon those opposed to his religion and to deliver his kingdom unto God. The phrase "with clouds" signifies change. For example, if we see clouds on the horizon, we know that a change in weather is coming.

Matthew 26:64; Jesus saith unto him, *Thou hast said: nevertheless I say unto you, Hereafter shall ye see the Son of man sitting on the right hand of power, and coming in the clouds of heaven.*

The phrases "every eye shall see him" and "all kindreds of the earth shall wail because of him" implies that this change will affect everyone, both good and evil. All people will be aware of this fact and those that opposed him will wail and express grief for their fate. The phrase "Even so, Amen" means: It is true, so, be it.

Revelation 1:8; I am Alpha and Omega, the beginning and the ending, saith the Lord, which is, and which was, and which is to come, the Almighty.

Verse eight *"I am Alpha and Omega"* signifies that the Lord is the beginning and the ending of all things. This describes the eternal nature of the Lord using the first and last letters of the Greek alphabet. The phrase, *"The Lord, which is, and which was, and which is to come, the Almighty"* shows the eternal existence and the power with which to control all things, including time. Verse eight following verse seven shows that the Lord is coming with this power on judgment day to end the world as we know it.

Isaiah 44:6; Thus saith the Lord the King of Israel, and his redeemer the Lord of hosts; I am the first, and I am the last; and beside me there is no God.

Revelation 1:9; I John, who also am your brother, and companion in tribulation, and in the kingdom and patience of Jesus Christ, was in the isle that is called Patmos, for the word of God, and for the testimony of Jesus Christ.

John states that he is their 'brother and companion in tribulation' meaning that he was a fellow Christian and was also suffering the same persecution as many of the early Christians. He also states that he was in 'the kingdom and patience of Jesus Christ' that indicates his status as a fellow Christian and shows that the Kingdom of Christ was already established. The ministry of Jesus Christ led to the church that is Christ's Kingdom being established in Jerusalem at Pentecost. John also states that he was exiled to the isle of Patmos for teaching and preaching the word of God and the testimony of Jesus Christ. The word patience indicates that he was enduring all tribulations for the sake and after the example of Christ.

John 15:20; Remember the word that I said unto you, The servant is not greater than his lord. If they have persecuted me, they will also persecute you; if they have kept my saying, they will keep yours also.
Revelation 1:10; I was in the Spirit on the Lords' day, and heard behind me a great voice, as of a trumpet,

John stating that he "was in the Spirit" indicates that he was guided by the Holy Spirit while the vision was being given to him. "On the Lord's day" means it was the first day of the week which is observed by Christians as their Holiday as Jesus arose on the first day of the week effectively replacing the Jewish Sabbath that was observed on the seventh day. Also, the church was established on this day as this was the day that the Holy Ghost descended upon the disciples since Pentecost was always on the first day of the week. Acts 20:7 confirms this is the day of the week the disciples met for communion service and also I Corinthians 16:1, 2 sets the example that our collection should be on the first day of the week in order to further Gods' Word.

Acts 20:7; And upon the first day of the week, when the disciples came together to break bread, Paul preached unto them, ready to depart on the morrow; and continued his speech until midnight.

The phrase "on the Lord's day" could also simply signify the Lord being in control.

Zechariah 14:1; Behold, the day of the LORD cometh, and thy spoil shall be divided in the midst of thee.

Isaiah 13:9; Behold, the day of the LORD cometh, cruel both with wrath and fierce anger, to lay the land desolate: and he shall destroy the sinners thereof out of it.

John heard behind him "a great voice, as of a trumpet". A trumpet was used to make announcements or to garner attention. The book of Exodus shows this was done in the same manner that God prepared Moses to receive the law on Mount Sinai.

Exodus 19:16,19; And it came to pass on the third day in the morning, that there were thunders and lightnings, and a thick cloud upon the mount, and the voice of the trumpet exceeding loud; so that all the people that was in the camp trembled. And when the voice of the trumpet sounded long, and waxed louder and louder, Moses spake, and God answered him by a voice.

Revelation 1:11; Saying, *I am Alpha and Omega, the first and the last: and, What thou seest, write in a book, and send it unto the seven churches which are in Asia; unto Ephesus, and unto Smyrna, and unto Pergamos, and unto Thyatira, and unto Sardis, and unto Philadelphia, and unto Laodicea.*

The voice instructed John as to it's identity, saying: *"I am Alpha and Omega, the first and the last"*, meaning the Lord. John was then told to write what he saw in a book, and send it to the seven churches that are in Asia. These churches are stated to be *Ephesus, Smyrna, Pergamos, Thyatira, Sardis, Philadelphia, and Laodicea.* However, we know that there were more churches in that area such as Heriopolis, and Troas.

Revelation 1:12; And I turned to see the voice that spake with me. And being turned, I saw seven golden candlesticks;

John turned to see the voice that spoke to him. Upon turning, John saw seven golden candlesticks. Seven is an adjective used to describe the noun candlesticks indicating perfection that is an apt description of the church that Christ established. This is God's perfect plan for defeating Satan and overcoming evil. The descriptive term "golden" indicates great value. The seven candlesticks are identified in verse twenty as the seven churches with the word "candlesticks" being symbolical representing the

churches bringing the gospel of Christ unto the world, that is, they are to bring light unto the world.

Candlesticks were not used in the worship services under the Mosaic Law, but rather a single lampstand with seven arms that used oil for the lamps.

Exodus 25:31,32,37; And thou shalt make a candlestick of pure gold: of beaten work shall the candlestick be made: his shaft, and his branches, his bowls, his knops, and his flowers, shall be of the same. And six branches shall come out of the sides of it; three branches of the candlestick out of the one side, and three branches of the candlestick out of the other side: And thou shalt make the seven lamps thereof: and they shall light the lamps thereof, that they may give light over against it.

Revelation 1:13; And in the midst of the seven candlesticks one like unto the Son of man, clothed with a garment down to the foot, and girt about the paps with a golden girdle.

Christ being in the midst of the Seven Golden Candlesticks shows that he is with his church directing the ministry and also indicating that his Word is being brought to light from the church which is his kingdom that he established on earth. The church is the light or candlestick from which the Gospel of Christ is being brought or shown to the rest of the world. This is accomplished through the preaching and teaching of his Word which will overcome Satan.

Mark 16:15-16; And he said unto them, *Go ye into all the world, and preach the gospel to every creature. He that believeth and is baptized shall be saved; but he that believeth not shall be damned.*

This also shows how the battle with Satan is being fought. This is why Jesus is referred to as "The Lamb of God" instead of a fierce beast like a lion, tiger or bear, for instance, which indicates that the ongoing battle between Christ and Satan is not a physical battle, but rather a spiritual battle and that Christ did not come to set up a physical kingdom as some people expected, but rather a spiritual kingdom. Jesus confirmed this viewpoint in his reply to Pilate when questioned if he were the King of the Jews.

John 18:36-37; Jesus answered, *My kingdom is not of this world: if my kingdom were of this world, then would my servants fight, that I should not be delivered to the Jews: but now is my kingdom not from hence.* Pilate therefore said unto him, Art thou a king then? Jesus answered, *Thou sayest that I am a king. To this end was I born, and for this cause came I into the world, that I should bear witness unto the truth. Every one that is of the truth heareth my voice.*

Notice Jesus said: "*heareth my voice*". That old adage, "The pen is mightier than the sword", shows that the written or spoken word is much more powerful, effective, and everlasting than a physical battle and that our Lord's spiritual kingdom will ultimately achieve victory. Christ and his Church triumphing over Satan with the goal of obtaining residence in heaven is the overall theme of the book of Revelation. This is further proof that Christ will not physically reign a second time on earth.

The phrase, "one like unto the Son of Man", is a term used to describe Jesus Christ as being with the churches spiritually during this Christian dispensation of the churches bringing "light" unto the world. The phrase "clothed with a garment down to the foot" has a threefold description. First, it is a description of the high priest while performing his duty of offering sacrifices unto the Lord. Secondly, it is used to describe a garment worn by a king which suggests that Christ is not only the high priest of his church but also King over his Kingdom. Jesus is our high priest representing us in heaven before the throne of God while overseeing his kingdom here on earth. Thirdly, it is used in the Old Testament to describe the garment worn by a prophet. This garment is unique to three groups of people: priests, kings, and prophets and it indicates his relationship to his church as a king and high priest obtaining atonement for his followers and as a prophet, revealing and teaching. The word "golden" signifies great value while the word "girdle" reflects a garment that was worn by priests under the Mosaic Law and suggests that he is dressed and ready to perform his duty of atonement.

Exodus 28:2,4-5; And thou shalt make holy garments for Aaron thy brother for glory and for beauty. And these are the garments which they shall make; a breastplate, and an ephod, and a robe, and a broidered coat, a mitre, and a girdle: and they shall make holy garments for Aaron thy brother, and his sons, that he may minister unto me in the priest's office. And they shall take gold, and blue, and purple, and scarlet, and fine linen.

Revelation 1:14; His head and his hairs were white like wool, as white as snow; and his eyes were as a flame of fire;

The word "white" is a term used in the book of Daniel. This not only indicates ancient age reflecting eternal existence and wisdom, but also is evidence of his glory and his divine purity without blemish or spot. This reference to white like snow and wool is found in:

Isaiah 1:18; Come now, and let us reason together, saith the Lord: though your sins be as scarlet, they shall be as white as snow; though they be red like crimson, they shall be as wool.

Daniel 7:9; I beheld till the thrones were cast down, and the Ancient of days did sit, whose garment was white as snow, and the hair of his head like the pure wool: his throne was like the fiery flame, and his wheels as burning fire.

This is a description of the eternal, sinless Jesus as the ancient, pure, and holy one. The phrase "his eyes were as a flame of fire" denotes the omniscient and all-penetrating nature of Christ. This all-seeing quality is described in:

Hebrews 4:13; Neither is there any creature that is not manifest in his sight: but all things are naked and opened unto the eyes of him with whom we have to do.

Revelation 1:15; And his feet like unto fine brass, as if they burned in a furnace; and his voice as the sound of many waters.

The phrase in verse fifteen "And his feet like unto fine brass, as if they burned in a furnace" is used to convey the idea of speed and strength in judgment while denoting the ability to move forward and accomplish his mission. This is indicated in the books of Daniel 10 and Ezekiel 1. This also is an emblem indicating stability and eternity as brass at the time this book was written was considered to be one of the most durable of all metallic substances.

Daniel 10:6; His body also was like the beryl, and his face as the appearance of lightning, and his eyes as lamps of fire, and his arms and his feet like in colour to polished brass, and the voice of his words like the voice of a multitude.

The phrase "and his voice as the sound of many waters" demands reverence as it implies a loud and huge volume of knowledge being imparted. The same description is found in:
EZEKIEL 43:2; And, behold, the glory of the God of Israel came from the way of the east: and his voice was like a noise of many waters: and the earth shined with his glory.
Revelation 1:16; And he had in his right hand seven stars: and out of his mouth went a sharp two-edged sword: and his countenance was as the sun shineth in his strength.

The seven stars are interpreted in verse twenty as the angels of the seven churches. The stars being held in his right hand shows that they are under his authority and control. Also, being in the right hand displays a place of prominence in the church's relationship with Christ.

The phrase "and out of his mouth went a sharp two-edged sword" represents the spoken Spiritual Word of God as the means of spreading the gospel throughout the world and through this action triumphing over Satan and his evil forces. Reference:
Ephesians 6:17; And take the helmet of salvation, and the sword of the Spirit, which is the word of God.
II Thessalonians 2:8; And then shall that Wicked be revealed, whom the Lord shall consume with the spirit of his mouth, and shall destroy with the brightness of his coming:
Hebrews 4:12; For the word of God is quick, and powerful, and sharper than any two-edged sword, piercing even to the dividing asunder of soul and spirit, and of the joints and marrow, and is a discerner of the thoughts and intents of the heart.

The sword having two edges indicates God's Word either unto salvation or unto judgment with punishment. The phrase "and his countenance was as the sun shineth in his strength" is indicative of his reverential glory and his status as the Son of God bringing religion unto the world. A similar form of expression can be found in the transfiguration of Jesus while in the presence of Moses, Elijah, and three of the apostles in:

Matthew 17:2,5; And was transfigured before them: and his face did shine as the sun, and his raiment was white as the light. While he yet spake, behold, a bright cloud overshadowed them: and behold a voice out of the cloud, which said, This is my beloved Son, in whom I am well pleased; hear ye him.

Revelation 1:17; And when I saw him, I fell at his feet as dead. And he laid his right hand upon me, saying unto me, *Fear not; I am the first and the last:*

John relates that when he saw Jesus Christ, he fell at his feet as dead. This represents complete reverence on John's part in regard to Jesus Christ. Christ's action of comforting John reveals that he loves us and that we have nothing to fear with him as our Lord. Laying his right hand upon John represents the status or prominence of disciples of Christ. The phrase *"Fear not, I am the first and the last"* reassures the writer John that Christ is all-powerful and that John has nothing to fear.

Ezekiel 1:28; As the appearance of the bow that is in the cloud in the day of rain, so was the appearance of the brightness round about. This was the appearance of the likeness of the glory of the LORD. And when I saw it, I fell upon my face, and I heard a voice of one that spake.

Revelation 1:18; I am he that liveth, and was dead; and, behold, I am alive for evermore, Amen; and have the keys of hell and of death.

This statement shows that he died for mankind and being raised from the dead to die no more was the great sacrifice being consummated. The statement that he has the keys of hell and death assures John that Christ has those things under his control as the key signifies his power and authority over life and death.

Romans 6:9; Knowing that Christ being raised from the dead dieth no more; death hath no more dominion over him.

Revelation 1:19; Write the things which thou hast seen, and the things which are, and the things which shall be hereafter;

John is told to write those things that have been revealed to him. The phrase *"Write the things which thou hast seen"* indicates the past. The phrase *"the things which are"* indicates those things occurring during the time period of John's day.

The phrase *"the things which shall be hereafter"* proves that this vision also applies to the prophecy of the future.

Revelation 1:20; The mystery of the seven stars which thou sawest in my right hand, and the seven golden candlesticks. The seven stars are the angels of the seven churches: and the seven candlesticks which thou sawest are the seven churches.

John is given the interpretation of the seven stars as being the angels of the seven churches and the seven candlesticks are the seven churches. The seven stars or angels in Christ's right hand are the messengers of God's Word from Christ to each of the seven churches while the candlestick or the church was the instrument for dispensing light (God's Word) unto the world.

CHAPTER 2

The letters to the seven churches follow a similar format with each of the letters addressed to, *"the angel of the church"* followed by Christ's various self-introductions with a reminder of his omniscient ability by the phrase *"I know thy works"* coupled with various words of praise to all of the churches with the exception of Laodicea which seemed to be indifferent and described as lukewarm. All of the churches received various statements of dissatisfaction with the exceptions of Smyrna and Philadelphia referencing their struggles with the Jews.

As we study these seven letters to the churches in Asia, we need to keep in mind the application of the principles involved, both the commendations and the condemnations, as pertains to our church and our lives today.

Revelation 2:1; Unto the angel of the church of Ephesus write; These things saith he that holdeth the seven stars in his right hand, who walketh in the midst of the seven golden candlesticks.

This message is directed to the angel of the church of Ephesus. This probably refers to the minister or presiding officer of that church whose duties included preaching, praying, and/or teaching. This would be similar to the duties of the minister in our church today. The message is from Christ introducing himself as he that holds the seven stars in his right hand. Holding the stars indicates that Christ is in control and has total authority of the angels or messengers that relay instructions unto the churches. Holding them in his right hand also shows the relationship of the churches in regard to Christ as the privilege of being on the right side is considered an honor and designates the prominence enjoyed in that relationship.

Jesus Christ walking in the midst of the seven golden candlesticks indicates that he is always with them during the ministry of God's Word which provides assurance and comfort to the churches as they move forward in their teaching and spreading of the truth. During the Mosaic dispensation there was a visible unity displayed in the tabernacle with one candlestick having seven arms displaying seven lights. The churches of the new dispensation find their spiritual unity in Christ who is ever present and active among them in and through his Spirit. Reference:

Matthew 18:20; *For where two or three are gathered together in my name, there am I in the midst of them.*

Revelation 2:2; I know thy works, and thy labour, and thy patience, and how thy canst not bear them which are evil: and thou hast tried them which say they are apostles, and are not, and hast found them liars:

This church was recognized for their works, their patient endurance under persecution, and commended for not allowing false prophets to create dissension within the church as it tried those which were evil and exposed them. By adhering to the true and proper message of Christ they taught the Word of God and became a proper example for not only their own members but also other churches.

Acts 20:28-29; Take heed therefore unto yourselves, and to all the flock, over the which the Holy Ghost hath made you overseers, to feed the church of God, which he hath purchased with his own blood. For I know this, that after my departing shall grievous wolves enter in among you, not sparing the flock.

II Corinthians 11:13; For such are false apostles, deceitful workers, transforming themselves into the apostles of Christ.

I John 4:1; Beloved, believe not every spirit, but try the spirits whether they are of God: because many false prophets are gone out into the world.

Revelation 2:3; And hast borne, and hast patience, and for my name's sake hast laboured, and hast not fainted.

This church was recognized for supporting the doctrine of Christ with patience during a trying period of tribulation and having done so without failing.

Galations 6:9; And let us not be weary in well-doing: for in due season we shall reap, if we faint not.

Revelation 2:4; Nevertheless I have somewhat against thee, because thou hast left thy first love.

Christ condemned the church with the phrase, *"because thou hast left thy first love"*. This means that their devotion to Christ had suffered somewhat from when they first gained knowledge of the truth. Remember that they had tried and exposed false apostles. It could also mean that their unity and devotion toward each other had deteriorated.

Revelation 2:5; Remember therefore from whence thou art fallen, and repent, and do the first works; or else I will come unto thee quickly, and will remove thy candlestick out of his place, except thou repent.

They were reminded to remember their previous satisfactory works as being urged to repent meant to seek forgiveness for becoming less diligent in keeping the ordinances of the Christian doctrine that had been taught to them and to do the first works meant to return to their original zeal and diligence. For Christ to come quickly meant to come in judgment as the phrase to *"remove the candlestick out of his place"* probably refers to the candlestick in the tabernacle and temple. All of the furniture used in the worship service under the Mosaic Law was required to be in place and as this church was referred to as a candlestick, this meant the punishment of losing the church.

Matthew 21:43; Therefore say I unto you, The kingdom of God shall be taken from you, and given to a nation bringing forth the fruits thereof.

Revelation 2:6; But this thou hast, that thou hatest the deeds of the Nicolaitans, which I also hate.

The warning in verse five is followed by words of encouragement showing that Christ agreed with them in hating the deeds of the Nicolaitans. Christ dislikes any compromise that is adverse to his message, therefore, he praised the church at

Ephesus for opposing the false doctrine of the Nicolaitans. These appeared to be a sect of people who promoted impure doctrines by teaching that adultery and the eating of meats offered to idols was acceptable and they also introduced some pagan rites unto the Christians. These Nicolaitans may possibly have been followers of a proselyte of Antioch.

Acts 6:5; And the saying pleased the whole multitude: and they chose Stephen, a man full of faith and of the Holy Ghost, and Philip, and Prochorus, and Nicanor, and Timon, and Parmenas, and Nicolas a proselyte of Antioch:

Revelation 2:7; He that hath an ear, let him hear what the Spirit saith unto the churches; To him that overcometh will I give to eat of the tree of life, which is in the midst of the paradise of God.

Christ gave the admonition to *"hear what the Spirit saith unto the churches"*. The word church is used in the plural form indicating that these letters were intended for instruction unto all churches. To heed these words was followed with a promise of heaven to the one who overcomes and that is the one who resists all evil anti-Christian doctrine and remains steadfast in the faith amidst tribulations and persecutions. To *"eat of the tree of life"* meant the reward of salvation in heaven. This promise of the reward of heaven is worded in a separate manner to each of the seven churches.

Proverbs 13:12; Hope deferred maketh the heart sick: but when the desire cometh, it is a tree of life.

Proverbs 15:4; A wholesome tongue is a tree of life: but perverseness therein is a breach in the spirit.

Revelation 2:8; And unto the angel of the church in Smyrna write; These things saith the first and the last, which was dead, and is alive;

The introduction to the angel of the church in Smyrna describes Christ as the first and the last proving his eternal existence as he that was dead, and is alive which also reflects his sacrifice and his power over death. Smyrna was the church of Polycarp who became martyred for his refusal to offer incense and proclaim the emperor of Rome as Lord.

Revelation 2:9; I know thy works, and tribulation, and poverty, (but thou art rich) and I know the blasphemy of them which say they are Jews, and are not, but are the synagogue of Satan.

The phrase *"I know thy works, and tribulation, and poverty"* indicates the omniscient power of Christ who understood the conditions that they were suffering under, mainly persecution and poverty, but also even including death as noted in verse ten. Becoming a Christian often meant loss of employment as they couldn't work for the Romans because they refused to take the oath of allegiance that required them to worship an emperor. The Jews would not employ them either as they also were opposed to Christianity and brought charges against the Christians unto Roman officials in order to persecute them. Other unbelievers also despised the Christians to the point that it became extremely difficult to earn a living wage.

Hebrews 10:34; For ye had compassion of me in my bonds, and took joyfully the spoiling of your goods, knowing in yourselves that ye have in heaven a better and an enduring substance.

The phrase, *"(but thou art rich)"*, signifies their spiritual wealth and the blessings that they would receive if they were faithful to the end. This was encouragement for them to endure these hardships.

The statement *"I know the blasphemy of them which say they are Jews, and are not"* refers to Christ recognizing the immoral values of those who said that they were Jews and pretended to worship God but in reality were minions of Satan because of their persecution of the Christians and for not showing love for their fellow man.

Romans 2:17,28-29; Behold, thou art called a Jew, and restest in the law, and makest thy boast of God, For he is not a Jew, which is one outwardly; neither is that circumcision, which is outward in the flesh: But he is a Jew, which is one inwardly; and circumcision is that of the heart, in the spirit, and not in the letter; whose praise is not of men, but of God.

Revelation 2:10; Fear none of those things which thou shalt suffer: behold, the devil shall cast some of you into prison, that ye may be tried; and ye shall have tribulation ten days: be thou faithful unto death, and I will give thee a crown of life.

The phrase *"Fear none of those things which thou shalt suffer"* indicates their physical suffering but that their tormentors would be unable to harm their spiritual health. They were told that some of them would be cast into prison that would try their faith. The phrase, *"ye shall have tribulation ten days"* indicates a period of time that the righteous would suffer this persecution by men. The numeral ten is a multiple of five and indicates deeds by mankind. By being deeds of men this period of time would have an ending and those who were faithful unto death could expect the reward of a crown of life signifying their entrance into heaven.

Hebrews 10:32-33;But call to remembrance the former days, in which, after ye were illuminated, ye endured a great fight of afflictions; Partly, whilst ye were made a gazingstock both by reproaches and afflictions; and partly, whilst ye became companions of them that were so used.

James 1:12; Blessed is the man that endureth temptation: for when he is tried, he shall receive the crown of life, which the Lord hath promised to them that love him.

II Peter 2:9; The Lord knoweth how to deliver the godly out of temptations, and to reserve the unjust unto the day of judgment to be punished:

Revelation 2:11; He that hath an ear, let him hear what the Spirit saith unto the churches; He that overcometh shall not be hurt of the second death.

This again repeats the message for those that will *"hear what the Spirit saith unto the churches"* will receive the reward of heaven. This promise is worded for the phrase *"He that overcometh"* reflecting those that have resisted all temptations, endured all persecutions, and remained faithful unto death. The first death is the physical death of the mortal body and the second death is a spiritual death.

Revelation 2:12; And to the angel of the church in Pergamos write; These things saith he which hath the sharp sword with two edges;

This identifies Christ by the manner in which he is doing battle with Satan. The battle is being fought with the Word of God through the preaching and spreading of the Gospel of Christ. The two edges represents that the word of God will save those who obey and condemn those who will not. This judgment will be for the quick and the dead.

Hebrews 4:12; For the word of God is quick, and powerful, and sharper than any twoedged sword, piercing even to the dividing asunder of soul and spirit, and of the joints and marrow, and is a discerner of the thoughts and intents of the heart.

Revelation 2:13; I know thy works and where thou dwellest, even where Satan's seat is: and thou holdest fast my name, and hast not denied my faith, even in those days wherein Antipas was my faithful martyr, who was slain among you, where Satan dwelleth.

The phrase *"I know thy works"* is in each of the seven letters to the churches reflecting the omniscient ability of Christ. The phrase *"Where thou dwellest, even where Satan's seat is"* indicates that Satan's seat is where evil reigns and to dwell there usually meant to partake of Satan's evil, anti-Christian doctrine or be persecuted for refusing to do so. The phrase *"Antipas was my faithful martyr, who was slain among you, where Satan dwelleth"* indicates that this evil included persecution unto death, but yet these Christians held fast to Christ's name and he was praising them for remaining faithful under those perilous conditions.

Even though Antipas had been put to death as a martyr, Christians at Pergamos held steadfast to their faith as reflected by the phrases, *"and thou holdest fast my name, and hast not denied my faith"* earning the commendations of Christ.

Revelation 2:14; But I have a few things against thee, because thou hast there them that hold the doctrine of Balaam, who taught Balac to cast a stumblingblock before the children of Israel, to eat things sacrificed unto idols, and to commit fornication.

The condemnation in verse fourteen probably refers to some Christians in this church attending pagan festivals and partaking of meats that had been offered to false gods and they also probably participated in some of the immoral rites and ceremonies that were common at these feasts as the comparison was

made to Balac and Balaam regarding the children of Israel who had become compromised by intermarrying with the descendants of Moab.

Numbers 25:1-2; And Israel abode in Shittim, and the people began to commit whoredom with the daughters of Moab. And they called the people unto the sacrifices of their gods: and the people did eat, and bowed down to their gods.

Numbers 31:16; Behold, these caused the children of Israel, through the counsel of Balaam, to commit trespass against the LORD in the matter of Peor, and there was a plague among the congregation of the LORD.

Remember the story of Balaam, who had been commissioned by Balak, the king of Moab, to pronounce a curse upon the children of Israel. He tried, but God would not let him, so he told Balak to have his people intermarry with the children of Israel and through this means of compromise he would eventually win them over.

To retain employment, these early Christians were placed in the position of having to participate in these feasts, eating meats dedicated to false gods, then participating in their immoral rites and ceremonies. Refusal meant that a person could lose their employment leaving them with limited means to support themselves and their families. Therefore, some people began the doctrine of compromise drawing this condemnation from Christ comparing them to the incident regarding Balaam and Balac. The church needed to remain more strongly committed to opposing these pagan festivals and ceremonies by disciplining those Christians who had participated in the worship of their false gods.

Revelation 2:15; So hast thou also them that hold the doctrine of the Nicolaitans, which thing I hate.

Christ condemnation of those members of the church at Pergamos goes further by comparing them to the Nicolaitans who believed and taught that eating meats offered to false gods was allowed and also participated in several pagan ceremonies that encouraged adultery and fornication.

Revelation 2:16; Repent; or else I will come unto thee quickly, and will fight against them with the sword of my mouth.

This admonition from Christ shows that the evil practices of the Nicolaitans will not be tolerated among Christians. Christ urges them to repent or he would quickly judge them. The phrase *"come unto them quickly"* **means swift judgment and punishment. To fight against them with** *"the sword of my mouth"* **meant either edification or judgment by God's word.**

Isaiah 49:2; And he hath made my mouth like a sharp sword; in the shadow of his hand hath he hid me, and made me a polished shaft; in his quiver hath he hid me;

Hosea 6:5; Therefore have I hewed them by the prophets; I have slain them by the words of my mouth: and thy judgments are as the light that goeth forth.

Revelations 2:17; He that hath an ear, let him hear what the Spirit saith unto the churches; To him that overcometh will I give to eat of the hidden manna, and will give him a white stone, and in the stone a new name written, which no man knoweth saving he that receiveth it.

The phrase *"He that hath an ear, let him hear what the Spirit saith unto the churches"* **is repeated in each of the letters to the seven churches advising them to heed the message that was given to them by the Spirit. The phrase** *"To him that overcometh"* **means remaining steadfast in the faith by the ability to withstand temptations and persecutions. The phrase** *"give to eat of the hidden manna, and will give him a white stone"* **represents spiritual life unto heavenly salvation. Christ has the power to grant this blessing as reflected in:**

Psalms 78:24; And had rained down manna upon them to eat, and had given them of the corn of heaven.

John 6:33,35,58; For the bread of God is he which cometh down from heaven, and giveth life unto the world. And Jesus said unto them, I am the bread of life: he that cometh to me shall never hunger; and he that believeth on me shall never thirst. This is that bread which came down from heaven: not as your fathers did eat manna, and are dead: he that eateth of this bread shall live for ever.

A white stone signifies innocence, purity, and/or durability representing eternity and it was given to a person found innocent of a crime as in a judicial trial. The *"new name written"* in the stone implies that this person had dedicated their life to Christ.

Revelation 3:12; *and I will write upon him my new name.*

Revelation 19:12; and he had a name written, that no man knew, but he himself.

The symbolism of writing a name was also reflected by the high priest during his sacrificial duties in the tabernacle or temple as he wore a mitre on his forehead with a reference to the Lord which implied his servitude and worship.

Exodus 28:36-38; And thou shalt make a plate of pure gold, and grave upon it, like the engravings of a signet, HOLINESS TO THE LORD. And thou shalt put it on a blue lace, that it may be upon the mitre; upon the forefront of the mitre it shall be. And it shall be upon Aaron's forehead, that Aaron may bear the iniquity of the holy things, which the children of Israel shall hallow in all their holy gifts; and it shall be always upon his forehead, that they may be accepted before the Lord.

Isaiah 62:2; And the Gentiles shall see thy righteousness, and all kings thy glory: and thou shalt be called by a new name, which the mouth of the LORD shall name.

Revelation 2:18; And unto the angel of the church in Thyatira write; These things saith the Son of God, who hath his eyes like unto a flame of fire, and his feet are like fine brass;

This introduction unto the angel of the church in Thyatira describes Christ as *"the Son of God"* reflecting his royal status and his power. The phrase *"his eyes like unto a flame of fire"* denotes the omniscient nature of Christ and his ability to penetrate and know a person's innermost thoughts.

Zechariah 4:10; For who hath despised the day of small things? for they shall rejoice, and shall see the plummet in the hand of Zerubbabel with those seven; they are the eyes of the LORD, which run to and fro through the whole earth.

Hebrews 4:13; Neither is there any creature that is not manifest in his sight: but all things are naked and opened unto the eyes of him with whom we have to do.

The phrase, *"his feet are like fine brass"*, indicates a refined or an improved product that was tried by tribulation referring to the method of making brass. Also indicates beauty, stability, and permanence with the ability to move forward and accomplish his mission.

Revelation 2:19; I know thy works, and charity, and service, and faith, and thy patience, and thy works; and the last to be more than the first.

"Thy works" meant their *"charity, service, faith, and patience,"* while maintaining their obedience to the Gospel of Christ. Christ does know their works through his omniscient nature and he next mentions their charity which is their love of God and benevolence toward others, probably those that were destitute or in need of aid. Next, he commends their service toward the ministry of the Gospel of Christ and their faith indicating their fidelity to this doctrine. This was followed by a commendation for their patience which indicates their perseverance under persecutions and tribulations. The phrase, *"the last to be more than the first"*, meant that they had improved their good works and in that respect had become better Christians.

Revelation 2:20; Notwithstanding I have a few things against thee, because thou sufferest that woman Jezebel, which calleth herself a prophetess, to teach and to seduce my servants to commit fornication, and to eat things sacrificed unto idols.

This verse starts with a condemnation in reference to *""that woman Jezebel, which calleth herself a prophetess,"* indicating that she was a teacher and probably a leader by example. Christ accused her of leading his followers astray by teaching and seducing them *"to commit fornication, and to eat things sacrificed unto idols"* which probably alludes to the rituals associated with trade guilds. As the city of Thyatira was a trading center, it probably had trade guilds that required participation by its members putting those early Christians under tremendous pressure of either complying or suffering the risk of losing their

employment. **Not removing this Jezebel from the church drew the condemnation of Christ. This appears to be a compromise of tolerating false teachers to avoid hardships.**
Isaiah 57:3; But draw near hither, ye sons of the sorceress, the seed of the adulterer and the whore.

Use of the name, Jezebel, could also allude to the wife of King Ahab as Ahab and Jezebel promoted worship unto false gods.
I Kings 16:30-31; And Ahab the son of Omri did evil in the sight of the LORD above all that were before him. And it came to pass, as if it had been a light thing for him to walk in the sins of Jeroboam the son of Nebat, that he took to wife Jezebel the daughter of Ethbaal king of the Zidonians, and went and served Baal, and worshipped him.

Thyatira was also the home of Lydia, the "seller of purple".
Acts 16:14-15; And a certain woman named Lydia, a seller of purple, of the city of Thyatira, which worshipped God, heard us: whose heart the Lord opened, that she attended unto the things which were spoken of Paul. And when she was baptized, and her household, she besought us, saying, If ye have judged me to be faithful to the Lord, come into my house, and abide there. And she constrained us.

Revelation 2:21; And I gave her space to repent of her fornication; and she repented not.

This verse indicates that this Jezebel had the opportunity to repent of her deeds, but did not, therefore, condemnation came from Christ against this church for allowing this behavior.

Revelation 2:22; Behold, I will cast her into a bed, and them that commit adultery with her into great tribulation, except they repent of their deeds.

The word *"bed"* is used in the Scriptures as a symbol of punishment, therefore, to cast them into bed unless they repented of their deeds signified punishment.
Job 33:19; He is chastened also with pain upon his bed, and the multitude of his bones with strong pain:

The following verses describes the punishment of Ahaziah, son of Jezebel, as described in the books of First and Second Kings who had been corrupted by her and did not repent. The punishment of *"cast her into a bed"* refers to Ahaziah, whose

117

punishment of being bedridden from which he would not recover, was because of his idolatry worship from the example of his mother, Jezebel. Elijah was sent by God to inform Ahaziah of his punishment for the lack of repentance. The phrase *"that commit adultery"* means the worship of idolatry or false gods.

I Kings 22:51-53; Ahaziah the son of Ahab began to reign over Israel in Samaria the seventeenth year of Jehoshaphat king of Judah, and reigned two years over Israel. And he did evil in the sight of the LORD, and walked in the way of his father, and in the way of his mother, and in the way of Jeroboam the son of Nebat, who made Israel to sin: For he served Baal, and worshipped him, and provoked to anger the LORD God of Israel, according to all that his father had done.

II Kings 1:2-4; And Ahaziah fell down through a lattice in his upper chamber that was in Samaria, and was sick: and he sent messengers, and said unto them, Go, enquire of Baalzebub the god of Ekron whether I shall recover of this disease. But the angel of the LORD said to Elijah the Tishbite, Arise, go up to meet the messengers of the king of Samaria, and say unto them, Is it not because there is not a God in Israel, that ye go to enquire of Baalzebub the god of Ekron? Now therefore thus saith the LORD, Thou shalt not come down from that bed on which thou art gone up, but shalt surely die. And Elijah departed.

Revelation 2:23; And I will kill her children with death; and all the churches shall know that I am he which searcheth the reins and hearts: and I will give unto every one of you according to your works.

Christ states that this punishment will progress to future generations of this evil person as proof that he controls his church with the ability to know their innermost thoughts and that everyone will be judged according to their deeds.

Joram, a second son of Jezebel, wife of King Ahab, was slain by Jehu as recorded in the book of Second Kings:

II Kings 9:22-24; And it came to pass, when Joram saw Jehu, that he said, Is it peace, Jehu? And he answered, What peace, so long as the whoredoms of thy mother Jezebel and her witchcrafts are so many? And Joram turned his hands, and fled, and said to Ahaziah, There is treachery, O Ahaziah. And Jehu drew a bow with his full strength, and smote Jehoram between his arms, and the arrow went out at his heart, and he sunk down in his chariot.

King Ahab's seventy sons were slain along with the forty-two brethren of Ahaziah as recorded in:
II Kings 10:7,13-14; And it came to pass, when the letter came to them, that they took the king's sons, and slew seventy persons, and put their heads in baskets, and sent him them to Jezreel. Jehu met with the brethren of Ahaziah king of Judah, and said, Who are ye? And they answered, We are the brethren of Ahaziah; and we go down to salute the children of the king and the children of the queen. And he said, Take them alive. And they took them alive, and slew them at the pit of the shearing house, even two and forty men; neither left he any of them.

The phrase *"I am he which searcheth the reins and hearts: and I will give unto every one of you according to your works"* **describes the omniscient ability of Christ along with his promise of judgment.**
Hebrews 4:12; For the word of God is quick, and powerful, and sharper than any twoedged sword, piercing even to the dividing asunder of soul and spirit, and of the joints and marrow, and is a discerner of the thoughts and intents of the heart.
Revelation 2:24; But unto you I say, and unto the rest in Thyatira, as many as have not this doctrine, and which have not known the depths of Satan, as they speak; I will put upon you none other burden.

The phrase, *"depths of Satan"*, **signifies participating in evil, anti-Christian acts. Christ is stating that he will not punish others who have not participated in this evil doctrine of committing fornication, eating meats sacrificed unto idols, or worshiping false gods.**

The term *"burden"* **used in many Scriptures refers to the Lord laying a burden upon King Ahab as referenced in:**
II Kings 9:25; Then said Jehu to Bidkar his captain, Take up, and cast him in the portion of the field of Naboth the Jezreelite: for remember how that, when I and thou rode together after Ahab his father, the LORD laid this burden upon him;
Isaiah 13:1; The burden of Babylon, which Isaiah the son of Amoz did see.

Acts 15:28-29; For it seemed good to the Holy Ghost, and to us, to lay upon you no greater burden than these necessary things; That ye abstain from meats offered to idols, and from blood, and from things strangled, and from fornication: from which if ye keep yourselves, ye shall do well. Fare ye well.

Revelation 2:25; But that which ye have already hold fast till I come.

This means to continue their good works and remain stead-fast in their faith until Christ comes to reward those found worthy and to execute punishment upon those that are found unworthy.

Revelation 2:26; And he that overcometh, and keepeth my works unto the end, to him will *I give power over the nations:*

The phrase, *"And he that overcometh, and keepeth my works unto the end"* **implies the person that resists all temptations, endures all tribulations and persecutions, and continues to obey all of the commandments of Christ will receive the reward of heaven as reflected by the phrase to** *"give power over the nations"* **which also implies having the power to teach the correct doc-trine that will overcome and condemn all of the false doctrines of the nations over the world.**

Psalms 2:8; Ask of me, and I shall give thee the heathen for thine inheritance, and the uttermost parts of the earth for thy possession.

Revelation 2:27; And he shall rule them with a rod of iron; as the vessels of a potter shall they be broken to shivers: even as I received of my Father.

This means to restrict and control evil with complete power and authority to the point that those who participate in acts adverse to the Gospel of Christ will be broken and destroyed like the vessels of a potter. A rod of iron would completely destroy the clay vessels of a potter. They will receive this power even as Christ received it from God.

Psalms 2:9; Thou shalt break them with a rod of iron; thou shalt dash them in pieces like a potter's vessel.

Proverbs 10:13; In the lips of him that hath understanding wisdom is found: but a rod is for the back of him that is void of understanding.

Revelation 2:28; And I will give him the morning star.

This refers to Christ himself as the morning star indicating the salvation of heaven through him.

Revelation 22:16. I Jesus have sent mine angel to testify unto you these things in the churches. I am the root and the offspring of David, and the bright and morning star.

The star is also the symbol of royalty.

Matthew 2:2; Saying, Where is he that is born King of the Jews? For we have seen his star in the east, and are come to worship him.

Numbers 24:17; I shall see him, but not now: I shall behold him, but not nigh: there shall come a Star out of Jacob, and a Sceptre shall rise out of Israel, and shall smite the corners of Moab, and destroy all the children of Sheth.

Ezekiel 43:2; And, behold, the glory of the God of Israel came from the way of the east: and his voice was like a noise of many waters: and the earth shined with his glory.

Revelation 2:29; He that hath an ear, let him hear what the Spirit saith unto the churches.

This phrase in verse twenty-nine is used in each of the seven letters to the various churches as a closing that is intended for all that will heed and obey the words of the Spirit.

I John 3:22-24; And whatsoever we ask, we receive of him, because we keep his commandments, and do those things that are pleasing in his sight. And this is his commandment, That we should believe on the name of his Son Jesus Christ, and love one another, as he gave us commandment. And he that keepeth his commandments dwelleth in him, and he in him. And hereby we know that he abideth in us, by the Spirit which he hath given us.

CHAPTER 3

*R*evelation 3:1; And unto the angel of the church in Sardis write:
*These things saith he that hath the seven Spirits of God, and
the seven stars; I know thy works, that thou hast a name that thou
livest, and art dead.*

This introduction of the letter to the church in Sardis reflects
Christ with a self description as *"he that hath the seven Spirits of
God, and the seven stars"* indicating that he is in control of the
spirits of each of the churches with the stars being the angels or
messengers of Christ's will and instructions to the churches. The
"seven Spirits of God" reflects his omniscient ability to see and
know everything throughout the world.
Zechariah 4:10; For who hath despised the day of small things?
for they shall rejoice, and shall see the plummet in the hand of
Zerubbabel with those seven; they are the eyes of the LORD, which
run to and fro through the whole earth.

The phrase, *"I know thy works"*, shows that Christ is ever
aware of their deeds while the phrase *"thou hast a name that
thou livest, and art dead"* reveals that they were recognized as
Christians on earth but were dead because they were falling
short of having their works being acceptable before God. They
had not performed consistently with the true attributes of
Christians.
*Revelation 3:2; Be watchful, and strengthen the things which
remain, that are ready to die: for I have not found thy works perfect
before God.*

This church was warned to remain alert and strengthen those attributes that had become weaker and they were about to lose as reflected by the phrase *"strengthen the things which remain, that are ready to die"* because their works were not found perfect before God. They needed to return to a life of obedience with the diligence, sincerity, and brotherly love that they had previously possessed when they first obeyed the Gospel of Christ.

I Peter 5:8-9; Be sober, be vigilant; because your adversary the devil, as a roaring lion, walketh about, seeking whom he may devour: Whom resist stedfast in the faith, knowing that the same afflictions are accomplished in your brethren that are in the world.

Revelation 3:3; Remember therefore how thou hast received and heard, and hold fast, and repent. If therefore thou shalt not watch, I will come on thee as a thief, and thou shalt not know what hour I will come upon thee.

They were cautioned to remember what they had previously been taught and heard, hold fast to that doctrine and repent of their actions. If they did not watch and control their actions accordingly, Christ would come when they were not expecting him and they would then be judged and punished for their actions.

Matthew 24:42,44; Watch therefore: for ye know not what hour your Lord doth come. Therefore be ye also ready: for in such an hour as ye think not the Son of man cometh.

Revelation 3:4; Thou hast a few names even in Sardis which have not defiled their garments; and they shall walk with me in white: for they are worthy.

This verse indicates that some members of the church had remained true to Christ by promoting the true Christian Doctrine and not committing evil acts or deeds. The word *"white"* reflects holiness and purity as in freedom from sin and the phrase *"they shall walk with me in white"* describes their clothing being clean as sins implied soiled or stained clothing. The phrase, *"for they are worthy"*, refers to those Christians who had refrained from sin and kept themselves pure. Being worthy meant that they had met the expectations of Christ and were still worthy of the crown of life that they had earned.

Zechariah 3:3-5;Now Joshua was clothed with filthy garments, and stood before the angel. And he answered and spake unto those that stood before him, saying, Take away the filthy garments from him. And unto him he said, Behold, I have caused thine iniquity to pass from thee, and I will clothe thee with change of raiment. And I said, Let them set a fair mitre upon his head. So they set a fair mitre upon his head, and clothed him with garments. And the angel of the LORD stood by.

Revelation 3:5; He that overcometh, the same shall be clothed in white raiment; and I will not blot out his name out of the book of life, but I will confess his name before my Father, and before his angels.

The phrase, *"He that overcometh"*, refers to those who remain steadfast in the faith of Christ through the persecutions, afflictions, and tribulations will be allowed to *"be clothed in white raiment"* which is a symbol of purity, righteousness, and worthiness.

The phrase *"and I will not blot out his name out of the book of life"* indicates that Christ will accept their earthly deeds as being worthy of the honor of achieving their place in heaven. The phrase, *"I will confess his name before my Father, and before his angels"*, indicates that Christ will acknowledge that person before God and His angels as his disciple and a member of his church or kingdom thereby earning his reward of eternal salvation.

Hebrews 12:23; To the general assembly and church of the firstborn, which are written in heaven, and to God the Judge of all, and to the spirits of just men made perfect,

Revelation 19:8; And to her was granted that she should be arrayed in fine linen, clean and white: for the fine linen is the righteousness of saints.

Revelation 3:6; He that hath an ear, let him hear what the Spirit saith unto the churches.

This refers to those that choose to listen and heed the words of caution in this letter that is intended as instructions and requirements for all churches.

Revelation 3:7; And to the angel of the church in Philadelphia write; These things saith he that is holy, he that is true, he that hath the key

of David, he that openeth, and no man shutteth; and shutteth, and no man openeth;

The introduction to the church in Philadelphia describes Christ as *"he that is holy"* referring to him as being perfectly pure and undefiled. The phrase *"he that is true"* refers to Christ as strictly adhering to the truth and will not lie affirming that his message can be believed. A key is an emblem of authority with the power or control over whatever the key refers to. The Kingdom or Church of Christ is under the power of Christ and he can open or shut it to whomsoever he pleases. If he opens it, no man can shut it and if he shuts it, no man can open it.

Through this phrase, *"he that hath the key of David"*, Christ is establishing the fact that he has the authority over the church and that the disbelieving Jews who had been causing trouble by their philosophy had no power or authority to continue their disruption within his church.

An example would be the key of David which represented the royal status and authority of David as he could allow whomsoever he wished to enter the kingdom of Israel and also even control of who became his successor. Isaiah promised Eliakim, his servant, the control over the government under the symbol of the key of the house of David.

Isaiah 22:22; And the key of the house of David will I lay upon his shoulder; so he shall open, and none shall shut; and he shall shut, and none shall open.

Revelation 3:8; I know thy works: behold, I have set before thee an open door, and no man can shut it: for thou hast a little strength, and hast kept my word, and hast not denied my name.

Christ first establishes that he knows their deeds and that he had the power to set before them an open door, not the disbelieving Jews, as signified by the phrase, *"no man can shut it"*. An open door signifies an opportunity to promote the Gospel of Christ even though the Jews were creating stumbling-blocks. Reference the apostle Paul in:

I Corinthians 16:9; For a great door and effectual is opened unto me, and there are many adversaries.

Christ was encouraging this church that they still had the power to promote the Christian doctrine by the phrase *"for thou hast a little strength"*. They received words of commendation in the phrase, *"and hast kept my word, and hast not denied my name"*. Their little strength may refer to their being few in number, their lack of material wealth, or the restrictions and persecution by the government and the Jews. The phrase, *"hast kept my word"*, shows that they adhered to the true doctrine while the phrase, *"hast not denied my name"*, suggests that they held fast to the faith of Christ while being persecuted.

Revelation 3:9; Behold, I will make them of the synagogue of Satan, which say they are Jews, and are not, but do lie; behold, I will make them to come and worship before thy feet, and to know that I have loved thee.

This verse shows that the persecuting Jews are only pretending to be true worshipers of God, but in reality, are doing the work of Satan by persecuting their fellow man. Christ will make them respect and worship Christianity and to know that the grace of God which formerly had been given to the Jews is now also being offered to the Gentiles. Christ accuses the Jews of lying as they had forsaken the true meaning of one of the main principles of their religion which was love toward their fellow man. This principle had been abandoned in their pursuit of adhering only to the letter of the Mosaic Law.

Matthew 5:20; For I say unto you, That except your righteousness shall exceed the righteousness of the scribes and Pharisees, ye shall in no case enter into the kingdom of heaven.

Matthew 15:9; But in vain they do worship me, teaching for doctrines the commandments of men.

Matthew 23:23,27-28; Woe unto you, scribes and Pharisees, hypocrites! for ye pay tithe of mint and anise and cummin, and have omitted the weightier matters of the law, judgment, mercy, and faith: these ought ye to have done, and not to leave the other undone. Woe unto you, scribes and Pharisees, hypocrites! for ye are like unto whited sepulchres, which indeed appear beautiful outward, but are within full of dead men's bones, and of all uncleanness. Even so ye also outwardly appear righteous unto men, but within ye are full of hypocrisy and iniquity.

Revelation 3:10; Because thou hast kept the word of my patience, I also will keep thee from the hour of temptation, which shall come upon all the world, to try them that dwell upon the earth.

This refers to their remaining faithful to the Christian doctrine that had exposed them to tremendous persecution requiring much patience on their part to endure. Because of that enduring patience, Christ promised to protect them from the hour of temptation which would be a short period of time that temptation and tribulation would affect the entire world and its inhabitants. This *"hour of temptation"* could refer to Satan's dominion of evil being spread throughout the world in this ongoing battle with Christ or it possibly could refer to that short period of time when Satan will rule as described in chapter eleven as three and one-half days.

John 17:15; I pray not that thou shouldest take them out of the world, but that thou shouldest keep them from the evil.

II Peter 2:9; The Lord knoweth how to deliver the godly out of temptations, and to reserve the unjust unto the day of judgment to be punished:

Revelation 3:11; Behold, I come quickly: hold that fast which thou hast, that no man take thy crown.

Christ tells them that He is coming quickly and to remain steadfast in their faith so that no man could take away their crown. Coming quickly means with no forewarning. The crown meant their reward of eternal salvation.

Revelation 3:12; Him that overcometh will I make a pillar in the temple of my God, and he shall go no more out: and I will write upon him the name of my God, and the name of the city of my God, which is new Jerusalem, which cometh down out of heaven from my God: and I will write upon him my new name.

The phrase *"Him that overcometh"* refers to those who endure the afflictions and persecutions of Christians and still remain faithful to Christ and his doctrine. The phrase, *"a pillar in the temple of my God"*, refers to a supporting structure that is permanent in the house of God. A pillar is an emblem of strength

used to support other parts of a building and to *"go no more out"* means that this building block will remain in the house of God permanently and refers to the soul of that person. To *"write upon him the name of my God"* signifies that this person had been accepted as a disciple of God. Under Mosaic Law the priest had written on a mitre, "Holiness to the Lord", which was to be worn on the forehead during his duties in the tabernacle or temple. The priest also wore a breastplate with the names of the twelve tribes engraved upon it and with the temple being in Jerusalem this was the center of their worship service. The phrase *"the name of the city of my God"* is called *"New Jerusalem"* which represents a new center of religious worship of God. This is the "new heaven and a new earth" that John saw in Revelation 21:1. The phrase *"I will write upon him my new name"* refers to Christ which replaced the Mosaic Law.

Revelation 3:13; He that hath an ear, let him hear what the Spirit saith unto the churches.

These are repeated words of warning for the reader regarding the dissertations to each of the seven churches.

Revelation 3:14; And unto the angel of the church of the Laodiceans write; These things saith the Amen, the faithful and true witness, the beginning of the creation of God;

In the address to the angel of the church in Laodicea the phrase *"These things saith the Amen"* and *"the faithful and true witness"* refers to other names for Christ with the intention of impressing upon them his all-powerful nature. The phrase *"the beginning of the creation of God"* is another name showing that Christ is eternal and the Supreme Lord over all of the earth and its creatures.

Colossians 1:16-18; For by him were all things created, that are in heaven, and that are in earth, visible and invisible, whether they be thrones, or dominions, or principalities, or powers: all things were created by him, and for him: And he is before all things, and by him all things consist. And he is the head of the body, the church: who is the beginning, the firstborn from the dead; that in all things he might have the preeminence.

Revelation 3:15; I know thy works, that thou art neither cold nor hot: I would thou wert cold or hot.

These phrases show that God is ever aware of all of their activities including their indifference and lack of zeal for following and promoting the doctrine of Christianity. The phrase *"I would thou wert cold or hot"* reveals that Christ desires sincerity in their pursuit of the Gospel of Christ and the salvation being offered.

Revelation 3:16; So then because thou art lukewarm, and neither cold nor hot, I will spue thee out of my mouth.

Verse sixteen reflects the displeasure of Christ in regard to their insincerity to the extent that He contemplates rejecting them.

Revelation 3:17; Because thou sayest, I am rich, and increased with goods, and have need of nothing; and knowest not that thou art wretched, and miserable, and poor, and blind, and naked:

Christ acknowledges their material wealth in which they have placed their faith at the expense of their spiritual salvation. The adjectives wretched, miserable, poor, blind, and naked reflects their state of spiritual condition. Wretched and miserable indicates an undesirable and deplorable condition while poor refers to the lack of spiritual wealth. Blind shows their inability to see and understand their spiritual state that is in need of improvement while naked means that they are not clothed in holiness.

Revelation 3:18; I counsel thee to buy of me gold tried in the fire, that thou mayest be rich; and white raiment, that thou mayest be clothed, and that the shame of thy nakedness do not appear; and anoint thine eyes with eye-salve, that thou mayest see.

This advice indicates they were instructed to obtain from Christ the grace that would allow them to seek spiritual salvation through the Christian religion with faith strong enough to withstand tribulations without falling away. The phrase *"gold tried in the fire"* refers to the great value of salvation with all of its impurities removed and proven to be more valuable than earthly wealth. This is purchased by accepting and having faith in Christ.

II Corinthians 8:9; For ye know the grace of our Lord Jesus Christ, that, though he was rich, yet for your sakes he became poor, that ye through his poverty might be rich.

The phrase *"that thou mayest be rich"* **represents spiritual wealth.**

Hosea 12:8; And Ephraim said, Yet I am become rich, I have found me out substance: in all my labours they shall find none iniquity in me that were sin.

The phrase, *"white raiment, that thou mayest be clothed"*, **reflects the state of ultimate spiritual purity and holiness in order that they may be clothed in righteousness worthy of the reward of heaven.**

II Corinthians 5:2; For in this we groan, earnestly desiring to be clothed upon with our house which is from heaven:

The phrase *"that the shame of thy nakedness do not appear"* **refers to their loss of spiritual salvation.**

II Corinthians 5:3; If so be that being clothed we shall not be found naked.

The phrase *"anoint thine eyes with eye-salve, that thou mayest see"* **means to realize the truth and do whatever is necessary to achieve that state of spiritual purity acceptable to Christ and to overcome spiritual blindness.**

Psalms 19:8; The statutes of the LORD are right, rejoicing the heart: the commandment of the LORD is pure, enlightening the eyes.

Revelation 3:19; As many as I love, I rebuke and chasten: be zealous therefore, and repent.

This means that Christ will reprehend and correct those whom He loves. They are instructed to be earnest and diligent in their pursuit of spiritual salvation while seeking forgiveness for their sins.

Job 5:17; Behold, happy is the man whom God correcteth: therefore despise not thou the chastening of the Almighty:

Hebrews 12:6; For whom the Lord loveth he chasteneth, and scourgeth every son whom he receiveth.

Relevation 3:20; Behold, I stand at the door, and knock: if any man hear my voice, and open the door, I will come in to him, and will sup with him, and he with me.

This is Christ's invitation to any one who will acknowledge him as being sent by God, accept His offer of repentance and salvation, and join Him in His Kingdom. To *"stand at the door"* indicates that Christ is awaiting a response to his invitation. To *"knock"* means that by grace an offer has been extended through the preaching of God's word and also through blessings and mercies being bestowed upon us. The phrase *"If any man hear my voice, and open the door"* reveals that it is up to the individual to accept this invitation.

Matthew 7:7-8; Ask, and it shall be given you; seek, and ye shall find; knock, and it shall be opened unto you: For every one that asketh receiveth; and he that seeketh findeth; and to him that knocketh it shall be opened.

The phrase *"I will come in to him, and will sup with him, and he with me"* means that Christ will pardon the person's iniquities, commune with him by giving him the 'bread of life' and accepting him in his Kingdom.

Revelation 3:21; To him that overcometh will I grant to sit with me in my throne, even as I also overcame, and am set down with my Father in his throne.

"To him that overcometh" means that if that person withstands all of the persecutions, trials, and tribulations thrust upon them as Christians and yet remain faithful then Christ will accept that person into his Kingdom. The reward of heaven is reflected by the phrase *"will I grant to sit with me in my throne"*. Matthew 19:28; *And Jesus said unto them, Verily I say unto you, That ye which have followed me, in the regeneration when the Son of man shall sit in the throne of his glory, ye also shall sit upon twelve thrones, judging the twelve tribes of Israel.*

The phrase, *"even as I also overcame"*, shows that Christ also endured the same hardships and overcame them with his reward of being with God in everlasting glory. The phrase *"ye also shall sit upon twelve thrones, judging the twelve tribes of Israel"* implies the reward of heaven in the kingdom of Christ.

Revelation 3:22: He that hath an ear, let him hear what the Spirit saith unto the churches.

These words of counsel and warning are for the benefit of the reader and were given at the end of each letter to the various churches. In the first three letters to the seven churches they were given before the promise of salvation and in the last four letters they were given after the promise of salvation. This again reflects the three plus four formula signifying that the Trinity (Father, Son, and the Holy Spirit) are in control of all of earth.

CHAPTER 4

This chapter is of John's vision of God in all of His power and glory pictured sitting on His throne in heaven with complete control of all earth and all things therein that were also created by this Supreme Lord over the universe. God on His throne is surrounded by the twenty-four elders and the saints in heaven as represented by the four living creatures called beasts in the KJV.

Revelation 4:1; After this I looked, and, behold, a door was opened in heaven: and the first voice which I heard was as it were of a trumpet talking with me; which said, Come up hither, and I will shew thee things which must be hereafter.

John saw a door which indicates the ability to enter or obtain something. In this case, it was to see a glorious vision of God on His throne and in His regal status as the supreme controlling power over everything. John heard a voice likened unto a trumpet talking with him. The trumpet indicates that John was to hear a command from one of authority. The message imparted to John was to come up hither which meant to come up to heaven and be shown things that were to happen in the future.

Revelation 4:2; And immediately I was in the spirit; and, behold, a throne was set in heaven, and one sat on the throne.

John states that he was in the spirit which proves that this was a vision. The vision that John saw was of God sitting on His throne which clearly indicates that He is in control with all power and authority.

Isaiah 6:1; In the year that king Uzziah died I saw also the LORD sitting upon a throne, high and lifted up, and his train filled the temple. Revelation 4:3; And he that sat was to look upon like a jasper and a sardine stone: and there was a rainbow round about the throne, in sight like unto an emerald.

The description that John gives of God is of the color of the beautiful precious stones jasper and sardine. The jasper stone is a bright green color suggesting a rebirth or new beginning and is also very hard indicating durability or everlasting while the sardine (sardius-ruby) stone is a deep blood-red color implying the price paid for our salvation.

Exodus 28 relates that the breastplate of judgment worn by the high priest had twelve precious gems embedded in it representing each of the twelve tribes of Israel. The jasper stone represented Benjamin with the sardius (ruby) stone representing Reuben. I believe the significance, other than the colors, of these two stones in this description is that they represent the youngest to the oldest sons of Israel which would encompass all twelve tribes.

John further relates that "there was a rainbow round about the throne, in sight like unto an emerald." The rainbow consisting of seven colors symbolizes complete perfection and that the Father, Son, and the Holy Spirit are in control of all of earth.

The rainbow represents the token of God's covenant with all living creatures upon the earth as reflected in Genesis, chapter nine, and being described "in sight like unto an emerald" which is green in color also suggests that this represents a renewal of life like unto springtime when herbs and plants come alive after a winter.

Ezekiel 1:28; As the appearance of the bow that is in the cloud in the day of rain, so was the appearance of the brightness round about. This was the appearance of the likeness of the glory of the LORD. And when I saw it, I fell upon my face, and I heard a voice of one that spake.

Revelation 4:4; And round about the throne were four and twenty seats: and upon the seats I saw four and twenty elders sitting, clothed in white raiment; and they had on their heads crowns of gold.

The twenty-four seats being round about the throne show the prominence and regal status enjoyed by the elders. These twenty-four elders represent the twelve tribes of Israel under the Mosaic Law and the twelve apostles under the New Covenant of Jesus Christ.

The numeral twelve signifies organized religion and as the numeral two represents confirmation of the truth then the establishment of the Mosaic Law with the twelve tribes followed by the establishment of Christianity by Christ with the twelve apostles reflects the validity of the worship of the Lord God as Supreme Ruler over the Universe.

The elders being in a sitting position reveals their subjection to the One on the throne and being clothed in white raiment reflects their purity, holiness, righteousness, and worthiness of being in heaven. The crowns of gold on their heads reveal their royal status as elders under God with gold denoting their great value to the One on the throne.

Revelation 4:5; And out of the throne proceeded lightnings and thunderings and voices: and there were seven lamps of fire burning before the throne, which are the seven Spirits of God.

The phrase "out of the throne proceeded lightnings and thunderings and voices" represent judgments by the edicts of God being brought upon those on earth in answer to the prayers of the saints. The "seven lamps of fire burning before the throne" are identified as "the seven Spirits of God" reflecting God's omniscient ability to observe and control everything throughout the whole earth as the number seven denotes completeness unto perfection and the lamps of "fire burning before the throne" suggests continuous activity with the word "fire" also denoting the ability to penetrate into innermost parts and discern thoughts.

Isaiah 66:6; A voice of noise from the city, a voice from the temple, a voice of the LORD that rendereth recompence to his enemies.

Zechariah 3:9; For behold the stone that I have laid before Joshua; upon one stone shall be seven eyes: behold, I will engrave the graving thereof, saith the LORD of hosts, and I will remove the iniquity of that land in one day.

Zechariah 4:2,10; And said unto me, What seest thou? And I said, I have looked, and behold a candlestick all of gold, with a bowl upon the top of it, and his seven lamps thereon, and seven pipes to the seven lamps, which are upon the top thereof: For who hath despised the day of small things? for they shall rejoice, and shall see the plummet in the hand of Zerubbabel with those seven; they are the eyes of the Lord, which run to and fro through the whole earth.

Revelation 4:6; And before the throne there was a sea of glass like unto crystal: and in the midst of the throne, and round about the throne, were four beasts full of eyes before and behind.

The phrase "sea of glass like unto crystal" may refer to immense calmness, serenity, and beauty in the presence of God. Jesus calmed the waters in:

Mark 4:39; And he arose, and rebuked the wind, and said unto the sea, Peace, be still. And the wind ceased, and there was a great calm.

It also could possibly refer to the sea of brass called the laver that contained water for the priests to cleanse themselves before performing their duties in the temple.

I Kings 7:23; And he made a molten sea, ten cubits from the one brim to the other: it was round all about, and his height was five cubits: and a line of thirty cubits did compass it round about.

These are the preferred interpretations of many scholars, however, as glass and crystal are transparent, I believe that this alludes to the veil of separation being removed from the temple with saints now having the ability to approach God in prayer whereas before under the Mosaic Law only the high priest could enter the holy place in the temple on behalf of the disciples of the Lord.

The phrase "In the midst of the throne, and round about the throne, were four living creatures full of eyes before and behind." The KJV describes these as beasts but living creatures in other translations would probably be a more apt description. As the numeral four implies all of earth, the four living creatures would represent all of God's disciples from earth.

Revelation 4:7; And the first beast was like a lion, and the second beast like a calf, and the third beast had a face as a man, and the fourth beast was like a flying eagle.

These living creatures represent disciples of the Lord and are explained by the pattern of travel and encampment of the children of Israel during their forty years in the wilderness as described in the book of Numbers, Chapters One and Two. The Levites pitched their tents round about the tabernacle of testimony in the midst of the encampment. The tribes of Judah, Issachar, and Zebulun pitched their tents on the east side of the encampment with the ensign or standard of Judah being the lion. The tribes of Reuben, Simeon, and Gad pitched their tents on the south side of the encampment with the ensign or standard of Reuben being the face of a man. The tribes of Ephraim, Manasseh, and Benjamin pitched their tents on the west side of the encampment with the ensign or standard of Ephraim being a calf or ox. The tribes of Dan, Asher, and Naphtali pitched their tents on the north side of the encampment with the ensign or standard of Dan being the flying eagle. Christian tradition passed these emblems on to each of four apostles with the flying eagle being given to John, the ox to Luke, the lion to Mark, and the man to Matthew.

The description by John of these four living creatures closely resembles the vision of Ezekiel by the river of Chebar as described in Ezekiel, Chapter One. Ezekiel Chapter 10 identifies these creatures as cherubims which are guardians and servants of God.

Genesis 3:24; So he drove out the man; and he placed at the east of the garden of Eden Cherubims, and a flaming sword which turned every way, to keep the way of the tree of life.

Exodus 25:20; And the cherubims shall stretch forth their wings on high, covering the mercy seat with their wings, and their faces shall look one to another; toward the mercy seat shall the faces of the cherubims be.

Each of the descriptions of these four living creatures could be reconciled to Jesus Christ in that Christ was described as "the Lion of the tribe of Judah".

Revelation 5:5; And one of the elders saith unto me, Weep not: behold, the Lion of the tribe of Judah, the Root of David, hath prevailed to open the book, and to loose the seven seals thereof.

Genesis 49:9; Judah is a lion's whelp: from the prey, my son, thou art gone up: he stooped down, he couched as a lion, and as an old lion; who shall rouse him up?

A male calf was used as a sacrifice for atonement under the Mosaic Law.

Numbers 15:24-26; Then it shall be, if ought be committed by ignorance without the knowledge of the congregation, that all the congregation shall offer one young bullock for a burnt offering, for a sweet savour unto the LORD, with his meat offering, and his drink offering, according to the manner, and one kid of the goats for a sin offering. And the priest shall make an atonement for all the congregation of the children of Israel, and it shall be forgiven them; for it is ignorance: and they shall bring their offering, a sacrifice made by fire unto the LORD, and their sin offering before the LORD, for their ignorance: And it shall be forgiven all the congregation of the children of Israel, and the stranger that sojourneth among them; seeing all the people were in ignorance.

The description of the face of a man could be represented as denoting that Christ was sent to earth in a human body and self-designated as the Son of Man.

Matthew 12:8; For the Son of man is Lord even of the sabbath day.

Matthew 16:27-28; For the Son of man shall come in the glory of his Father with his angels; and then he shall reward every man according to his works. Verily I say unto you, There be some standing here, which shall not taste of death, till they see the Son of man coming in his kingdom.

Matthew 18:11; For the Son of man is come to save that which was lost.

Matthew 20:28; Even as the Son of man came not to be ministered unto, but to minister, and to give his life a ransom for many.

Matthew 24:27,30; For as the lightning cometh out of the east, and shineth even unto the west; so shall also the coming of the Son of man be. And then shall appear the sign of the Son of man in heaven: and then shall all the tribes of the earth mourn, and they shall see the Son of man coming in the clouds of heaven with power and great glory.

The description of a flying eagle denotes swiftness and is reflected in many Scriptures with the phrase *"Behold, I come quickly"*.

Revelation 3:11; Behold, I come quickly: hold that fast which thou hast, that no man take thy crown.

Revelation 22:7; Behold, I come quickly: blessed is he that keepeth the sayings of the prophecy of this book.

Revelation 22:12; And, behold, I come quickly; and my reward is with me, to give every man according as his work shall be.

Revelation 4:8; And the four beasts had each of them six wings about him; and they were full of eyes within: and they rest not day and night, saying, Holy, holy, holy, Lord God Almighty, which was, and is, and is to come.

These four beasts represent the children of Israel during their time of forty years in the wilderness and as they are praising the Lord God before His throne in heaven reflects their presence and salvation in heaven. The numeral four implies all of earth with the numeral six referring to mankind which represents all of mankind over the entire earth that has achieved salvation. The phrase "which was, and is, and is to come" signifies the Lord God as existing through all eternity.

Isaiah 6:2-3; Above it stood the seraphims: each one had six wings; with twain he covered his face, and with twain he covered his feet, and with twain he did fly. And one cried unto another, and said, Holy, holy, holy, is the Lord of hosts: the whole earth is full of his glory.

Revelation 4:9; And when those beasts give glory and honour and thanks to him that sat on the throne, who liveth for ever and ever,

This verse is acknowledgment of all of the saints in heaven praising and honoring the Lord God as the supreme ruler over all creation. The phrase "who liveth for ever and ever" is another description of the eternal existence of God. This description of the Lord upon His throne comes from Isaiah 6:1-3 when Isaiah saw the Lord sitting upon a throne, high and lifted up, and his train filled the temple.

Psalms 30:12; To the end that my glory may sing praise to thee, and not be silent. O LORD my God, I will give thanks unto thee for ever.

Revelation 4:10; The four and twenty elders fall down before him that sat on the throne, and worship him that liveth for ever and ever, and cast their crowns before the throne, saying,

The twenty-four elders are symbolic of all organized religion under God. Their falling down and casting their crowns before Him reveals their total submission and recognition of Him as the Supreme Ruler over the universe.

Psalms 95:6; O come, let us worship and bow down: let us kneel before the LORD our maker.

Revelation 4:11; Thou art worthy, O Lord, to receive glory and honour and power: for thou hast created all things, and for thy pleasure they are and were created.

The twenty-four elders are representative of the twelve tribes under Mosaic Law and the twelve apostles under Christ. In verse nine all creatures praise and give glory and honor and thanks to Him that sat on the throne, so also, do the twenty-four elders fall down and worship Him likewise. This shows that all creation honors God as the Supreme Power and the Creator of all things.

Psalms 75:1; Unto thee, O God, do we give thanks, unto thee do we give thanks: for that thy name is near thy wondrous works declare.

Psalms 118:28; Thou art my God, and I will praise thee: thou art my God, I will exalt thee.

CHAPTER 5

As in chapter four, John's vision is still before the throne of God but is now focused on Christ as the only one worthy to open the sealed book of God that is sealed with the seven seals. The seven seals are reflective of God's judgments in regard to the prayers of the saints. Christ became worthy through God's plan of redemption by His sacrifice on our behalf.

Revelation 5:1; And I saw in the right hand of him that sat on the throne a book written within and on the backside, sealed with seven seals.

With the book being held in the hand of God shows that God is in control and being held with the right hand reflects the significance and importance of the event. At the time this was recorded by John the book was probably a scroll on which was written the future events that were to occur as directed by God. Only God had the power and authority to determine what these events were to be and when they were to take place. With the book being written on both sides indicates how comprehensive the instructions were. As the numeral seven means completeness, therefore, being sealed with seven seals proves that the book was completely sealed to keep hidden God's plan for mankind until its implementation.

Revelation 5:2; And I saw a strong angel proclaiming with a loud voice, Who is worthy to open the book, and to loose the seals thereof?

Being a strong angel evidently means that there must be a hierarchy among angels. We know that the Greek word for archangel means chief angel which also adds confirmation to there being a hierarchy among angels. With the angel proclaiming his question in a loud voice implies that everyone will hear and also indicates the importance and significance of the necessity for loosing the seals and opening the book.

Revelation 5:3; And no man in heaven, nor in earth, neither under the earth, was able to open the book, neither to look thereon.

No mortal human was worthy enough to execute God's plan of bringing to fruition the Kingdom of Christians that was established by the sacrifice of Christ.

Revelation 5:4; And I wept much, because no man was found worthy to open and to read the book, neither to look thereon.

John was greatly disturbed that no man was found worthy because he knew of the persecutions and dire circumstances that he and all of his fellow Christians were suffering and having to endure. John realizes that the opening of the seals would begin the implementation of God's plan for mankind on earth.

Revelation 5:5; And one of the elders saith unto me, Weep not: behold, the Lion of the tribe of Juda, the Root of David, hath prevailed to open the book, and to loose the seven seals thereof.

John was comforted by one of the elders as he was told to "Weep not". The phrase "the Lion of the tribe of Juda" refers to Jesus Christ who descended from that tribe through the seed of David. Christ alone was qualified to open the book and carry out God's plan for mankind. The loosing of the seven seals means that the time has arrived for the implementation of God's plan for mankind bringing about the final judgment day.

Revelation 5:6; And I beheld, and, lo, in the midst of the throne and of the four beasts, and in the midst of the elders, stood a Lamb as it had been slain, having seven horns and seven eyes, which are the seven Spirits of God sent forth into all the earth.

Being in the midst of the throne and the four beasts and the elders signify spiritual unity as this totals three entities. The slain Lamb is Christ and being in the midst indicates that He is ever with us.

Matthew 18:20; For where two or three are gathered together in my name, there am I in the midst of them.

The phrase "stood a Lamb as it had been slain" refers to Christ as the Son of God and being worthy to open the seven seals because he was slain for our redemption and that he had established his kingdom upon earth. The phrase "having seven horns" refers to Christ as having complete power with the phrase "seven eyes" reflecting the ability to see and know everything that is occurring upon earth. The phrase, "the seven Spirits of God", refers to the omniscient ability of God and Christ having complete knowledge and control of all on earth. (Reference the explanation in Revelation chapter 4, verse 5.)

Zechariah 4:10; For who hath despised the day of small things? for they shall rejoice, and shall see the plummet in the hand of Zerubbabel with those seven; they are the eyes of the LORD, which run to and fro through the whole earth.

Revelation 5:7; And he came and took the book out of the right hand of him that sat upon the throne.

Taking the book shows that Christ is being designated to fulfill God's plan for mankind and by receiving the book out of the right hand signifies the prominence of Christ in relation to God and also as having been given the authority and power to carry out the mission. The phrase "Him that sat upon the throne" refers to God as the Supreme Power in the universe.

Revelation 5:8; And when he had taken the book, the four beasts and four and twenty elders fell down before the Lamb, having every one of them harps, and golden vials full of odours, which are the prayers of saints.

Christ taking the book shows that He had accepted the assignment of fulfilling God's plan for mankind on earth. The four beasts indicate all of the saints that were saved from the earth and the twenty-four elders represent organized religion as formed by God with the twelve tribes under the Mosaic Law and the twelve apostles under Christ. With all falling down before the Lamb (Christ) reveals that they recognized Him as having received the authority from God and being worthy of this honor. As harps were used as recognition and to honor achievement or royalty, this act reveals Christ receiving the honor that was due Him for being worthy. The "golden vials full of odours" are the prayers of saints with the word "golden" signifying great value and the word "odours" revealing that incense had accompanied the prayers to heaven thereby making them more palatable and acceptable unto God.

Psalm 144:9; will sing a new song unto thee, O God: upon a psaltery and an instrument of ten strings will I sing praises unto thee.

Psalms 141:2; Let my prayer be set forth before thee as incense; and the lifting up of my hands as the evening sacrifice.

Revelation 5:9; And they sung a new song, saying, Thou art worthy to take the book, and to open the seals thereof: for thou wast slain, and hast redeemed us to God by thy blood out of every kindred, and tongue, and people, and nation;

To sing a new song means to honor someone for a significant achievement or to recognize royalty. The phrase "Thou art worthy to take the book, and to open the seals thereof: for thou wast slain" refers to Christ paying the ultimate sacrifice to make it possible for all to achieve eternal spiritual salvation. By this deed, redemption was made possible for everyone regardless of ethnic background, language, or national origin. This act was part of the reason for being honored with harps and a new song. Being designated by God for this mission of establishing religion upon earth was another reason for being recognized and honored. The phrase "every kindred, and tongue, and people, and nation" totals four entities indicating all of the redeemed from peoples over the entire earth.

Psalms 96:1; O sing unto the LORD a new song: sing unto the LORD, all the earth.

Isaiah 42:10; Sing unto the LORD a new song, and his praise from the end of the earth, ye that go down to the sea, and all that is therein; the isles, and the inhabitants thereof.

Revelation 5:10; And hast made us unto our God kings and priests: and we shall reign on the earth.

Being kings and priests or a kingdom of priests reveals that we are no longer obligated to have a Mosaic priest make sacrifices for us as Christ, by his sacrifice, has now made it possible for us to pray directly unto God through Him without animal

or vegetable offerings. **Through Christ our status has been ele-
vated to that of priests.**
Exodus 19:6; And ye shall be unto me a kingdom of priests, and an
holy nation.
**The phrase "we shall reign on the earth" reveals that Christ's
kingdom will eventually conquer all evil adversaries.**
I Peter 2:5,9; Ye also, as lively stones, are built up a spiritual house,
an holy priesthood, to offer up spiritual sacrifices, acceptable to God
by Jesus Christ. But ye are a chosen generation, a royal priesthood,
an holy nation, a peculiar people; that ye should shew forth the
praises of him who hath called you out of darkness into his marvellous light;
Revelation 5:11; And I beheld, and I heard the voice of many angels
round about the throne and the beasts and the elders: and the number
of them was ten thousand times ten thousand, and thousands of
thousands;
**John heard "the voice of many angels" surrounding the
throne, the beasts, and the elders. Endeavoring to place a numerical value upon them as they are innumerable is also reflected in:**
Psalms 68:17; The chariots of God are twenty thousand, even thousands of angels: the Lord is among them, as in Sinai, in the holy
place.
Daniel 7:10; A fiery stream issued and came forth from before him:
thousand thousands ministered unto him, and ten thousand times
ten thousand stood before him: the judgment was set, and the books
were opened.
Revelation 5:12; Saying with a loud voice, Worthy is the Lamb that
was slain to receive power, and riches, and wisdom, and strength,
and honour, and glory, and blessing.
**The term "loud voice" reveals that the volume was loud
enough for all to hear. Christ is worthy of receiving every honor
and all praise and power possible because of his sacrifice on
our behalf and also because his kingdom will eventually defeat
all evil adversaries and bring us unto the new heaven and new
earth. Notice that these accolades total seven virtues revealing
completeness and perfection. There are many instances in the
Book of Revelation totaling seven by using entities, activities,**

and/or adjectives. I will mention several of them during our study of this book.

Philippians 2:10-11; That at the name of Jesus every knee should bow, of things in heaven, and things in earth, and things under the earth; And that every tongue should confess that Jesus Christ is Lord, to the glory of God the Father.

Revelation 5:13; And every creature which is in heaven, and on the earth, and under the earth, and such as are in the sea, and all that are in them, heard I saying, Blessing, and honour, and glory, and power, be unto him that sitteth upon the Throne, and unto the Lamb for ever and ever.

John heard the due recognition for Christ throughout all eternity and described it with four nouns identifying places and four adjectives describing Christ which indicates that everything regarding heaven and earth has been placed under the jurisdiction and kingdom of Christ.

Psalms 24:1; The earth is the LORD's, and the fulness thereof; the world, and they that dwell therein.

I Chronicles 29:11-12; Thine, O LORD is the greatness, and the power, and the glory, and the victory, and the majesty: for all that is in the heaven and in the earth is thine; thine is the kingdom, O LORD, and thou art exalted as head above all. Both riches and honour come of thee, and thou reignest over all; and in thine hand is power and might; and in thine hand it is to make great, and to give strength unto all.

Revelation 5:14; And the four beasts said, Amen. And the four and twenty elders fell down and worshipped him that liveth for ever and ever.

The act of falling down to worship is the ultimate show of respect made by all of the saints and elders in heaven and they also acknowledged him as existing throughout all eternity. The word "Amen" means agreement indicating that all of the saints in heaven agreed with all of the events that placed Christ in control over everything.

I Chronicles 16:34; O give thanks unto the LORD; for he is good; for his mercy endureth for ever.

Psalms 30:12; To the end that my glory may sing praise to thee, and not be silent. O LORD my God, I will give thanks unto thee for ever. Psalms 118:28; Thou art my God, and I will praise thee: thou art my God, I will exalt thee.

Psalms 135:1; Praise ye the LORD. Praise ye the name of the LORD; praise him, O ye servants of the LORD.

CHAPTER 6

T his chapter shows the opening of four of the seals revealing the beginning of the battle between Christ and Satan and is reflected by symbols of different colored horses and the consequences of each of those seals. The tremendous persecution of the Christians is revealed by the fifth seal while the sixth seal is symbolized as an earthquake destroying Satan's dominion of evil. Horses symbolize warfare as they gave many important military advantages when used as instruments in battle.

Isaiah 31:1; Woe to them that go down to Egypt for help; and stay on horses, and trust in chariots, because they are many; and in horsemen, because they are very strong; but they look not unto the Holy One of Israel, neither seek the LORD!

The four different colored horses are identified in Zechariah chapter six, verses one through eight revealing God's control of all of earth.

Zechariah 6:1-8; And I turned, and lifted up mine eyes, and looked, and, behold, there came four chariots out from between two mountains; and the mountains were mountains of brass. In the first chariot were red horses; and in the second chariot black horses; And in the third chariot white horses; and in the fourth chariot grisled and bay horses. Then I answered and said unto the angel that talked with me, What are these, my Lord? And the angel answered and said unto me, These are the four spirits of the heavens, which go forth from standing before the Lord of all the earth. The black horses which are therein go forth into the north country; and the white go forth after them; and the grisled go forth toward the south country. And the bay

went forth, and sought to go that they might walk to and fro through the earth: and he said, Get you hence, walk to and fro through the earth. So they walked to and fro through the earth. Then cried he upon me, and spake unto me, saying, Behold, these that go toward the north country have quieted my spirit in the north country.
Revelation 6:1; And I saw when the Lamb opened one of the seals, and I heard, as it were the noise of thunder, one of the four beasts saying, Come and see.

John observed when Christ opened one of the seals and heard as it were the noise of thunder which indicates the Lord bringing forth judgment with punishment upon the earth. One of the four living creatures told John to come and see the event taking place as he was instructed to record everything that he observed.
Revelation 6:2; And I saw, and behold a white horse: and he that sat on him had a bow; and a crown was given unto him: and he went forth conquering, and to conquer.

Christ sitting on a white horse signifies his purity and holiness while the horse reflects strength in warfare. Being armed with a bow indicates the onset of a battle as the bow was usually the first weapon to be used as it was capable of striking the enemy from a longer distance. This indicates the beginning of the spiritual battle between Christ and Satan and the crown signifies the regal status and authority of Christ given to him by God to conduct this warfare while the phrase "he went forth conquering, and to conquer" reveals the eventual outcome of this battle. This verse has three entities and four activities totaling seven. Many verses may be construed as having a combination of three and four totaling seven using entities, activities, or adjectives.
Revelation 6:3; And when he had opened the second seal, I heard the second beast say, Come and see.

John was instructed by the second beast to observe what had been hidden by the second seal which was a red horse with Christ as the rider whose mission was to wage warfare on earth against Satan as indicated by the color red and under the symbol of a horse.

Matthew 10:34; Think not that I am come to send peace on earth: I came not to send peace, but a sword.

Revelation 6:4; And there went out another horse that was red: and power was given to him that sat thereon to take peace from the earth, and that they should kill one another: and there was given unto him a great sword.

The red horse signifies warfare with bloodshed. This is Christ establishing His kingdom on earth and doing battle with Satan resulting in much persecution of Christianity. The phrase "power was given unto him that sat thereon" reveals that Christ had been given the authority by God to conduct this battle with evil.

Ephesians 1:20-22; Which he wrought in Christ, when he raised him from the dead, and set him at his own right hand in the heavenly places, Far above all principality, and power, and might, and dominion, and every name that is named, not only in this world, but also in that which is to come: And hath put all things under his feet, and gave him to be the head over all things to the church,

"To take peace from the earth" describes the ongoing battle with Satan and his evil forces. The phrase "that they should kill one another" denotes that death, both physical and spiritual, will result from this warfare. The phrase "there was given unto him a great sword" which is a symbol of God's word indicating the manner in how this battle is being waged. In this case the sword is a machaira which is the short sacrificial sword indicating that this battle was to establish the religion of Christ upon earth which resulted in the warfare with Satan and his doctrine of evil. A side effect of this battle resulted in the religious persecution of the Christians by Satan and his forces of evil.

Genesis 22:6,10; And Abraham took the wood of the burnt offering, and laid it upon Isaac his son; and he took the fire in his hand, and a knife; and they went both of them together. And Abraham stretched forth his hand, and took the knife to slay his son.

The knife that Abraham had in his hand was the machaira and this was also the knife used by the Levites in their duties as priests.

Matthew 10:34-35; Think not that I am come to send peace on earth: I came not to send peace, but a sword. For I am come to set a man at variance against his father, and the daughter against her mother, and the daughter in law against her mother in law.

Ezekiel 26:11; With the hoofs of his horses shall he tread down all thy streets: he shall slay thy people by the sword, and thy strong garrisons shall go down to the ground.

Zechariah 1:8-10; I saw by night, and behold a man riding upon a red horse, and he stood among the myrtle trees that were in the bottom; and behind him were there red horses, speckled, and white. Then said I, O my Lord, what are these? And the Angel that talked with me said unto me, I will shew thee what these be. And the man that stood among the myrtle trees answered and said, These are they whom the Lord hath sent to walk to and fro through the earth.

Revelation 6:5; And when he had opened the third seal, I heard the third beast say, Come and see. And I beheld, and lo a black horse; and he that sat on him had a pair of balances in his hand.

When Christ opened the third seal John was summoned by the third living creature to observe the upcoming event. The black horse denotes mourning brought about by severe famine and despair. We know that the Christians during John's time were denied the right to work by the trade guilds because of their refusal to participate in idolatry worship at these pagan feasts held by the trade guilds resulting in poverty. This idolatry worship included eating meats that had been sacrificed to false idols. Also, the Roman government had the power to deny employment to those who refused to declare the Roman emperor as lord. The phrase "he that sat on him had a pair of balances in his hand" shows that food was to be purchased by weight indicating famine probably through lack of employment.

Jeremiah 8:21; For the hurt of the daughter of my people am I hurt; I am black; astonishment hath taken hold on me.

Jeremiah 14:1-2; The word of the LORD that came to Jeremiah concerning the dearth. Judah mourneth, and the gates thereof languish; they are black unto the ground; and the cry of Jerusalem is gone up.

Acts 11:28; And there stood up one of them named Agabus, and signified by the Spirit that there should be great dearth throughout all the world: which came to pass in the days of Claudius Caesar.
Revelation 6:6; And I heard a voice in the midst of the four beasts say, A measure of wheat for a penny, and three measures of barley for a penny; and see thou hurt not the oil and the wine.

This verse indicates famine through economic hardship as at the time this book was written the Roman denarius was the ordinary day's pay for a person which would only allow for a bare subsistence. The KJV translates this Roman denarius as the English penny. The sale of food by weight with the price comparison of wheat to the less desirable barley indicates either the scarcity of food or the lack of money with which to purchase it leading to famine. The oil and wine were not a necessity, therefore, they were to be used sparingly.

Ezekiel 4:10,16; And thy meat which thou shalt eat shall be by weight, twenty shekels a day: from time to time shalt thou eat it. Moreover he said unto me, Son of man, behold, I will break the staff of bread in Jerusalem: and they shall eat bread by weight, and with care; and they shall drink water by measure, and with astonishment:
Revelation 6:7; And when he had opened the fourth seal, I heard the voice of the fourth beast say, Come and see.

When Christ opened the fourth seal, John was summoned by the fourth beast to observe what was to transpire.

Revelation 6:8; And I looked, and behold a pale horse: and his name that sat on him was Death, And Hell followed with him. And power was given unto them over the fourth part of the earth, to kill with sword, and with hunger, and with death, and with the beasts of the earth.

The pale horse symbolizes death as it resembles the complexion of a dead person. The word Hell in the KJV means Hades which is the state of being in the grave prior to judgment indicating physical death. Physical hardship revealing the power of God is sometimes necessary to impress upon people the need to accept Christ into their lives resulting in their conversion from evil pursuits unto spiritual salvation. The phrase "power was given unto them over the fourth part of the earth"

indicates that authority was given to slaughter a significant portion of mankind over the entire earth as signified by the term
"fourth". The phrase "to kill with sword, and with hunger, and
with death, and with the beasts of the earth" describes God's
four judgments in Ezekiel denoting four types of persecution
designed to bring about conversion unto God.

Ezekiel 14:21; For thus saith the Lord God; How much more when
I send my four sore judgments upon Jerusalem, the sword, and the
famine, and the noisome beast, and the pestilence, to cut off from it
man and beast?

The sword in this verse is the rhomphaia which is the long,
heavy sword used in physical warfare, therefore, this sword
indicates death by various means of warfare between good and
evil throughout this Christian Dispensation period. The word
"hunger" means famine as in chapter fourteen, verse twenty-
one of the book of Ezekiel. The noisome beast refers to beasts of
the earth. Pestilence is described as "death" in the Scriptures.
Being four judgments means that all woes of mankind are covered as the numeral four is used to indicate the entire earth.
This reflects God's displeasure with all of His adversaries which
include those who worship idolatry and it also implies judgments by God upon unbelievers of Christianity and/or persecutions of Christians by those unbelievers.

Revelation 6:9; And when he had opened the fifth seal, I saw under
the altar the souls of them that were slain for the word of God, and
for the testimony which they held:

This verse is intended to impart comfort unto those Christians
during their time of distress for many of them had been slain
for their belief and testimony of the Gospel of Christ. The Jews
believed that the life of the flesh was in the blood, therefore, it was
poured out under the altar symbolizing the ultimate sacrifice.

Leviticus 8:15; And he slew it; and Moses took the blood, and put it
upon the horns of the altar round about with his finger, and purified
the altar, and poured the blood at the bottom of the altar, and sanctified it, to make reconciliation upon it.

Leviticus 17:11; For the life of the flesh is in the blood: And I have given it to you upon the altar to make an atonement for your souls: for it is the blood that maketh an atonement for the soul.

The souls being under the altar indicate early entrance into heaven representing the first resurrection and also confirming to the Christians that heaven would be their reward if they held steadfast to the faith. Being "slain for the word of God, and for the testimony which they held" reveals that those saints were martyred and now reigning in heaven with Christ. This verse corresponds with verse four, chapter twenty, reflecting the prayers unto God made by previously persecuted saints as recorded in Psalms ninety, verse four and verses fourteen through seventeen.

Psalms 90:4,14-17; For a thousand years in thy sight are but as yesterday when it is past, and as a watch in the night. O satisfy us early with thy mercy; that we may rejoice and be glad all our days. Make us glad according to the days wherein thou hast afflicted us, and the years wherein we have seen evil. Let thy work appear unto thy servants, and thy glory unto their children. And let the beauty of the LORD our God be upon us: and establish thou the work of our hands upon us; yea, the work of our hands establish thou it.

Revelation 6:10; And they cried with a loud voice, saying, How long, O Lord, holy and true, dost thou not judge and avenge our blood on them that dwell on the earth?

These saints, who had given their lives as martyrs for the Word of God, are acknowledging the Lord as holy and true and questioning when their blood would be avenged and judgment brought upon their persecutors. These saints had achieved their ultimate goal of heaven while God was the one being impugned.

Acts 7:59-60; And they stoned Stephen, calling upon God, and saying, Lord Jesus, receive my spirit. And he kneeled down, and cried with a loud voice, Lord, lay not this sin to their charge. And when he had said this, he fell asleep.

Deuteronomy 32:35-36,43; To me belongeth vengeance and recompence; their foot shall slide in due time: for the day of their calamity is at hand, and the things that shall come upon them make haste. For the LORD shall judge his people, and repent himself for his servants, when he seeth that their power is gone, and there is none shut up, or left. Rejoice, O ye nations, with his people: for he will avenge the blood of his servants, and will render vengeance to his adversaries, and will be merciful unto his land, and to his people.

Luke 18:7-8; And shall not God avenge his own elect, which cry day and night unto him, though he bear long with them? I tell you that he will avenge them speedily. Nevertheless when the Son of man cometh, shall he find faith on the earth?

Revelation 6:11; And white robes were given unto every one of them; and it was said unto them, that they should rest yet for a little season, until their fellow-servants also and their brethren, that should be killed as they were, should be fulfilled.

The white robes indicate purity, holiness, and worthiness symbolizing achieving their reward of heaven. They were advised to wait for a period of time until other Christians could join them as more were to be slain. Some saints had already been accepted into heaven as they were martyred for the Word of God as shown by verse nine. This is reflected by the prayer unto God as recorded in the book of Psalms. Other disciples will be raised on the final judgment day plus God is allowing more time for others to be reached by the Christian Gospel prior to the final judgment day. Early entrance into heaven was granted unto martyrs and is also reflected again in chapter twenty, verse four and identified as the first resurrection.

Psalms 90:14-15; O satisfy us early with thy mercy; that we may rejoice and be glad all our days. Make us glad according to the days wherein thou hast afflicted us, and the years wherein we have seen evil.

Matthew 5:10-12; Blessed are they which are persecuted for righteousness' sake: for theirs is the kingdom of heaven. Blessed are ye, when men shall revile you, and persecute you, and shall say all manner of evil against you falsely, for my sake. Rejoice, and be exceeding glad: for great is your reward in heaven: for so persecuted they the prophets which were before you.

Revelation 6:12; And I beheld when he had opened the sixth seal, and, lo, there was a great earthquake; and the sun became black as sackcloth of hair, and the moon became as blood;

The earthquake signifies judgment by the Lord with this verse referring to the final judgment day and the second coming of Christ. The phrase "the sun became black as sackcloth of hair" reflects the end of Christian religious polity here on earth. The phrase "the moon became as blood" signifies the end of Mosaic Law and their government upon earth.

Joel 2:10,31; The earth shall quake before them; the heavens shall tremble: the sun and the moon shall be dark, and the stars shall withdraw their shining: The sun shall be turned into darkness, and the moon into blood, before the great and the terrible day of the Lord come.

Revelation 6:13; And the stars of heaven fell unto the earth, even as a fig tree casteth her untimely figs, when she is shaken of a mighty wind.

The phrase "the stars of heaven fell unto the earth" reflects the falling of all leaders and those in authority of both religious and civil polity. The phrase "even as a fig tree casteth her untimely figs" shows the day of destruction happening when unexpected while the phrase "when she is shaken of a mighty wind" reveals the immense power of the Lord causing this destruction.

Isaiah 34:4; And all the host of heaven shall be dissolved, and the heavens shall be rolled together as a scroll: and all their host shall fall down, as the leaf falleth off from the vine, and as a falling fig from the fig tree.

Revelation 6:14; And the heaven departed as a scroll when it is rolled together; and every mountain and island were moved out of their places.

This refers to the destruction of our first heaven and first earth to be replaced by a new heaven and a new earth as reflected in chapter twenty-one, verse one. Mountains symbolize kingdoms and nations while islands denote faraway places indicating wide-spread complete destruction.

Revelation 21:1; And I saw a new heaven and a new earth: for the first heaven and the first earth were passed away; and there was no more sea.

Revelation 6:15; And the kings of the earth, and the great men, and the rich men, and the chief captains, and the mighty men, and every bondman, and every free man, hid themselves in the dens and in the rocks of the mountains;

This verse discloses that Gods judgment will fall upon all mankind of every walk in life. Seven different types of mankind are reflected in this verse indicating completeness meaning that all mankind will be affected.

Isaiah 2:19; And they shall go into the holes of the rocks, and into the caves of the earth, for fear of the Lord, and for the glory of his majesty, when he ariseth to shake terribly the earth.

Revelation 6:16; And said to the mountains and rocks, Fall on us, and hide us from the face of him that sitteth on the throne, and from the wrath of the Lamb:

This verse reflects the terror and fear of those who had not accepted Christ by judgment day as mankind will tremble and try to hide from the wrath of the Lord.

Hosea 10:8; The high places also of Aven, the sin of Israel, shall be destroyed: the thorn and the thistle shall come up on their altars; and they shall say to the mountains, Cover us; and to the hills, Fall on us.

Revelation 6:17; For the great day of his wrath is come; and who shall be able to stand?

This is the final judgment day and no one will be exempt for all will be held accountable for their actions.

Psalms 76:7; Thou, even thou, art to be feared: and who may stand in thy sight when once thou art angry?

CHAPTER 7

This chapter reflects the disciples of God that are found worthy of heaven and being signified as sealed indicates that their salvation has been secured. The seals of God being placed in their foreheads is open proclamation to the world of their allegiance to God.

Revelation 7:1; And after these things I saw four angels standing on the four corners of the earth, holding the four winds of the earth, that the wind should not blow on the earth, nor on the sea, nor on any tree.

The quantity of angels symbolized by the numeral four represents angels deployed over the entire earth poised to implement the Lord's command to destroy those adversaries of the Gospel Dispensation. Notice that the instruction given to the four angels is to not let the four winds blow on the three entities: earth, sea, and tree. Adding the numerals four plus three totaling seven indicates that The Holy Trinity (three) is in control of all of the earth (four) with the numeral seven representing completeness unto perfection.

Revelation 7:2; And I saw another angel ascending from the east, having the seal of the living God: and he cried with a loud voice to the four angels, to whom it was given to hurt the earth and the sea,

"Ascending from the east" identifies Christ as this angel as God and Christ always approach from the east.

Ezekiel 43:2; And, behold, the glory of the God of Israel came from the way of the east: and his voice was like a noise of many waters: and the earth shined with his glory.

Matthew 2:2; Saying, Where is he that is born King of the Jews? for we have seen his star in the east, and are come to worship him.

"Ascending from the east" also refers to Christ being called the dayspring (east) by Luke in chapter one, verse seventy-eight. Crying in a loud voice means the proclamation was made loud enough for all on earth to hear demonstrating his power and authority as Christ was designated by God to implement his plan for mankind.

Luke 1:78-79; Through the tender mercy of our God; whereby the dayspring from on high hath visited us; To give light to them that sit in darkness and in the shadow of death, to guide our feet into the way of peace.

Revelation 2:28; And I will give him the morning star.

Revelation 22:16; I Jesus have sent mine angel to testify unto you these things in the churches. I am the root and the offspring of David, and the bright and morning star.

The phrase "having the seal of the living God" designates the allegiance of Christ unto God and the reason he was entrusted with the power and authority to control his kingdom and offer salvation to whomsoever he pleased.

Matthew 16:19; And I will give unto thee the keys of the kingdom of heaven: and whatsoever thou shalt bind on earth shall be bound in heaven: and whatsoever thou shalt loose on earth shall be loosed in heaven.

Ephesians 1:13; In whom ye also trusted, after that ye heard the word of truth, the gospel of your salvation: in whom also after that ye believed, ye were sealed with that holy Spirit of promise,

Revelation 7:3; Saying, Hurt not the earth, neither the sea, nor the trees, till we have sealed the servants of our God in their foreheads.

The angels were commanded to wait until all of the disciples of God had been distinguished from the adversaries of Christ. The mark on the forehead refers to the custom of marking servants indicating their servitude unto and their ownership by a master.

Matthew 13:49; So shall it be at the end of the world: the angels shall come forth, and sever the wicked from among the just,

Ezekiel 9:4; And the Lord said unto him, Go through the midst of the city, through the midst of Jerusalem, and set a mark upon the foreheads of the men that sigh and that cry for all the abominations that be done in the midst thereof.

The four angels in verse two added to the three entities in verse three totals seven indicating completeness and designating all of those servants of God that became sealed.

Revelation 7:4: And I heard the number of them which were sealed: and there were sealed an hundred and forty and four thousand of all the tribes of the children of Israel.

This symbolizes all of those redeemed by the Lord from the twelve tribes of Israel as the numeral twelve indicates religion and when multiplied by the number one-thousand symbolizing a complete number from each tribe then multiplied by the twelve tribes totals 144,000 sealed. This total number is symbolic of all those children of Israel found worthy and is a symbolic number only as the total number is innumerable as reflected in verse nine.

Revelation 7:5; Of the tribe of Juda were sealed twelve thousand. Of the tribe of Reuben were sealed twelve thousand. Of the tribe of Gad were sealed twelve thousand.

Revelation 7:6; Of the tribe of Aser were sealed twelve thousand. Of the tribe of Nepthalim were sealed twelve thousand. Of the tribe of Manasses were sealed twelve thousand.

Revelation 7:7; Of the tribe of Simeon were sealed twelve thousand. Of the tribe of Levi were sealed twelve thousand. Of the tribe of Issachar were sealed twelve thousand.

Revelation 7:8; Of the tribe of Zabulon were sealed twelve thousand. Of the tribe of Joseph were sealed twelve thousand. Of the tribe of Benjamin were sealed twelve thousand.

To be sealed means acceptance into heaven with their salvation being secured. Even though the tribes of Levi and Joseph did not own land they were included in these verses. The tribes of Dan and Ephraim were not included and no reason was given for their being omitted. In all probability, their being omitted was simply to keep the number at twelve indicating organized religion. This same pattern was followed earlier with the seven

letters to the seven churches. There were actually more than seven churches but only seven were used thereby keeping the number at seven indicating perfection and completeness.

Revelation 7:9; After this I beheld, and, lo, a great multitude, which no man could number, of all nations, and kindreds, and people, and tongues, stood before the throne, and before the Lamb, clothed with white robes, and palms in their hands;

The great multitude of all nations, kindreds, people, and tongues indicates that everyone throughout earth had been offered salvation through the Christian Gospel Dispensation which indicates that Gentiles have now been included. Standing before the throne and the Lamb indicates their acceptance by Christ. Clothed with white robes means they were free from sin and found worthy of heaven. With "palms in their hands" reveals their acknowledgment of Christ and honoring him as their king. Again, "the great multitude" is divided into four groups reflecting all of earth.

Leviticus 23:40; And ye shall take you on the first day the boughs of goodly trees, branches of palm trees, and the boughs of thick trees, and willows of the brook; and ye shall rejoice before the LORD your God seven days.

John 12:13; Took branches of palm trees, and went forth to meet him, and cried, Hosanna: Blessed is the King of Israel that cometh in the name of the Lord.

Revelation 7:10; And cried with a loud voice, saying, Salvation to our God which sitteth upon the throne, and unto the Lamb.

The phrase "cried with a loud voice" signifies a voice loud enough insuring that all will hear that they are honoring God as the Supreme Power worthy of occupying the throne and as the only one who could provide salvation. They also honored Christ who provided their access to salvation as the sacrificial Lamb.

Psalms 3:8: Salvation belongeth unto the Lord: thy blessing is upon thy people. Selah.

Revelation 7:11; And all the angels stood round about the throne, and about the elders and the four beasts, and fell before the throne on their faces, and worshipped God,

Again, there are four activities with three groups totaling seven implying completeness indicating that all of the disciples are worshiping God.

Revelation 7:12; Saying, Amen: Blessing, and glory, and wisdom, and thanksgiving, and honour, and power, and might, be unto our God for ever and ever. Amen.

All of the deserving accolades given to God by all of the angels, elders, and living creatures total seven virtues of praise signifying perfection and completeness. This praise comes from all of the saints in heaven, with the word "Amen" signifying that all were in agreement.

Revelation 7:13; And one of the elders answered, saying unto me, What are these which are arrayed in white robes? And whence came they?

The elder is bringing John's attention to this great multitude of various peoples that are standing before the throne praising God. Their holiness and purity was achieved by their being free from sin is indicated by their white robes. They came from different nations as salvation had been made available to all.

Revelation 7:14; And I said unto him, Sir, thou knowest. And he said to me, These are they which came out of great tribulation, and have washed their robes, and made them white in the blood of the Lamb.

John's reply to the elder was that the elder knew the answers to his own questions. The elder's reply confirmed that the people had been made free from sin by the sacrifice of Christ as reflected symbolically by the phrases "have washed their robes, and made them white in the blood of the Lamb". The great tribulation reveals they also had been persecuted on earth and had remained faithful.

Revelation 1:5; And from Jesus Christ, who is the faithful witness, and the first begotten of the dead, and the prince of the kings of the earth. Unto him that loved us, and washed us from our sins in his own blood,

Isaiah 1:18; Come now, and let us reason together, saith the Lord: though your sins be as scarlet, they shall be as white as snow; though they be red like crimson, they shall be as wool.

The Jews symbolically believed that sins were stains upon their clothing with the color red signifying that those sins could cause spiritual death. The color scarlet was symbolic of their sins being doubled or multiplied as the color scarlet was achieved by the process of dying their clothing twice.

Revelation 7:15; Therefore are they before the throne of God, and serve him day and night in his temple: and he that sitteth on the throne shall dwell among them.

Because these people had accepted Christ and were made free from sin, had endured the hardships imposed upon them and remained faithful, they had earned their reward in paradise and were now before the throne of God serving him day and night with God now dwelling among them.

John 14:2; In my Father's house are many mansions: if it were not so, I would have told you. I go to prepare a place for you.

Revelation 7:16; They shall hunger no more, neither thirst any more; neither shall the sun light on them, nor any heat.

The words hunger and thirst are symbolic for the desire of spiritual salvation. Religion was referred to as the sun and heat as travails through sin and false worship. Their religion is protection from this heat of sinful behavior.

John 4:14; But whosoever drinketh of the water that I shall give him shall never thirst; but the water that I shall give him shall be in him a well of water springing up into everlasting life.

Isaiah 4:6; And there shall be a tabernacle for a shadow in the daytime from the heat, and for a place of refuge, and for a covert from storm and from rain.

Isaiah 25:4; For thou hast been a strength to the poor, a strength to the needy in his distress, a refuge from the storm, a shadow from the heat, when the blast of the terrible ones is as a storm against the wall.

Isaiah 49:10; They shall not hunger nor thirst; neither shall the heat nor sun smite them: for he that hath mercy on them shall lead them, even by the springs of water shall he guide them.

Revelation 7:17; For the Lamb which is in the midst of the throne shall feed them, and shall lead them unto living fountains of waters: and God shall wipe away all tears from their eyes.

This refers to Christ who is on the right hand of God and always in the midst of his followers supplying their spiritual needs by His sacrifice and teachings of the Christian Doctrine and also referring to God who will eliminate all of their sorrows. Isaiah 25:8; He will swallow up death in victory; and the Lord God will wipe away tears from off all faces; and the rebuke of his people shall he take away from off all the earth: for the Lord hath spoken it. Hosea 13:14; I will ransom them from the power of the grave; I will redeem them from death: O death, I will be thy plagues; O grave, I will be thy destruction: repentance shall be hid from mine eyes.

CHAPTER 8

$\mathbf{T}$ his chapter begins with the opening of the seventh seal signifying the onset of God's judgments as indicated by the casting of fire from the altar unto the earth with a golden censer. These judgments appear to be designed to influence people to turn away from evil unto the worship of God as only a "third part" of the various entities were affected proving that these were not the final judgments that are to be associated with the earth and mankind being completely destroyed. This is followed by the sounding of the seven trumpets which are a warning that these events are imminent. The consequence of each judgment is revealed by the sounding of each of the seven trumpets.

Revelation 8:1; And when he had opened the seventh seal, there was silence in heaven about the space of half an hour.

The opening of the seventh seal by Christ (The Lamb) indicates that these judgments are to begin. As God does not willingly afflict the wicked, a short period of silence is observed. The observance of this period of silence reflects the importance and significance of these events brought by God while furnishing every opportunity for people to repent and accept Christ. The period of silence is also a sign of respect that honors God while He is in His temple upon His Holy throne.

Ezekiel 33:11; Say unto them, As I live, saith the Lord God, I have no pleasure in the death of the wicked; but that the wicked turn from his way and live: turn ye, turn ye from your evil ways; for why will ye die, O house of Israel?

Lamentations 3:33; For he doth not afflict willingly nor grieve the children of Men.

Zephaniah 1:7; Hold thy peace at the presence of the Lord God: for the day of the Lord is at hand: for the Lord hath prepared a sacrifice, he hath bid his guests.

Habakkuk 2:20; But the Lord is in his holy temple: let all the earth keep silence before him.

Zechariah 2:13; Be silent, O all flesh, before the Lord: for he is raised up out of his holy habitation.

Revelation 8:2; And I saw the seven angels which stood before God; and to them were given seven trumpets.

These are the seven Spirits referred to in chapter one, verse four, that were before the throne being referred to as seven angels before God. These are the eyes of the Lord reflecting His omnipresence throughout the whole earth. Being given seven trumpets means that these angels were assigned the tasks of notification by trumpet of each of the seven plagues that were to be dispersed.

Zechariah 4:10; For who hath despised the day of small things? for they shall rejoice, and shall see the plummet in the hand of Zerubbabel with those seven; they are the eyes of the LORD, which run to and fro through the whole earth.

Revelation 8:3; And another angel came and stood at the altar, having a golden censer; and there was given unto him much incense, that he should offer it with the prayers of all saints upon the golden altar which was before the throne.

This angel is Christ as He is the one with authority to act as the mediator between the prayers of the saints and the golden altar before the throne of God. Having a golden censer and much incense indicates his great value unto God and the honor due him as associated with royalty.

I Timothy 2:5; For there is one God, and one mediator between God and men, the man Christ Jesus;

Revelation 8:4; And the smoke of the incense, which came with the prayers of the saints, ascended up before God out of the angel's hand.

The prayers of the saints are represented as being offered with the smoke of the incense carrying them up unto God. The burning of incense produced sweet odors thought to be pleasing unto God in order to make God more receptive to their pleas of mercy while the smoke rising from this procedure was to carry the prayers up unto God.

Psalms 141:2; Let my prayer be set forth before thee as incense; and the lifting up of my hands as the evening sacrifice.

Revelation 8:5; And the angel took the censer, and filled it with fire of the altar, and cast it into the earth: and there were voices, and thunderings, and lightnings, and an earthquake.

Under Mosaic Law, it was the custom of the priests to take fire from the altar in a silver censer except on the 'day of atonement' when the high priest took fire from the altar with a golden censer. While the high priest was accomplishing this ritual, the people prayed outside the temple. Casting the fire into the earth accompanied with the voices, thunderings, lightnings, and an earthquake indicates the onset of God's plan for mankind.

The phrase "voices, and thunderings, and lightnings, and an earthquake" imply that God's edicts and judgments upon earth and mankind represent an answer to the prayers of the saints as reflected in verse four.

Exodus 20:18; And all the people saw the thunderings, and the lightnings, and the noise of the trumpet, and the mountain smoking: and when the people saw it, they removed, and stood afar off.

Isaiah 66:6; A voice of noise from the city, a voice from the temple, a voice of the LORD that rendereth recompence to his enemies.

Luke 1:9-10; According to the custom of the priest's office, his lot was to burn incense when he went into the temple of the Lord. And the whole multitude of the people were praying without at the time of incense.

Revelation 8:6; And the seven angels which had the seven trumpets prepared themselves to sound.

The seven angels being ready to sound the trumpets indicates that preparation was being made to warn of the onset of events to take place upon earth and all therein.

Revelation 8:7; The first angel sounded, and there followed hail and fire mingled with blood, and they were cast upon the earth: and the third part of trees was burnt up, and all green grass was burnt up.

"Hail and fire" indicate destruction and punishment upon earth while the phrase "mingled with blood" shows that lives were being lost. "The third part of trees and grass" reveal that a great number of leaders and common people were affected even though they had been forewarned by God as indicated by the phrase "The first angel sounded".
Genesis 19:24; Then the LORD rained upon Sodom and upon Gomorrah brimstone and fire from the LORD out of heaven;
Exodus 9:23; And Moses stretched forth his rod toward heaven: and the Lord sent thunder and hail, and the fire ran along upon the ground; and the Lord rained hail upon the land of Egypt.
II Kings 19:23; By thy messengers thou hast reproached the LORD, and hast said, With the multitude of my chariots I am come up to the height of the mountains, to the sides of Lebanon, and will cut down the tall cedar trees thereof, and the choice fir trees thereof: and I will enter into the lodgings of his borders, and into the forest of his Carmel.
Isaiah 40:7; The grass withereth, the flower fadeth: because the spirit of the LORD bloweth upon it: surely the people is grass.
Daniel 4:20,22; The tree that thou sawest, which grew, and was strong, whose height reached unto the heaven, and the sight thereof to all the earth; It is thou, O king, that art grown and become strong: for thy greatness is grown, and reacheth unto heaven, and thy dominion to the end of the earth.
Revelation 8:8; And the second angel sounded, and as it were a great mountain burning with fire was cast into the sea: and the third part of the sea became blood;

A great mountain burning with fire being cast into the sea indicates that a huge catastrophe was happening with many people being affected. The "great mountain" is Satan's kingdom or dominion of evil while the phrase "burning with fire" reveals active destruction by this evil and is also indicative of God's warning affecting the nations upon earth. The "third part" is phraseology used by Jewish rabbi's to indicate a large portion

of any given number and as the word "sea" represents a multitude of nations or an immense number of people, therefore, the phrase "the third part of the sea became blood" reveals spiritual death for many people by this evil entity. **Satan's kingdom or dominion of evil will affect many people as indicated by the word "sea".**

Psalms 18:7; Then the earth shook and trembled; the foundations also of the hills moved and were shaken, because he was wroth.

Nahum 1:5; The mountains quake at him, and the hills melt, and the earth is burned at his presence, yea, the world, and all that dwell therein.

Habakkuk 3:6; He stood, and measured the earth: he beheld, and drove asunder the nations; and the everlasting mountains were scattered, the perpetual hills did bow: his ways are everlasting.

Jeremiah 51:25; Behold, I am against thee, O destroying mountain, saith the LORD, which destroyest all the earth: and I will stretch out mine hand upon thee, and roll thee down from the rocks, and will make thee a burnt mountain.

The word "mountains" was used in Hebrew phraseology to symbolize kingdoms. This would indicate that many people were being affected.

Revelation 8:9; And the third part of the creatures which were in the sea, and had life, died; and the third part of the ships were destroyed.

The "third part" simply means a large portion of a great number while the phrase, "in the sea" alludes to many people, therefore, many people died from this "great mountain burning with fire". The phrase "and had life" refers to those that previously were disciples of God but lost their spiritual life because they had succumbed to the evils of Satan even though they were forewarned by God. The phrase "third part of the ships" represents that a large volume of the trafficking and commerce of religious doctrines has ceased.

Revelation 8:10; And the third angel sounded, and there fell a great star from heaven, burning as it were a lamp, and it fell upon the third part of the rivers, and upon the fountains of waters;

The great star falling from heaven is Satan and the phrase "burning as it were a lamp" indicates Satan actively promoting

evil. The word "lamp" implies that Satan is the source of that evil being imparted unto others. The word "rivers" indicates Satan imparting or the flowing of his evil doctrine unto people while the phrase "fountains of waters" reveals that many people became a source for his evil doctrine. The phrase "fountains of waters" refers to the source of knowledge with the word "rivers" indicating the flowing of that knowledge, which, in this case, is evil knowledge.

Isaiah 8:6-8; Forasmuch as this people refuseth the waters of Shiloah that go softly, and rejoice in Rezin and Remaliah's son; Now therefore, behold, the Lord bringeth up upon them the waters of the river, strong and many, even the king of Assyria, and all his glory: and he shall come up over all his channels, and go over all his banks: And he shall pass through Judah; he shall overflow and go over, he shall reach even to the neck; and the stretching out of his wings shall fill the breadth of thy land, O Immanuel.

Revelation 8:11; And the name of the star is called Wormwood: and the third part of the waters became wormwood; and many men died of the waters, because they were made bitter.

The word "wormwood" means "bitters or poison". The phrase "the name of the star is called Wormwood" reveals that this is Satan and the phrase "the third part of the waters became wormwood" indicates that many people accepted and taught Satan's evil doctrine. The phrase "many men died of the waters" implies that they lost their spiritual life because of this evil "bitter" doctrine.

Jeremiah 9:15; Therefore thus saith the LORD of hosts, the God of Israel; Behold, I will feed them, even this people, with wormwood, and give them water of gall to drink.

Jeremiah 23:15; Therefore thus saith the LORD of hosts concerning the prophets; Behold, I will feed them with wormwood, and make them drink the water of gall: for from the prophets of Jerusalem is profaneness gone forth into all the land.

Revelation 8:12; And the fourth angel sounded, and the third part of the sun was smitten, and the third part of the moon, and the third part of the stars; so as the third part of them was darkened, and the day shone not for a third part of it, and the night likewise.

With the fourth angel sounding the trumpet, another portion of the occurrences on earth begin to take place. The phrase "third part" means a large portion of a great number will be affected with the "sun" representing the light of God's Word through Christ, the "moon" indicating the light of God's Word through the Mosaic Law, "stars" reflecting leaders, and being "darkened" indicating God's Word being obscured throughout various walks of life by being influenced with Satan's evil doctrine. The phrase "the day shone not for a third part of it, and the night likewise" reveals that much of God's Word became obscured by Satan's evil agenda with many people being lost from the true Word of salvation.

Revelation 8:13; And I beheld, and heard an angel flying through the midst of heaven, saying with a loud voice, Woe, woe, woe, to the inhabiters of the earth by reason of the other voices of the trumpet of the three angels, which are yet to sound!

This angel was a messenger of God with a warning loud enough insuring all on earth would hear of the upcoming judgments of God yet to be revealed by the last three trumpets. The three woes indicate three judgments left to be inflicted upon mankind. The term "loud voice" implies a warning that was loud enough that this message was heard by all of the people on earth.

CHAPTER 9

This chapter continues the same theme as chapter eight in that the judgments of God are being used to impress upon people the fallacy of being swayed by Satan's evil wiles. This chapter begins with Satan being cast from heaven and establishing his dominion of evil represented as a bottomless pit. His doctrine of evil is symbolized as smoke partially obscuring God's Word and his evil minions are represented as locusts devouring this dispensation and causing many people to be deceived and led astray from the light of God's Word. Scorpions reflect the spiritual pain being inflicted upon the peoples of the earth. Many of the symbols presented by John will be found in the book of Isaiah and the book of Joel.

Revelation 9:1; And the fifth angel sounded, and I saw a star fall from heaven unto the earth: and to him was given the key of the bottomless pit.

The star falling from heaven is Satan and being given the key indicates that Satan had authority over the bottomless pit which signifies never-ending evil.

Luke 10:18; And he said unto them, *I beheld Satan as lightning fall from heaven.*

Revelation 12:7-9; And there was war in heaven: Michael and his angels fought against the dragon; and the dragon fought and his angels, And prevailed not; neither was their place found any more in heaven. And the great dragon was cast out, that old serpent, called the Devil, and Satan, which deceiveth the whole world: he was cast out into the earth, and his angels were cast out with him.

172

Revelation 9:2; And he opened the bottomless pit; and there arose a smoke out of the pit, as the smoke of a great furnace; and the sun and the air were darkened by reason of the smoke of the pit.

Opening the bottomless pit means that Satan is loosing evil into the world. The phrase "as the smoke of a great furnace" reveals the enormity of evil being promoted by Satan. Smoke coming out of the pit with the sun being darkened indicates that this evil is obscuring God's Doctrine with false worship. The air being darkened is the actual practice of evil in the world as Satan is referred to as the prince of the air.

Joel 2:2; A day of darkness and of gloominess, a day of clouds and of thick darkness, as the morning spread upon the mountains: a great people and a strong; there hath not been ever the like, neither shall be any more after it, even to the years of many generations.

Ephesians 2:2; Wherein in time past ye walked according to the course of this world, according to the prince of the power of the air, the spirit that now worketh in the children of disobedience:

Revelation 9:3; And there came out of the smoke locusts upon the earth: and unto them was given power, as the scorpions of the earth have power.

The evil emanating from the bottomless pit is likened unto locusts in a symbolical spiritual battle as swarms of locusts devour everything in their path. The locusts were given power to impose their wickedness which is compared to a scorpion sting that inflicts great pain and needs to be avoided. This pain is symbolical of spiritual harm to the faith of the disciples of God as it is opposition to God's Doctrine.

Exodus 10:5,15; And they shall cover the face of the earth, that one cannot be able to see the earth: and they shall eat the residue of that which is escaped, which remainth unto you from the hail, and shall eat every tree which growth for you out of the field: For they covered the face of the whole earth, so that the land was darkened; and they did eat every herb of the land, and all the fruit of the trees which the hail had left: and there remained not any green thing in the trees, or in the herbs of the field, through all the land of Egypt.

Joel 2:3; A fire devoureth before them; and behind them a flame burneth: the land is as the garden of Eden before them, and behind them
a desolate wilderness; yea, and nothing shall escape them.

Revelation 12:13; And when the dragon saw that he was cast unto
the earth, he persecuted the woman which brought forth the man
child.

Revelation 9:4; And it was commanded them that they should not
hurt the grass of the earth, neither any green thing, neither any tree;
but only those men which have not the seal of God in their foreheads.

**It is customary in Hebrew literature to use nature as an
analogy with human endeavors and as green reflects a rebirth
or renewing of plant life in the springtime, therefore this color
is used as symbolical of spiritual life or salvation and as long
as we remain faithful, we are not subject to the evils of Satan.
The spiritual evil of Satan being spread throughout the world is
likened unto locusts consuming all plant life, but affecting only
those people who have not become disciples of God as expressed
by the phrase "but only those men which have not the seal of God
in their foreheads". The word "grass" represents the common
people while the word "trees" reflect leaders.**

Isaiah 40:7; The grass withereth, the flower fadeth: because the spirit
of the LORD bloweth upon it: surely the people is grass.

Daniel 4:20,22; The tree that thou sawest, which grew, and was
strong, whose height reached unto the heaven, and the sight thereof
to all the earth; It is thou, O king, that art grown and become strong:
for thy greatness is grown, and reacheth unto heaven, and thy
dominion to the end of the earth.

Revelation 9:5; And to them it was given that they should not kill
them, but that they should be tormented five months: and their torment was as the torment of a scorpion, when he striketh a man.

**The phrase "that they should not kill them" signifies that
the evil doctrine of Satan will cause tremendous spiritual suffering through deception and temptation but can be overcome
by remaining faithful to the Lord God. The numeral five relates
to mankind which reveals that this evil is limited in power with
man exposed to it during his physical life span. The phrase "torment was as the torment of a scorpion" also indicates the spiri-**

tual grief and suffering brought about through the wiles and actions of Satan.

Revelation 9:6; And in those days shall men seek death, and shall not find it; and shall desire to die, and death shall flee from them.

This is phraseology indicating the dire straits of those who are searching for satisfaction in their physical life with no success and finding human life is but vanity. Vanity, as explained by Job and Solomon, is the futile search for true happiness in your physical life as true riches are not to be found in material possessions, but rather, in spiritual salvation.

Job 3:20-22; Wherefore is light given to him that is in misery, and life unto the bitter in soul; Which long for death, but it cometh not; and dig for it more than for hid treasures; Which rejoice exceedingly, and are glad, when they can find the grave?

Job 7:3,16; So am I made to possess months of vanity, and wearisome nights are appointed to me. I loathe it; I would not live alway: let me alone; for my days are vanity.

Proverbs 21:6; The getting of treasures by a lying tongue is a vanity tossed to and fro of them that seek death.

Ecclesiastes 2:17-23; Therefore I hated life; because the work that is wrought under the sun is grievous unto me: for all is vanity and vexation of spirit. Yea, I hated all my labour which I had taken under the sun: because I should leave it unto the man that shall be after me. And who knoweth whether he shall be a wise man or a fool? yet shall he have rule over all my labour wherein I have laboured, and wherein I have shewed myself wise under the sun. This is also vanity. Therefore I went about to cause my heart to despair of all the labour which I took under the sun. For there is a man whose labour is in wisdom, and in knowledge, and in equity; yet to a man that hath not laboured therein shall he leave it for his portion. This also is vanity and a great evil. For what hath man of all his labour, and of the vexation of his heart, wherein he hath laboured under the sun? For all his days are sorrows, and his travail grief; yea, his heart taketh not rest in the night. This is also vanity.

Revelation 9:7; And the shapes of the locusts were like unto horses prepared unto battle; and on their heads were as it were crowns like gold, and their faces were as the faces of men.

Locusts represent evil emanating and spreading from the "bottomless pit" while horses are symbolical of warfare as this is a battle between good and evil. The phrase's "crowns like gold" and "faces of men" indicate kings, leaders, or teachers with false doctrine and worship. The word "gold" indicates great value unto their evil cause.

Joel 2:4; The appearance of them is as the appearance of horses; and as horsemen, so shall they run.

Revelation 9:8; And they had hair as the hair of women, and their teeth were as the teeth of lions.

Samson's power came from his uncut hair which would be likened as to a woman's long hair. Samson's uncut hair was the result of instructions to Samson's mother from an angel of God for Samson to be a Nazarite unto God, which required that his hair be not cut, and that he would deliver Israel out of the hand of the Philistines.

Judges 13:5; For, lo, thou shalt conceive, and bear a son; and no razor shall come on his head: for the child shall be a Nazarite unto God from the womb: and he shall begin to deliver Israel out of the hand of the Philistines.

Also, long hair is the trademark of women who generally use guile rather than physical strength to accomplish their goals. The spiritual battle between Christ and Satan is through varied means, but primarily through guile and deceit. The expression of fierce battles implied by the analogy of physical power is merely to illustrate the ferocity of the spiritual battle between good versus evil.

The phrase "their teeth were as the teeth of lions" implies ferocity and indicates a physically strong nation overpowering and forcing false worship upon true worshipers of God.

Joel 1:6; For a nation is come up upon my land, strong, and without number, whose teeth are the teeth of a lion, and he hath the cheek teeth of a great lion.

Revelation 9:9; And they had breastplates, as it were breastplates of iron; and the sound of their wings was as the sound of chariots of many horses running to battle.

Breastplates were armor used in battle for bodily protection, therefore, this indicates that penetration of the truth of God's Word into this false doctrine would be extremely difficult. The phrase "sound of chariots of many horses running to battle" expresses a great number of people worshiping false doctrines, combating the Word of God, and forcing Satan's evil doctrine upon others. The phrase "the sound of their wings was as the sound of chariots of many horses running to battle" reflects the swiftness of the promotion of evil by many minions of Satan.

Joel 2:5; Like the noise of chariots on the tops of mountains shall they leap, like the noise of a flame of fire that devoureth the stubble, as a strong people set in battle array.

Revelation 9:10; And they had tails like unto scorpions, and there were stings in their tails: and their power was to hurt men five months.

The phrase "hurt men five months" reflects evil deeds by mankind during his lifespan on earth while the phrase "tails like unto scorpions" means false teachers and the phrase "there were stings in their tails" indicates much spiritual damage and pain during man's lifetime.

Isaiah 9:14-15; Therefore the Lord will cut off from Israel head and tail, branch and rush, in one day. The ancient and honourable, he is the head; and the prophet that teacheth lies, he is the tail.

Revelation 9:11; And they had a king over them, which is the angel of the bottomless pit, whose name in the Hebrew tongue is Abaddon, but in the Greek tongue hath his name Apollyon.

These names "Abaddon and Apollyon" imply Satan who is the "angel of the bottomless pit" from which all evil emanates as he is king over all false teachers and these names translate into the word "Destroyer".

Ephesians 2:2; Wherein in time past ye walked according to the course of this world, according to the prince of the power of the air, the spirit that now worketh in the children of disobedience:

Revelation 9:12; One woe is past; and, behold, there come two woes more hereafter.

The sounding of the trumpet of the fifth angel reflected the ongoing spiritual battle between Christ and Satan that encom-

passed the events detailed in verses one through eleven of this chapter while the phrase "there come two woes more hereafter" reveals more spiritual battles await.

Revelation 9:13; And the sixth angel sounded, and I heard a voice from the four horns of the golden altar which is before God,

The four horns relate to the power given to mankind upon all of earth by God as indicated in verse fourteen while the voice from the golden altar refers to another judgment of God.

Revelation 9:14; Saying to the sixth angel which had the trumpet, Loose the four angels which are bound in the great river Euphrates.

The great river Euphrates refers to the flowing and imparting of evil knowledge from Babylon which is called the great harlot because of the varied false worship forced upon mankind from among the evil nations throughout history being headquartered in Babylon. The phrase "Loose the four angels which are bound" suggests that these angels are messengers from Satan whose duty is to spread this false worship throughout all of earth as indicated by the numeral four. This command came from God which reveals that God is in control of all events upon earth.

Revelation 9:15; And the four angels were loosed, which were prepared for an hour, and a day, and a month, and a year, for to slay the third part of men.

The numeral four used in the description of the quantity of angels and also their preparation time being divided into four parts indicate that their mission was to be the whole earth. "To slay the third part of men" represents that their goal was to lead a large number of people astray from the true spiritual worship of God.

Revelation 9:16; And the number of the army of the horsemen were two hundred thousand thousand: and I heard the number of them.

The use of numbers in the book of Revelation rarely indicates an actual mathematical value. This symbolically represents an extremely large number of people implementing evil upon the earth for Satan.

Psalms 68:17; The chariots of God are twenty thousand, even thousands of angels: the Lord is among them, as in Sinai, in the holy place.

Daniel 7:10; A fiery stream issued and came forth from before him: thousand thousands ministered unto him, and ten thousand times ten thousand stood before him: the judgment was set, and the books were opened.

Revelation 9:17; And thus I saw the horses in the vision, and them that sat on them, having breastplates of fire, and of jacinth, and brimstone: and the heads of the horses were as the heads of lions; and out of their mouths issued fire and smoke and brimstone.

The word "horses" reveal a battle with their riders being protected by "breastplates of fire" indicating false worship being difficult to penetrate with the truth. "The heads of the horses were as the heads of lions" shows that this is a fierce battle between good and evil. "Out of their mouths issued fire" implies false doctrine being taught with the word "smoke" representing the obscuring of God's Doctrine and the word "brimstone" symbolizing spiritual punishment unto those pursuing false doctrines. The word "jacinth" is a reddish-orange gemstone possibly resembling a burning flame which would indicate continuous activity.

Isaiah 9:18-19; For wickedness burneth as the fire: it shall devour the briers and thorns, and shall kindle in the thickets of the forest, and they shall mount up like the lifting up smoke. Through the wrath of the Lord of hosts is the land darkened, and the people shall be as the fuel of the fire: no man shall spare his brother.

Revelation 9:18; By these three was the third part of men killed, by the fire, and by the smoke, and by the brimstone, which issued out of their mouths.

The phrase, "By these three", fire, smoke, and brimstone indicate the various ways that people lose their spiritual salvation. "Fire" represents destruction by wickedness, "smoke" as deception, and "brimstone" reflects punishment. The phrase "which issued out of their mouths" proves this is a spiritual rather than physical battle between Christ and Satan.

Jeremiah 5:14; Wherefore thus saith the LORD God of hosts, Because ye speak this word, behold, I will make my words in thy mouth fire, and this people wood, and it shall devour them.

"Smoke" represents the obscuring of God's Word.

Revelation 9:2; And he opened the bottomless pit; and there arose a smoke out of the pit, as the smoke of a great furnace; and the sun and the air were darkened by reason of the smoke of the pit.

"Brimstone" is the punishment by God for those people accepting or believing false teaching and being guilty of evil practices.

Genesis 19:24; Then the LORD rained upon Sodom and upon Gomorrah brimstone and fire from the LORD out of heaven;

The "third part of men killed" reflects a large number of people losing their spiritual salvation because of the evil doctrine being taught by false prophets.

Revelation 9:19; For their power is in their mouth, and in their tails: for their tails were like unto serpents, and had heads, and with them they do hurt.

Power in their mouth represents false teaching as the words "tails" and "heads" imply false teachers and leaders while the phrase "they do hurt" means spiritual damage through false doctrine and false worship. The phrase "like unto serpents" reveals that this false teaching was influenced by Satan.

Isaiah 9:15; The ancient and honourable, he is the head; and the prophet that teacheth lies, he is the tail.

Hebrews 13:9; Be not carried about with divers and strange doctrines. For it is a good thing that the heart be established with grace; not with meats, which have not profited them that have been occupied therein.

II Peter 2:1-3; But there were false prophets also among the people, even as there shall be false teachers among you, who privily shall bring in damnable heresies, even denying the Lord that bought them, and bring upon themselves swift destruction. And many shall follow their pernicious ways; by reason of whom the way of truth shall be evil spoken of. And through covetousness shall they with feigned words make merchandise of you: whose judgment now of a long time lingereth not, and their damnation slumbereth not.

Revelation 9:20; And the rest of the men which were not killed by these plagues yet repented not of the works of their hands, that they should not worship devils, and idols of gold, and silver, and brass, and stone, and of wood: which neither can see, nor hear, nor walk:

This identifies those people that are guilty of worshiping false idols and still have the opportunity to accept the Christian Doctrine, yet have not. Being six different descriptions of false worship reflects sinister activities by mankind.

I Kings 21:24-26; Him that dieth of Ahab in the city the dogs shall eat; and him that dieth in the field shall the fowls of the air eat. But there was none like unto Ahab, which did sell himself to work wickedness in the sight of the LORD, whom Jezebel his wife stirred up. And he did very abominably in following idols, according to all things as did the Amorites, whom the LORD cast out before the children of Israel.

Revelation 9:21; Neither repented they of their murders, nor of their sorceries, nor of their fornication, nor of their thefts.

This refers to those that were yet alive with the time and opportunity to turn to the true worship of God but had not yet done so. They were still murdering others, worshiping false idolatry, practicing witchcraft, and stealing. Verse twenty-one lists these four entities indicating deeds on earth by man.

I Kings 22:40,52-53; So Ahab slept with his fathers; and Ahaziah his son reigned in his stead. And he did evil in the sight of the LORD, and walked in the way of his father, and in the way of his mother, and in the way of Jeroboam the son of Nebat, who made Israel to sin: For he served Baal, and worshiped him, and provoked to anger the LORD God of Israel, according to all that his father had done.

CHAPTER 10

This chapter begins with Christ, identified as a mighty angel clothed with a cloud, being sent to earth to accomplish God's plan for mankind as revealed by a little book being open in his hand. Setting his right foot upon the sea and his left foot upon the earth signifies that he has the authority and is control of all of earth while acknowledging God as the eternal Supreme Power.

Revelation 10:1; And I saw another mighty angel come down from heaven, clothed with a cloud: and a rainbow was upon his head, and his face was as it were the sun, and his feet as pillars of fire:

This is Christ being sent to earth to accomplish God's plan for mankind and being clothed with a cloud was symbolical of the Lord's appearance and presence bringing about change. The sun represents the Christian religion and with the rainbow upon his head reflects God's covenant with all creatures. The phrase "his feet as pillars of fire" reveals the ability to advance forward and accomplish His mission.

Numbers 16:42; And it came to pass, when the congregation was gathered against Moses and against Aaron, that they looked toward the tabernacle of the congregation: and, behold, the cloud covered it, and the glory of the Lord appeared.

Matthew 17:2; And was transfigured before them: and his face did shine as the sun, and his raiment was white as the light.

Revelation 1:15; And his feet like unto fine brass, as if they burned in a furnace; and his voice as the sound of many waters.

Genesis 9:14,16; And it shall come to pass, when I bring a cloud over the earth, that the bow shall be seen in the cloud: And the bow shall be in the cloud; and I will look upon it, that I may remember the everlasting covenant between God and every living creature of all flesh that is upon the earth.

Revelation 10:2; And he had in his hand a little book open: and he set his right foot upon the sea, and his left foot on the earth,

Having an open book in his hand reveals following the instructions for implementing God's plan of salvation and combating evil upon earth. Setting his feet upon the sea and the earth demonstrates Christ's power and authority over all of the earth. John 18:37; Pilate therefore said unto him, Art thou a king then? Jesus answered, Thou sayest that I am a king. To this end was I born, and for this cause came I into the world, that I should bear witness unto the truth. Every one that is of the truth heareth my voice.

Revelation 10:3; And cried with a loud voice, as when a lion roareth: and when he had cried, seven thunders uttered their voices.

The phrase, "cried with a loud voice" means a warning being given loud enough to be heard by everyone while the phrase, "as when a lion roareth" demonstrates power. The phrase, "and when he had cried, seven thunders uttered their voices" indicates complete authority and control over the events about to occur as the number seven indicates completeness. The numeral "seven" in the phrase "seven thunders" show God's complete approval of Christ as the instrument for implementing His complete plan of salvation for mankind and combating Satan's evil doctrine while the word "thunders" indicate God's judgments.

Revelation 10:4; And when the seven thunders had uttered their voices, I was about to write: and I heard a voice from heaven saying unto me, Seal up those things which the seven thunders uttered, and write them not.

John was instructed to not report what was to occur regarding the seven thunders as this knowledge was to remain concealed from mankind until God was ready to implement it upon earth. Daniel was also instructed to not report his vision in:

Daniel 8:26; And the vision of the evening and the morning which was told is true: wherefore shut thou up the vision; for it shall be for many days.

Daniel 12:4,9; But thou, O Daniel, shut up the words, and seal the book, even to the time of the end: many shall run to and fro, and knowledge shall be increased. And he said, Go thy way, Daniel: for the words are closed up and sealed till the time of the end.

Mankind is not privileged to know the intricacies of God's final judgment.

Matthew 24:36; But of that day and hour knoweth no man, no, not the angels of heaven, but my Father only.

Revelation 10:5; And the angel which I saw stand upon the sea and upon the earth lifted up his hand to heaven,

Christ standing upon the sea and the earth shows that He is in control and rules over the entire world and by the phrase "lifted up his hand to heaven" shows that he acknowledges God as the Supreme Ruler over everything.

Genesis 14:19,22; And he blessed him, and said, Blessed be Abram of the most high God, possessor of heaven and earth: And Abram said to the king of Sodom, I have lift up mine hand unto the LORD, the most high God, the possessor of heaven and earth,

Revelation 10:6; And sware by him that liveth for ever and ever, who created heaven, and the things that therein are, and the earth, and the things that therein are, and the sea, and the things which are therein, that there should be time no longer:

This is Christ acknowledging God as the eternal Supreme Being and Creator of all things and that He will fulfill God's judgment for all of mankind as reflected by the word "sea", then deliver His Christian Kingdom to God while bringing an end to this current heaven and earth as indicated by the phrase "that there should be time no longer".

Daniel 12:7; And I heard the man clothed in linen, which was upon the waters of the river, when he held up his right hand and his left hand unto heaven, and sware by him that liveth for ever that it shall be for a time, times, and a half; and when he shall have accomplished to scatter the power of the holy people, all these things shall be finished.

Revelation 10:7; But in the days of the voice of the seventh angel, when he shall begin to sound, the mystery of God should be finished, as he hath declared to his servants the prophets.

When the seventh angel sounds the last trump the mystery of God's plan will be revealed signaling the onset of the final judgment with the destruction of all evil forces along with this heaven and earth and the deliverance of Christ's kingdom to God as the new heaven and the new earth as foretold by the prophets.

Revelation 11:15; And the seventh angel sounded; and there were great voices in heaven, saying, The kingdoms of this world are become the kingdoms of our Lord, and of his Christ; and he shall reign for ever and ever.

Daniel 7:18; But the saints of the most High shall take the kingdom, and possess the kingdom for ever, even for ever and ever.

Revelation 10:8; And the voice which I heard from heaven spake unto me again, and said, Go and take the little book which is open in the hand of the angel which standeth upon the sea and upon the earth.

John was instructed to take the little book out of the hand of Christ who had power, dominion, and control over all earth as indicated by one foot upon the sea and one foot upon the earth. With the book being opened reveals that Christ was following and fulfilling God's plan for earth and mankind. The book being little implies that this was not the final judgment, but, rather, the plan for establishing the Gospel of Christ upon earth as Christ was the Son of God.

Revelation 10:9; And I went unto the angel, and said unto him, Give me the little book. And he said unto me, Take it, and eat it up; and it shall make thy belly bitter, but it shall be in thy mouth sweet as honey.

This is the Word of God establishing the plan of salvation which brings great joy for those that choose to partake of God's grace, but also opposition and persecution from Satan and his evil angels. The phrase, "in thy mouth sweet as honey", means salvation while the phrase, "make thy belly bitter" means suffering persecution as a disciple of Christ.

Jeremiah 15:16; Thy words were found, and I did eat them; and thy word was unto me the joy and rejoicing of mine heart: for I am called by thy name, O Lord God of hosts.

Ezekiel 2:8-10; But thou, son of man, hear what I say unto thee; Be not thou rebellious like that rebellious house: open thy mouth, and eat that I give thee. And when I looked, behold, an hand was sent unto me; and, lo, a roll of a book was therein; And he spread it before me; and it was written within and without: and there was written therein lamentations, and mourning, and woe.

Revelation 10:10; And I took the little book out of the angel's hand, and ate it up; and it was in my mouth sweet as honey: and as soon as I had eaten it, my belly was bitter.

The phrase "and it was in my mouth sweet as honey" reflects the love and benevolence of our Lord who extended the offer of eternal salvation in heaven and the phrase "my belly was bitter" represents the persecutions by Satan and his evil forces to be endured by those who accept this offer of our Lord.

Ezekiel 3:3; And he said unto me, Son of man, cause thy belly to eat, and fill thy bowels with this roll that I give thee. Then did I eat it; and it was in my mouth as honey for sweetness.

Psalms 119:103; How sweet are thy words unto my taste! yea, sweeter than honey to my mouth!

Revelation 10:11; And he said unto me, Thou must prophesy again before many peoples, and nations, and tongues, and kings.

John was instructed to teach the Word of God, the plan of salvation, and the Gospel of Christ to as many different people, nations, tongues, and kings as possible. The four entities of peoples, nations, tongues, and kings reveal that this prophesy was to be taught over the entire earth.

Ezekiel 3:4; And he said unto me, Son of man, go, get thee unto the house of Israel, and speak with my words unto them.

CHAPTER 11

This chapter reflects the preaching and teaching of God's Word by His two witnesses, the Mosaic Law and Christ while under severe persecution from Satan and his evil forces. It also reveals that there will be a short period of time symbolized as three days and an half during which Satan's dominion of evil will be in control and that God's Word will be temporarily extinguished.

Revelation 11:1; And there was given me a reed like unto a rod: and the angel stood, saying, Rise, and measure the temple of God, and the altar, and them that worship therein.

A reed was a measuring instrument used as a ruler in our terminology. To take measure of something implies future judgment or change to that entity and also to determine the ability or the vulnerability of that which was measured. To "measure the temple of God" and those "that worship therein" was to determine the ability of the temple and its worshipers to withstand the coming persecution of their enemies.

Ezekiel 40:3; And he brought me thither, and, behold, there was a man, whose appearance was like the appearance of brass, with a line of flax in his hand, and a measuring reed; and he stood in the gate;

Ezekiel 43:7; And he said unto me, Son of man, the place of my throne, and the place of the soles of my feet, where I will dwell in the midst of the children of Israel for ever, and my holy name, shall the house of Israel no more defile, neither they, nor their kings, by their whoredom, nor by the carcases of their kings in their high places.

Ezekiel 44:2; Then said the Lord unto me; This gate shall be shut, it shall not be opened, and no man shall enter in by it; because the Lord, the God of Israel, hath entered in by it, therefore it shall be shut. (Ezekiel 40, 41, 42, 43, 44.)

Habakkuk 3:6; He stood, and measured the earth: he beheld, and drove asunder the nations; and the everlasting mountains were scattered, the perpetual hills did bow: his ways are everlasting.

Revelation 11:2; But the court which is without the temple leave out, and measure it not; for it is given unto the Gentiles: and the holy city shall they tread under foot forty and two months.

The instruction to measure the temple of God was to keep and insure separation between disciples of God versus the followers of Satan. To not measure the outer court suggests that the Gentiles would be allowed a period of time to persecute the temple of God. The phrase "the holy city shall they tread under foot forty and two months" reveals persecution by the Gentiles for this period of time. The forty-two months is the period of time designated by God to accomplish the preaching and teaching of His Word throughout earth and is also the period of time designated by God for the battle between good and evil for the souls of mankind. Also, to not measure the outer court of the Gentiles implies that God's disciples must not use physical force to impart God's Word.

Psalms 79:1; O God, the heathen are come into thine inheritance; thy holy temple have they defiled; they have laid Jerusalem on heaps.

Ezekiel 42:20; He measured it by the four sides: it had a wall round about, five hundred reeds long, and five hundred broad, to make a separation between the sanctuary and the profane place.

Luke 21:24; And they shall fall by the edge of the sword, and shall be led away captive into all nations: and Jerusalem shall be trodden down of the Gentiles, until the times of the Gentiles be fulfilled.

Revelation 11:3; And I will give power unto my two witnesses, and they shall prophesy a thousand two hundred and threescore days, clothed in sackcloth.

The two witnesses were: firstly, the law given on Mount Sinai to the children of Israel through Moses commonly called "The Mosaic Law" and the second witness is the Christian

Gospel dispensation through the teachings of Christ. Through the preaching and teaching of these two witnesses the testimony of God was brought unto earth. God empowered His two witnesses to bring His Word unto mankind to combat evil brought into the world by Satan. Under the Mosaic Law, two witnesses were necessary for confirmation of the truth. Christ also dispatched seventy disciples two by two in advance of his ministry throughout the cities and places in advance of his coming as the second person was confirmation of the truth.

Deuteronomy 19:15; One witness shall not rise up against a man for any iniquity, or for any sin, in any sin that he sinneth: at the mouth of two witnesses, or at the mouth of three witnesses, shall the matter be established.

II Corinthians 13:1; This is the third time I am coming to you. In the mouth of two or three witnesses shall every word be established.

Matthew 18:16; But if he will not hear thee, then take with thee one or two more, that in the mouth of two or three witnesses every word may be established.

Luke 10:1; After these things the LORD appointed other seventy also, and sent them two and two before his face into every city and place, whither he himself would come.

The thousand two hundred sixty days is the same as the forty-two month time period and the time, times, and half a time which is the period of time designated by God to spread His Word throughout earth.

Daniel 12:7; And I heard the man clothed in linen, which was upon the waters of the river, when he held up his right hand and his left hand unto heaven, and sware by him that liveth for ever that it shall be for a time, times, and an half; and when he shall have accomplished to scatter the power of the holy people, all these things shall be finished.

Being "clothed in sackcloth" implies the duress under which the spreading of God's Word will be accomplished.

Mark 1:4; John did baptize in the wilderness, and preach the baptism of repentance for the remission of sins.

Revelation 11:4; These are the two olive trees, and the two candlesticks standing before the God of the earth.

The two olive trees and the two candlesticks are symbolic for the two witnesses and they represent the oil for the lamps and the source of energy which brings the light of God's Word unto earth.

Zechariah 4:1-3,6,12-14; And the angel that talked with me came again, and waked me, as a man that is wakened out of his sleep, And said unto me, What seest thou? And I said, I have looked, and behold a candlestick all of gold, with a bowl upon the top of it, and his seven lamps thereon, and seven pipes to the seven lamps, which are upon the top thereof: And two olive trees by it, one upon the right side of the bowl, and the other upon the left side thereof. Then he answered and spake unto me, saying, This is the word of the Lord unto Zerubbabel, saying, Not by might, nor by power, but by my spirit, saith the Lord of hosts. And I answered again, and said unto him, What be these two olive branches which through the two golden pipes empty the golden oil out of themselves? And he answered me and said, Knowest thou not what these be? And I said, No, my lord. Then said he, These are the two anointed ones, that stand by the Lord of the whole earth.

Revelation 11:5; And if any man will hurt them, fire proceedeth out of their mouth, and devoureth their enemies: and if any man will hurt them, he must in this manner be killed.

This is a judgment of God for retribution upon the enemies of His Word being enforced by His Word out of the mouths of His witnesses.

II Kings 1:10; And Elijah answered and said to the captain of fifty, If I be a man of God, then let fire come down from heaven, and consume thee and thy fifty. And there came down fire from heaven, and consumed him and his fifty.

Jeremiah 5:14: Wherefore thus saith the LORD God of hosts, Because ye speak this word, behold, I will make my words in thy mouth fire, and this people wood, and it shall devour them.

Revelation 11:6; These have power to shut heaven, that it rain not in the days of their prophecy: and have power over waters to turn them to blood, and to smite the earth with all plagues, as often as they will.

This means that God, through His two witnesses, has empowered his servants to preach and teach His Word throughout earth and the phrase "have power to shut heaven, that it rain not in the days of their prophecy" means they were given power and authority over devils, diseases, and the elements.

James 5:17; Elias was a man subject to like passions as we are, and he prayed earnestly that it might not rain: and it rained not on the earth by the space of three years and six months.

I Kings 17:1; And Elijah the Tishbite, who was of the inhabitants of Gilead, said unto Ahab, As the Lord God of Israel liveth, before whom I stand, there shall not be dew nor rain these years, but according to my word.

Matthew 16:19; And I will give unto thee the keys of the kingdom of heaven: and whatsoever thou shalt bind on earth shall be bound in heaven: and whatsoever thou shalt loose on earth shall be loosed in heaven.

As the word "waters" represents a multitude of people or nations, the phrase "turn waters into blood" implies the ability to impose spiritual death upon their opposition as the word "blood" symbolizes loss of spiritual life.

John 20:23; Whose soever sins ye remit, they are remitted unto them; and whose soever sins ye retain, they are retained.

Matthew 10:7-8,11-14; And as ye go, preach, saying, The kingdom of heaven is at hand. Heal the sick, cleanse the lepers, raise the dead, cast out devils: freely ye have received, freely give. And into whatsoever city or town ye shall enter, enquire who in it is worthy; and there abide till ye go thence. And when ye come into an house, salute it. And if the house be worthy, let your peace come upon it: but if it be not worthy, let your peace return to you. And whosoever shall not receive you, nor hear your words, when ye depart out of that house or city, shake off the dust of your feet.

Mark 6:11; And whosoever shall not receive you, nor hear you, when ye depart thence, shake off the dust under your feet for a testimony against them. Verily I say unto you, It shall be more tolerable for Sodom and Gomorrha in the day of judgment, than for that city.

Luke 9:1-2,5; Then he called his twelve disciples together, and gave them power and authority over all devils, and to cure diseases. And he sent them to preach the kingdom of God, and to heal the sick. *And whosoever will not receive you, when ye go out of that city, shake off the very dust from your feet for a testimony against them.*

Many wars have been fought over religion causing much physical and spiritual death and also, by strict Puritan standards, death, both physical and spiritual, has occurred. This has happened often throughout history as severe punishment has been imposed upon many people. An example was the edict issued upon the life of Martin Luther when he left the Catholic Church over differences of opinion in the Scriptures.

Exodus 7:20; And Moses and Aaron did so, as the Lord commanded; and he lifted up the rod, and smote the waters that were in the river, in the sight of Pharaoh, and in the sight of his servants; and all the waters that were in the river were turned to blood.

Revelation 11:7; And when they shall have finished their testimony, the beast that ascendeth out of the bottomless pit shall make war against them, and shall overcome them, and kill them.

This is a prophecy indicating that evil will eventually overwhelm Christian principles after the ceasing of the testimony of God's Word upon earth reflected as the "thousand years" bringing about the final judgment of God. This prophecy of a short time period that Satan will rule is symbolized as "three days and an half" that begins after the Gospel Dispensation period ends and is alluded to in Matthew, chapter twenty-four, verses fourteen and twenty-two and referenced again in Revelation, chapter twenty, verses three, seven, and eight.

Matthew 24:14,22; And this gospel of the kingdom shall be preached in all the world for a witness unto all nations; and then shall the end come. And except those days should be shortened, there should no flesh be saved: but for the elect's sake those days shall be shortened.

Revelation 13:7; And it was given unto him to make war with the saints, and to overcome them: and power was given him over all kindreds, and tongues, and nations.

Revelation 20:3,7-8; And cast him into the bottomless pit, and shut him up, and set a seal upon him, that he should deceive the nations no more, till the thousand years should be fulfilled: and after that he must be loosed a little season. And when the thousand years are expired, Satan shall be loosed out of his prison, And shall go out to deceive the nations which are in the four quarters of the earth, Gog, and Magog, to gather them together to battle: the number of whom is as the sand of the sea.

II Thessalonians 2:3; Let no man deceive you by any means: for that day shall not come, except there come a falling away first, and that man of sin be revealed, the son of perdition;

The preaching and teaching of God's Word induced warfare from Satan through various avenues of evil such as idolatry, false doctrines, and also by those with no religious morals allowing Satan to destroy many people through his evil doctrine.

Mosaic Law and Christianity have been and are under attack from many different avenues such as radical Islam which proscribes death to any other religion. Also, in efforts to further their agenda or political power, many leaders have forced upon these disciples abominations to God. This has been done throughout history with the Chaldean (Babylonian) Empire, the Medo-Persian Empire, the Alexandrian Empire, the Roman Empire, and also is in evidence today by our own government with the removal of references to Christianity from public forums and by the promotion of homosexuality.

Revelation 11:8; And their dead bodies shall lie in the street of the great city, which spiritually is called Sodom and Egypt, where also our Lord was crucified.

The phrase "and their dead bodies shall lie in the street" indicates that the ceasing of the testimony of God's Word will result in the loss of a moral voice causing much spiritual loss of life while the phrase, "the great city, which spiritually is called Sodom and Egypt", represents immoral values and persecution becoming dominant for a short period of time before the final judgment day. Sodom is synonymous with immorality while Egypt worshiped false gods and persecuted the children of Israel that were under their bondage.

Jeremiah 23:14; I have seen also in the prophets of Jerusalem an horrible thing: they commit adultery, and walk in lies: they strengthen also the hands of evildoers, that none doth return from his wickedness: they are all of them unto me as Sodom, and the inhabitants thereof as Gomorrah.

Revelation 11:9; And they of the people and kindreds and tongues and nations shall see their dead bodies three days and an half, and shall not suffer their dead bodies to be put in graves.

The four entities "people and kindreds and tongues and nations" listed imply that this covers all of the people on earth as the numeral four reflects all of earth. The "three days and an half" is the much shorter period of time designated by God from the end of the testimony of His two witnesses until the final judgment and destruction of Satan and his evil forces while the phrase "shall not suffer their dead bodies to be put in graves" proves that God's Word will never be destroyed.

Psalms 79:2-3; The dead bodies of thy servants have they given to be meat unto the fowls of the heaven, the flesh of thy saints unto the beasts of the earth. Their blood have they shed like water round about Jerusalem; and there was none to bury them.

Matthew 24:22; And except those days should be shortened, there should no flesh be saved: but for the elect's sake those days shall be shortened.

Revelation 11:10; And they that dwell upon the earth shall rejoice over them, and make merry, and shall send gifts one to another; because these two prophets tormented them that dwelt on the earth.

The phrase "they that dwelt on the earth" refers to those people who are in opposition to the religion established by the Lord God. The teaching of religious morals interferes with those who desire no restrictions on their lifestyle while the word "earth" signifies the battleground for the spiritual war between God and Satan. During the time of this writing by John it was customary to celebrate by sending gifts one to another. The phrase "these two prophets tormented them that dwelt on the earth" reflects the preaching and teaching of God's Word by the Mosaic Law and Christ tormenting those who refuse to accept this testimony.

Esther 9:22; As the days wherein the Jews rested from their enemies, and the month which was turned unto them from sorrow to joy, and from mourning into a good day: that they should make them days of feasting and joy, and of sending portions one to another, and gifts to the poor.

Revelation 11:11; And after three days and an half the Spirit of life from God entered into them, and they stood upon their feet; and great fear fell upon them which saw them.

The three days and a half is the much shorter period of time designated by God from the ceasing of the testimony of His Word upon earth to mankind until the final judgment day. The phrase "the Spirit of life from God entered into them" proves that God's Word will never be destroyed while the phrase "and they stood upon their feet" reveals their spiritual salvation as promised by God. This caused "great fear" among the people who believed that the voices of the two great witnesses, Mosaic Law and Christ, had been stopped. After this Christian Gospel Dispensation period and the short period of time that Satan will rule, Christ will return the second time to render judgment upon evil and deliver His Kingdom unto God causing extreme anguish "and great fear" among those that remain lost from spiritual salvation.

Ezekiel 37:14; And shall put my spirit in you, and ye shall live, and I shall place you in your own land: then shall ye know that I the LORD have spoken it, and performed it, saith the LORD.

This verse represents the children of Israel being brought out of bondage from Chaldea back into their own land by the hand of the Lord symbolizing this period of time.

I Peter 1:25; But the word of the Lord endureth for ever. And this is the word which by the gospel is preached unto you.

II Peter 3:7,12; But the heavens and the earth, which are now, by the same word are kept in store, reserved unto fire against the day of judgment and perdition of ungodly men. Looking for and hasting unto the coming of the day of God, wherein the heavens being on fire shall be dissolved, and the elements shall melt with fervent heat?

Revelation 11:12; And they heard a great voice from heaven saying unto them, Come up hither. And they ascended up to heaven in a cloud; and their enemies beheld them.

This salvation and transporting to heaven of these witnesses martyred for the testimony of God's Word will be heard and

observed by the enemies of the Lord God causing the heathens to recognize that the power of God's Word will never be extinguished. As these were martyrs for the testimony of God's Word, they were given early entrance into heaven called the first resurrection. This early acceptance into heaven was granted in answer to the prayer made as reflected by the book of Psalms, chapter ninety, verses fourteen through seventeen.

Matthew 24:30; And then shall appear the sign of the Son of man in heaven: and then shall all the tribes of the earth mourn, and they shall see the Son of man coming in the clouds of heaven with power and great glory.

II Peter 3:13-14; Nevertheless we, according to his promise, look for new heavens and a new earth, wherein dwelleth righteousness. Wherefore, beloved, seeing that ye look for such things, be diligent that ye may be found of him in peace, without spot, and blameless.

Revelation 11:13; And the same hour was there a great earthquake, and the tenth part of the city fell, and in the earthquake were slain of men seven thousand: and the remnant were affrighted, and gave glory to the God of heaven.

The phrase "same hour" implies an immediate response with this being another judgment of God as indicated by the symbol "earthquake" with a large portion of mankind suffering punishment causing others to become frightened and recognizing God as the Supreme Power. The tenth part of a city means a large portion of man made structures were destroyed. Seven thousand represents the complete number of those lost without salvation. The remnant being "affrighted" and giving "glory to the God of heaven" suggests that this judgment by God led to repentance among some people.

II Thessalonians 1:8-9; In flaming fire taking vengeance on them that know not God, and that obey not the gospel of our Lord Jesus Christ: Who shall be punished with everlasting destruction from the presence of the Lord, and from the glory of his power;

Revelation 11:14; The second woe is past; and, behold, the third woe cometh quickly.

There were three woes pronounced in Revelation 8:13 by an angel flying through the midst of heaven. The first woe was the evil warfare launched by Satan from the bottomless pit. The second woe was the retaliation by Satan's evil forces against the spreading of God's Word. The third woe is the warfare by Satan upon the man-child which is Christ.

Revelation 11:15; And the seventh angel sounded; and there were great voices in heaven, saying, The kingdoms of this world are become the kingdoms of our Lord, and of his Christ; and he shall reign for ever and ever.

The seventh angel sounding the trumpet signals the victory of the Lord and His Christ over the kingdoms of this world. The term "great voices in heaven" reflects the announcement of this change revealing that God's judgments had prevailed.

Daniel 7:14,18,27; And there was given him dominion, and glory, and a kingdom, that all people, nations, and languages, should serve him: his dominion is an everlasting dominion, which shall not pass away, and his kingdom that which shall not be destroyed. But the saints of the most High shall take the kingdom, and possess the kingdom for ever, even for ever and ever. And the kingdom and dominion, and the greatness of the kingdom under the whole heaven, shall be given to the people of the saints of the most High, whose kingdom is an everlasting kingdom, and all dominions shall serve and obey him.

Revelation 11:16; And the four and twenty elders, which sat before God on their seats, fell upon their faces, and worshiped God,

The twenty-four elders, twelve each from the children of Israel, representing the twelve tribes under Mosaic Law, and twelve each from the Christian Doctrine, representing the twelve apostles under Christ, totals twenty-four which represent all of the elders of God from both the Mosaic Law and Christianity falling upon their faces worshiping God.

Revelation 11:17; Saying, We give thee thanks, O Lord God Almighty, which art, and wast, and art to come; because thou hast taken to thee thy great power, and hast reigned.

The twenty-four elders, probably representing all of the saints, give thanks to God as the Supreme Power and acknowledge Him as being eternal who has and will continue to exist and reign forever.

Psalms 75:1; Unto thee, O God, do we give thanks, unto thee do we give thanks: for that thy name is near thy wondrous works declare.

Revelation 11:18; And the nations were angry, and thy wrath is come, and the time of the dead, that they should be judged, and that thou shouldest give reward unto thy servants the prophets, and to the saints, and them that fear thy name, small and great; and shouldest destroy them which destroy the earth.

The enemies of God and Christ are angry that the wrath of God is bringing judgment upon them with their time being finished upon earth and the rewards being given to the prophets, saints, and all that fear God while the foes of Christ suffer destruction.

II Thessalonians 1:8; In flaming fire taking vengeance on them that know not God, and that obey not the gospel of our Lord Jesus Christ:

II Thessalonians 2:8; And then shall that Wicked be revealed, whom the Lord shall consume with the spirit of his mouth, and shall destroy with the brightness of his coming:

II Thessalonians 3:2; And that we may be delivered from unreasonable and wicked men: for all men have not faith.

Revelation 11:19; And the temple of God was opened in heaven, and there was seen in his temple the ark of his testament: and there were lightnings, and voices, and thunderings, and an earthquake, and great hail.

The temple of God being opened in heaven indicates the acceptance of Christ's Church or Kingdom being delivered unto God. The phrase "ark of his testament" indicates God's Word which is the source of this immense power. The phrase "and there were lightnings, and voices, and thunderings, and an earthquake, and great hail" represent destruction of mankind upon earth by the judgments of God as there are five entities of destruction. The word "voices" indicate the edicts of God bringing about these judgments.

Isaiah 66:6; A voice of noise from the city, a voice from the temple, a voice of the LORD that rendereth recompence to his enemies.

CHAPTER 12

C hapter's twelve through fourteen give a brief synopsis of the main theme of the book of Revelation in dramatic, symbolic language with this chapter showing the Christian religion being established upon earth symbolized as a great wonder in heaven; a woman clothed with the sun, the moon under her feet, and upon her head a crown of twelve stars, and delivering a man child, which is Christ, while Satan, portrayed as a dragon, is cast from heaven and attempts to destroy Christ and his church. Revelation 12:1; And there appeared a great wonder in heaven; a woman clothed with the sun, and the moon under her feet, and upon her head a crown of twelve stars:

The phrase "A woman clothed with the sun" suggests the birth and coming establishment of the Christian Church as the word "woman" implies a beginning or birth of an entity. The entity in this case is the establishment of the Christian Church as indicated by the phrase "great wonder". The sun was used to represent the light of God's Word through Christ which was their worship of the Lord as their primary reason for existence. The moon was used to symbolize the light of God's Word through the Mosaic Law, therefore, with "the moon under her feet" implies that the Christian religion is replacing and has power over the Mosaic Law and also to redeem those that were under the law. The word "crown" reflects royalty while the numeral "twelve" indicates organized religion and coupled with the word "stars" which represent the twelve leaders (twelve apostles) of that religion.

Galatians 4:4-5; But when the fullness of the time was come, God sent forth his Son, made of a woman, made under the law, To redeem them that were under the law, that we might receive the adoption of sons.

Revelation 12:2; And she being with child cried, travailing in birth, and pained to be delivered.

This is symbolic of establishing a religion and is detailed in Isaiah 66 with the establishment of Jerusalem by the Lord for the children of Israel as their religious center.

Isaiah 66:7-9; Before she travailed, she brought forth; before her pain came, she was delivered of a man child. Who hath heard such a thing? Who hath seen such things? Shall the earth be made to bring forth in one day? Or shall a nation be born at once? For as soon as Zion travailed, she brought forth her children. Shall I bring to the birth, and not cause to bring forth? saith the Lord: shall I cause to bring forth, and shut the womb? saith thy God:

Revelation 12:3; And there appeared another wonder in heaven; and behold a great red dragon, having seven heads and ten horns, and seven crowns upon his heads.

The great red dragon is Satan with the color red indicating an evil, sinful nature bringing about bloodshed and warfare. The seven heads reveal Satan's complete authority over evil with the ten horns representing a succession of earthly kings among mankind as being given the power by Satan to be the instrument for this implementation of evil. The seven crowns upon his heads represent Satan's complete authority over these kings and the establishment of a complete period of time to accomplish his evil through this succession of evil forms of government.

Daniel 7:24; And the ten horns out of this kingdom are ten kings that shall arise: and another shall rise after them; and he shall be diverse from the first, and he shall subdue three kings.

Revelation 12:4; And his tail drew the third part of the stars of heaven, and did cast them to the earth: and the dragon stood before the woman which was ready to be delivered, for to devour her child as soon as it was born.

The phrase "his tail drew the third part of the stars of heaven " reveals that Satan influenced many rulers and leaders

to follow him in his pursuit of evil as the words "third part" indicate a large number while the word "stars" reflects leaders.

II Peter 2:4; For if God spared not the angels that sinned, but cast them down to hell, and delivered them into chains of darkness, to be reserved unto judgment;

Jude 6: And the angels which kept not their first estate, but left their own habitation, he hath reserved in everlasting chains under darkness unto the judgment of the great day.

Satan also attempted to get Christ to follow him by offering him power over all of the kingdoms of the world.

Luke 4:2; Being forty days tempted of the devil. And in those days he did eat nothing: and when they were ended, he afterward hungered.

Luke 4:5-8; And the devil, taking him up into an high mountain, shewed unto him all the kingdoms of the world in a moment of time. And the devil said unto him, All this power will I give thee, and the glory of them: for that is delivered unto me; and to whomsoever I will I give it. If thou therefore wilt worship me, all shall be thine. And Jesus answered and said unto him, *Get thee behind me, Satan: for it is written, Thou shalt worship the Lord thy God, and him only shalt thou serve.*

The phrase "to devour her child as soon as it was born" implies that Satan began his opposition to God's plan of religion immediately. One example of this opposition refers to King Herod being advised of the birth of the King of the Jews in Bethlehem and subsequently ordering the slaying of all the children under the age of two years in Bethlehem in an attempt to slay this King.

Matthew 2:16; Then Herod, when he saw that he was mocked of the wise men, was exceeding wroth, and sent forth, and slew all the children that were in Bethlehem, and in all the coasts thereof, from two years old and under, according to the time which he had diligently inquired of the wise men.

Revelation 12:5; And she brought forth a man child, who was to rule all nations with a rod of iron: and her child was caught up unto God, and to his throne.

The man-child is Christ who was sent by God to establish and rule His kingdom (church) here on earth. The "rod of iron" is

the strength of God's Word and the means by which Christ will eventually conquer and control all nations. The phrase "caught up unto God, and to his throne" implies strict allegiance to God by Christ with the eventual delivery of his kingdom to God.

Psalms 2:9; Thou shalt break them with a rod of iron; thou shalt dash them in pieces like a potter's vessel.

I John 3:8; He that committeth sin is of the devil; for the devil sinneth from the beginning. For this purpose the Son of God was manifested, that he might destroy the works of the devil.

Revelation 2:27; And he shall rule them with a rod of iron; as the vessels of a potter shall they be broken to shivers: even as I received of my Father.

Revelation 12:6; And the woman fled into the wilderness, where she hath a place prepared of God, that they should feed her there a thousand two hundred and threescore days.

The phrase "And the woman fled into the wilderness" suggests that the establishment of the church or kingdom of Christ on earth would be fraught with many perils compounded by evil challenges from Satan. One example would refer to Joseph and Mary fleeing into Egypt to escape the edict of King Herod. The "wilderness" is also virgin, unconquered, spiritual territory (earth) for establishing a religion and represents the battleground between Christ and Satan with the "thousand two hundred and threescore days" reflecting the period of time established by God for mankind to preach and teach His Word on earth while enduring persecution from followers of Satan.

Matthew 2:12-13; And being warned of God in a dream that they should not return to Herod, they departed into their own country another way. And when they were departed, behold, the angel of the Lord appeareth to Joseph in a dream, saying, Arise, and take the young child and his mother, and flee into Egypt, and be thou there until I bring thee word: for Herod will seek the young child to destroy him.

Isaiah 43:19-20; Behold, I will do a new thing; now it shall spring forth; shall ye not know it? I will even make a way in the wilderness, and rivers in the desert. The beast of the field shall honour me, the dragons and the owls: because I give waters in the wilderness, and rivers in the desert, to give drink to my people, my chosen.

Revelation 12:7; And there was war in heaven: Michael and his angels fought against the dragon; and the dragon fought and his angels,

This depicts the beginning of the warfare between good and evil with Satan being cast out of heaven unto earth to continue his pursuit of evil there.

Revelation 12:8; And prevailed not; neither was their place found any more in heaven,

Satan lost the war in heaven to Michael and his angels and was cast down unto earth to continue his opposition to religious morality here on earth.

Isaiah 14:12; How art thou fallen from heaven, O Lucifer, son of the morning! How art thou cut down to the ground, which didst weaken the nations!

Luke 10:18; And he said unto them, *I beheld Satan as lightning fall from heaven.*

Revelation 8:8-9; And the second angel sounded, and as it were a great mountain burning with fire was cast into the sea: and the third part of the sea became blood; And the third part of the creatures which were in the sea, and had life, died; and the third part of the ships were destroyed.

Revelation 12:9; And the great dragon was cast out, that old serpent, called the Devil, and Satan, which deceiveth the whole world: he was cast out into the earth, and his angels were cast out with him.

The result of Satan losing the war in heaven against Michael and his angels was his expulsion from heaven unto earth from which he began his dominion of evil with his minions deceiving and swaying a large number of people unto their spiritual death.

Revelation 8:10-11; And the third angel sounded, and there fell a great star from heaven, burning as it were a lamp, and it fell upon the third part of the rivers, and upon the fountains of waters; And the name of the star is called Wormwood: and the third part of the waters became wormwood; and many men died of the waters, because they were made bitter.

Revelation 9:1; And the fifth angel sounded, and I saw a star fall from heaven unto the earth: and to him was given the key to the bottomless pit.

Satan, the source of evil, being referred to as "that old serpent" originates in the book of Genesis as does the term "woman" that indicates the beginning of the religion established by God. Being given the "key to the bottomless pit" reveals that Satan has control over all of the evil in this world.

Genesis 3:14-15; And the Lord God said unto the serpent, Because thou hast done this, thou art cursed above all cattle, and above every beast of the field; upon thy belly shalt thy go, and dust shalt thou eat all the days of thy life: And I will put enmity between thee and the woman, and between thy seed and her seed; it shall bruise thy head, and thou shalt bruise his heel.

Revelation 12:10; And I heard a loud voice saying in heaven, Now is come salvation, and strength, and the kingdom of our God, and the power of his Christ: for the accuser of our brethren is cast down, which accused them before our God day and night.

The "loud voice" is indicative of authority with a volume loud enough for all to hear. This reflects the establishment of Christ's kingdom to combat and offer salvation against the evil brought upon earth by Satan which led to his ultimate defeat as God placed Christ upon earth to eventually conquer Satan and his forces of evil.

John 12:31; Now is the judgment of this world: now shall the prince of this world be cast out.

II Thessalonians 2:8; And then shall that Wicked be revealed, whom the Lord shall consume with the spirit of his mouth, and shall destroy with the brightness of his coming:

Revelation 12:11; And they overcame him by the blood of the Lamb, and by the word of their testimony; and they loved not their lives unto the death.

With Christ's sacrifice on our behalf, His blood became atonement for our sins and our promise of salvation became possible by our rejection of evil and acceptance of Him as the Son of God. The phrase "word of their testimony" reveals that the battle between Chris and Satan is being fought by the promo-

tion of God's Word. The phrase "and they loved not their lives unto the death" refers to those Christians that held steadfast to the faith of Christ even unto death.

Romans 8:33-34,37; Who shall lay any thing to the charge of God's elect? It is God that justifieth. Who is he that condemneth? It is Christ that died, yea rather, that is risen again, who is even at the right hand of God, who also maketh intercession for us. Nay, in all these things we are more than conquerors through him that loved us.

Revelation 12:12; Therefore rejoice, ye heavens, and ye that dwell in them. Woe to the inhabiters of the earth and of the sea! For the devil is come down unto you, having great wrath, because he knoweth that he hath but a short time.

Rejoicing is for those who have accepted Christ while others need to beware of the deception of Satan who is restricted to the promotion of evil for only a short time on earth.

Romans 16:20; And the God of peace shall bruise Satan under your feet shortly. The grace of our Lord Jesus Christ be with you. Amen.

Revelation 12:13; And when the dragon saw that he was cast unto the earth, he persecuted the woman which brought forth the man child.

The man child is Christ and as Satan's dominion of evil became restricted to earth, he first focused on the death of Christ as reflected in verse four with an example cited of the effort by King Herod. Satan next focused his attention upon the destruction of the Christian Church which was heavily persecuted by both the Roman Empire and the Jews during the time of this revelation to John.

John 16:11; Of judgment, because the prince of this world is judged.

Revelation 12:14; And to the woman were given two wings of a great eagle, that she might fly into the wilderness, into her place, where she is nourished for a time, and times, and half a time, from the face of the serpent.

The "two wings of a great eagle" are verification and confirmation that Christ's Church (Kingdom) is promoting the truth of God's Word as indicated by the numeral two. The word "wilderness" signifies earth which is unconquered spiritual territory and the battleground for the war between Christ and Satan. The

phrase "time, and times, and half a time" refers to the period of time that God's Word will be preached and taught throughout earth.

Daniel 12:7; And I heard the man clothed in linen, which was upon the waters of the river, when he held up his right hand and his left hand unto heaven, and sware by him that liveth for ever that it shall be for a time, times, and an half; and when he shall have accomplished to scatter the power of the holy people, all these things shall be finished.

The Lord's protection and preservation of His servants is compared to birds flying overhead.

Exodus 19:4; Ye have seen what I did unto the Egyptians, and how I bare you on eagle's wings, and brought you unto myself.

Isaiah 31:5; As birds flying, so will the Lord of hosts defend Jerusalem; defending also he will deliver it; and passing over he will preserve it.

The Lord renewing the strength of His servants is likened to wings as an eagle.

Isaiah 40:31; But they that wait upon the Lord shall renew their strength; they shall mount up with wings as eagles; they shall run, and not be weary; and they shall walk, and not faint.

The leadership of the Lord is of the analogy of an eagle caring for her young with an example in Deuteronomy of the Lord's direction and care of Jacob.

Deuteronomy 32:11-12; As an eagle stirreth up her nest, fluttereth over her young, spreadeth abroad her wings, taketh them, beareth them on her wings: So the Lord alone did lead him, and there was no strange god with him.

The Christian Church is achieving success during this Christian Gospel Age that has been designated by God to spread His Word. The phrases "fly into the wilderness, into her place, where she is nourished" and "from the face of the serpent" reflects the nourishment and protection of God during the Gospel Dispensation period.

Deuteronomy 1:31; And in the wilderness, where thou hast seen how that the LORD thy God bare thee, as a man doth bear his son, in all the way that ye went, until ye came into this place.

Psalms 78:5; For he established a testimony in Jacob, and appointed a law in Israel, which he commanded our fathers, that they should make them known to their children:

Psalms136:16; To him which led his people through the wilderness: for his mercy endureth for ever.

Isaiah 51:3; For the LORD shall comfort Zion: he will comfort all her waste places; and he will make her wilderness like Eden, and her desert like the garden of the LORD; joy and gladness shall be found therein, thanksgiving, and the voice of melody.

Revelation 12:15; And the serpent cast out of his mouth water as a flood after the woman, that he might cause her to be carried away of the flood.

This is symbolic of the immense volume of false doctrine and idolatry worship promoted by Satan to deceive people. The word "serpent" is symbolic for Satan and the phrase "cast out of his mouth" reflects false teaching or prophecy while the word "water" represents evil knowledge or deceit. The phrase "that he might cause her to be carried away of the flood" is reflective of the immense volume of evil doctrine put forth by the followers of Satan.

Psalms 18:4; The sorrows of death compassed me, and the floods of ungodly men made me afraid.

Isaiah 59:19; So shall they fear the name of the LORD from the west, and his glory from the rising of the sun. When the enemy shall come in like a flood, the Spirit of the LORD shall lift up a standard against him.

Isaiah 8:6-8; Forasmuch as this people refuseth the waters of Shiloah that go softly, and rejoice in Rezin and Remaliah's son: Now therefore, behold, the Lord bringeth up upon them the waters of the river, strong and many, even the king of Assyria, and all his glory: and he shall come up over all his channels, and go over all his banks: And he shall pass through Judah; he shall overflow and go over, he shall reach even to the neck; and the stretching out of his wings shall fill the breadth of thy land, O Immanuel.

Revelation 12:16; And the earth helped the woman, and the earth opened her mouth, and swallowed up the flood which the dragon cast out of his mouth.

   This is the truth of God's Word being promoted throughout earth that proves the path to spiritual destruction of false doctrine and idolatry. The analogy of this verse reflects the growth of the kingdom of Christ with the spreading of the Word of God exposing the fallacy of the doctrine of Satan and also being able to overcome his false doctrine.

Psalms 18:15-17; Then the channels of waters were seen, and the foundations of the world were discovered at thy rebuke, O LORD, at the blast of the breath of thy nostrils. He sent from above, he took me, he drew me out of many waters. He delivered me from my strong enemy, and from them which hated me: for they were too strong for me.

Isaiah 30:28,30-31; And his breath, as an overflowing stream, shall reach to the midst of the neck, to sift the nations with the sieve of vanity: and there shall be a bridle in the jaws of the people, causing them to err. And the Lord shall cause his glorious voice to be heard, and shall shew the lighting down of his arm, with the indignation of his anger, and with the flame of a devouring fire, with scattering, and tempest, and hailstones. For through the voice of the Lord shall the Assyrian be beaten down, which smote with a rod.

Revelation 12:17; And the dragon was wroth with the woman, and went to make war with the remnant of her seed, which keep the commandments of God, and have the testimony of Jesus Christ.

   As Satan was unable to destroy Christ or his church and has not effectively combated the Word of God, his attention is now directed toward attacking individual members of the Christian Church.

I Peter 5:8-9; Be sober, be vigilant; because your adversary the devil, as a roaring lion, walketh about, seeking whom he may devour: Whom resist stedfast in the faith, knowing that the same afflictions are accomplished in your brethren that are in the world.

I John 4:1,3; Beloved, believe not every spirit, but try the spirits whether they are of God: because many false prophets are gone out into the world. And every spirit that confesseth not that Jesus Christ is come in the flesh is not of God: and this is that spirit of anti-christ, whereof ye have heard that it should come; and even now already is it in the world.

CHAPTER 13

This chapter signifies the beginning and the establishment of Satan's dominion of evil along with detailing the methods employed by Satan to combat Christ and the Christian Doctrine which consists of a succession of evil empires and nations under the symbol of a sea beast promoting his evil doctrine and with false teachers/prophets under the symbol of an earth beast that uses sorcery and deception.

Revelation 13:1; And I stood upon the sand of the sea, and saw a beast rise up out of the sea, having seven heads and ten horns, and upon his horns ten crowns, and upon his heads the name of blasphemy.

The phrase, "And I stood upon the sand of the sea" indicates that the writer John was spiritually taken to a location enabling him to observe "a beast rise up out of the sea". As the word "sea" represents a multitude of people or nations and the word "beast" reflects anti-Christian doctrine then the phrase "beast rising up out of the sea" signifies a succession of evil, anti-Christian empires coming to power from a multitude of people and nations with the ability to control many of its subjects with false religious doctrine. Their false religious worship is adverse to and blasphemes the Lord.

Isaiah 57:20; But the wicked are like the troubled sea, when it cannot rest, whose waters cast up mire and dirt.

The "seven heads" implies complete control over its subjects. The "ten horns" reveal that its power is human with the "ten crowns" implying that its authority is also restricted to mankind while "the name of blasphemy" reveals its opposition and animosity to the Lord.

The crowns being upon the horns suggest these are earthly rulers subservient to Satan whereas in chapter twelve, verse three, the crowns were upon the seven heads which shows that Satan ruled and was in complete control with authority over all evil.

Revelation 13:2; And the beast which I saw was like unto a leopard, and his feet were as the feet of a bear, and his mouth as the mouth of a lion: and the dragon gave him his power, and his seat, and great authority.

John's comparison of this beast to a leopard, bear, and lion, all beasts of prey, would indicate the nature of this succession of evil empires. The leopard uses guile and stealth to subdue its prey while the bear's main weapon of power is its feet or paws and the lion not only uses its paws but also its mouth to rend its prey. The ferocity of these beasts of prey reflects the nature and determination of this evil opposition to Christ.

Hosea 13:7-8; Therefore I will be unto them as a lion: as a leopard by the way will I observe them: I will meet them as a bear that is bereaved of her whelps, and will rend the caul of their heart, and there will I devour them like a lion: the wild beast shall tear them.

Fierceness is also implied as David and his men are compared to a bear robbed of her whelps.

II Samuel 17:8; For, said Hushai, thou knowest thy father and his men, that they be mighty men, and they be chafed in their minds, as a bear robbed of her whelps in the field: and thy father is a man of war, and will not lodge with the people.

The dragon is Satan from which this beast derives its power, position, and authority.

From the book of Daniel, chapter seven, describing the vision and prophecy of Daniel, the interpretation of this sea beast is revealed as four great beasts which were the Chaldean Empire, the Medo-Persian Empire, the Macedonian Empire, and the Roman Empire, all of which practiced various false religions that controlled the religious worship practices of its subjects.

Daniel 7:2-4; Daniel spake and said, I saw in my vision by night, and, behold, the four winds of the heaven strove upon the great sea. And four great beasts came up from the sea, diverse one from another. The first was like a lion, and had eagle's wings: I beheld till the wings thereof were plucked, and it was lifted up from the earth, and made stand upon the feet as a man, and a man's heart was given to it.

This empire was compared to a lion and foretold in the books of Isaiah and Jeremiah as conquering Israel.

Isaiah 5:29; Their roaring shall be like a lion, they shall roar like young lions: yea, they shall roar, and lay hold of the prey, and shall carry it away safe, and none shall deliver it.

Jeremiah 4:7; The lion is come up from his thicket, and the destroyer of the Gentiles is on his way; he is gone forth from his place to make thy land desolate; and thy cities shall be laid waste, without an inhabitant.

The comparison to an eagle is also made in the books of Jeremiah and Ezekiel. The eagle is used to denote the swiftness with which these conquests are made.

Jeremiah 48:40; For thus saith the Lord; Behold, he shall fly as an eagle, and shall spread his wings over Moab.

Ezekiel 17:3,7; And say, Thus saith the Lord God; A great eagle with great wings, longwinged, full of feathers, which had divers colours, came unto Lebanon, and took the highest branch of the cedar: There was also another great eagle with great wings and many feathers: and, behold, this vine did bend her roots toward him, and shot forth her branches toward him, that he might water it by the furrows of her plantation.

Daniel 7:5; And behold another beast, a second, like to a bear, and it raised up itself on one side, and it had three ribs in the mouth of it between the teeth of it: and they said thus unto it, Arise, devour much flesh.

The second beast was the Medo-Persian Empire under Cyrus and Darius. Raising itself up on one side reflects that Cyrus was the primary ruler. The three ribs indicate the conquest of the Medes, Persians, and the Babylonians.

Daniel 7:6; After this I beheld, and lo another, like a leopard, which had upon the back of it four wings of a fowl; the beast had also four heads; and dominion was given to it.

This third beast was the Macedonian Empire with the four wings suggesting the speed of conquests by Alexander's four generals who represent the four heads with each governing a separate region after Alexander's death with the numeral four also indicating all of the known earth.

The four generals were Cassander who ruled over Macedon and Greece; Lysimachus who ruled over Thrace and Bithynia; Ptolemy who ruled over Egypt; and Seleucus who ruled over Syria.

Daniel 7:7; After this I saw in the night visions, and behold a fourth beast, dreadful and terrible, and strong exceedingly; and it had great iron teeth: it devoured and brake in pieces, and stamped the residue with the feet of it: and it was diverse from all the beasts that were before it; and it had ten horns.

The fourth beast was the Roman Empire and it was diverse from the others in that it had a republican form of government and it encompassed all forms of false religious worship.

Daniel 7:8; I considered the horns, and behold, there came up among them another little horn, before whom there were three of the first horns plucked up by the roots: and, behold, in this horn were eyes like the eyes of man, and a mouth speaking great things.

These four beasts are identified as kingdoms in:

Daniel 7:17; These great beasts, which are four, are four kings, which shall arise out of the earth. **(Reference Daniel 7:3).**

Revelation 13:3; And I saw one of his heads as it were wounded to death; and his deadly wound was healed: and all the world wondered after the beast.

This symbolically appears that one of the leaders of these evil empires allowed the disciples of the Lord to again freely worship Him for a period of time. Some Biblical scholars have proposed that this may have been Nero, emperor of Rome, who committed suicide which stopped the persecution of the Christians until Domitian came into power as the leader of Rome and the persecution resumed.

It may also have been Nebuchadnezzar, king over the Babylonian Empire, after Daniel, acknowledging the Lord as the revealer of secrets, interpreted his dream of the metallic image, with the king then acknowledging Daniel's God as the God of gods.

Daniel 2:28,47; But there is a God in heaven that revealeth secrets, and maketh known to the king Nebuchadnezzar what shall be in the latter days. Thy dream, and the visions of thy head upon thy bed, are these; The king answered unto Daniel, and said, Of a truth it is, that your God is a God of gods, and a Lord of kings, and a revealer of secrets, seeing thou couldest reveal this secret.

Also, Nebuchadnezzar attempted to slay Hananiah, Mishael, and Azariah for not worshiping a false image, but was unable to burn them in his fiery furnace causing him to acknowledge the power of God, and issued a decree in:

Daniel 3:29-30; Therefore I make a decree, That every people, nation, and language, which speak any thing amiss against the God of Shadrach, Meshach, and Abednego, shall be cut in pieces, and their houses shall be made a dunghill: because there is no other God that can deliver after this sort. Then the king promoted Shadrach, Meshach, and Abednego, in the province of Babylon.

Another dream of Nebuchadnezzar that was interpreted by Daniel proclaimed that the king would lose his sanity for a period of time, but his sanity and kingdom would be returned after the king acknowledged that God was in control.

Daniel 4:34,37; And at the end of the days I Nebuchadnezzar lifted up mine eyes unto heaven, and mine understanding returned unto me, and I blessed the most High, and I praised and honoured him that liveth forever, whose dominion is an everlasting dominion, and his kingdom is from generation to generation: Now I Nebuchadnezzar praise and extol and honour the King of heaven, all whose works are truth, and his ways judgment: and those that walk in pride he is able to abase.

It may possibly have been Cyrus, king of Persia, who issued the edict to rebuild the house of God in Jerusalem.

Ezra 1:1-2; Now in the first year of Cyrus king of Persia, that the word of the LORD by the mouth of Jeremiah might be fulfilled, the

LORD stirred up the spirit of Cyrus king of Persia, that he made a proclamation throughout all his kingdom, and put it also in writing, saying, Thus saith Cyrus king of Persia, The LORD God of heaven hath given me all the kingdoms of the earth; and he hath charged me to build him an house at Jerusalem, which is in Judah.

It may also have been King Artaxerxes of the Persian Empire, who allowed the Israelites under Nehemiah to return to Jerusalem, rebuild their temple, and resume their worship unto the Lord.

Nehemiah 2:6-8; And the king said unto me, (the queen also sitting by him,) For how long shall thy journey be? And when wilt thou return? So it pleased the king to send me; and I set him a time. Moreover I said unto the king, If it please the king, let letters be given me to the governors beyond the river, that they may convey me over till I come into Judah; And a letter unto Asaph the keeper of the king's forest, that he may give me timber to make beams for the gates of the palace which appertained to the house, and for the wall of the city, and for the house that I shall enter into. And the king granted me, according to the good hand of my God upon me.

The point being made is that it would be difficult to pinpoint any particular incident in history to adequately justify the interpretation of the deadly wound being healed.

My preference of the interpretation is that it is false religious doctrines that have remained dormant among the people of these evil empires for a period of time after the fall of their empires, then grew to become an evil force at a later time. The book of Daniel relates that these evil empires were cast down, the beast was slain, his body destroyed, and given to the burning flame, but yet, even though their dominion was taken away, the rest of the beast's lives were prolonged for a season and time. History confirms that the evil dominion of Satan has always progressed from the fall of one empire to a successive empire. Reference:

Daniel 7:9-15; I beheld till the thrones were cast down, and the Ancient of days did sit, whose garment was white as snow, and the hair of his head like the pure wool: his throne was like the fiery flame, and his wheels as burning fire. A fiery stream issued and came forth from before him: thousand thousands ministered unto him, and ten thousand times ten thousand stood before him: the judgment was set, and the books were opened. I beheld then because of the voice of the great words which the horn spake: I beheld even till the beast was slain, and his body destroyed, and given to the burning flame. As concerning the rest of the beasts, they had their dominion taken away: yet their lives were prolonged for a season and time. I saw in the night visions, and, behold, one like the Son of man came with the clouds of heaven, and came to the Ancient of days, and they brought him near before him. And there was given him dominion, and glory, and a kingdom, that all people, nations, and languages, should serve him: his dominion is an everlasting dominion, which shall not pass away, and his kingdom that which shall not be destroyed. I Daniel was grieved in my spirit in the midst of my body, and the visions of my head troubled me.

Some Biblical scholars have also theorized that this may be the Catholic Church that persecuted the laity with their doctrines and corruption. It may be the nation of Islam, but it probably is a general principle that continually re-occurs throughout history.

Revelation 13:4; And they worshiped the dragon which gave power unto the beast: and they worshiped the beast, saying, Who is like unto the beast? who is able to make war with him?

The people, under the jurisdiction of these evil empires, accepted the teaching and worship of these false doctrines put forth by Satan believing that their false gods were in control of their fate and fortune. They also believed that their false gods were all powerful and invincible.

Revelation 13:5; And there was given unto him a mouth speaking great things and blasphemies; and power was given unto him to continue forty and two months.

Satan empowered the rulers of these evil empires to disperse his evil doctrine as various false religions and teachings during this time period (forty and two months) established by God.

Daniel 7:8,11; I considered the horns, and, behold, there came up among them another little horn, before whom there were three of the first horns plucked up by the roots: and, behold, in this horn were eyes like the eyes of man, and a mouth speaking great things. I beheld then because of the voice of the great words which the horn spake: I beheld even till the beast was slain, and his body destroyed, and given to the burning flame.

Revelation 13:6; And he opened his mouth in blasphemy against God, to blaspheme his name, and his tabernacle, and them that dwell in heaven.

All of these false religions and anti-Christian doctrines under the symbol of the sea beast blaspheme God, Christ's Church, and His disciples as God's doctrine is in opposition to their false teachings.

Daniel 7:25; And he shall speak great words against the most High, and shall wear out the saints of the most High, and think to change times and laws: and they shall be given into his hand until a time and times and the dividing of time.

Revelation 13:7; And it was given unto him to make war with the saints, and to overcome them: and power was given him over all kindreds, and tongues, and nations.

God has designated this set period of time allowing Satan to reign on earth spreading his evil amid various false religions. This set period of time is also reflected as one thousand two hundred sixty days, forty-two months, three and one-half years, and also as time, times, and half-time and is the time period established by God for the spreading and teaching of His Word while under persecution by Satan's evil forces.

Daniel 7:21-22; I beheld, and the same horn made war with the saints, and prevailed against them; Until the Ancient of days came, and judgment was given to the saints of the most High; and the time came that the saints possessed the kingdom.

This reflects the second coming of Christ unto final judgment.

Revelation 13:8; And all that dwell upon the earth shall worship him, whose names are not written in the book of life of the Lamb slain from the foundation of the world.

Many people will be deceived and led astray by these various false doctrines and false religions put forth by Satan and his evil empires.

Philippians 3:18-19; (For many walk, of whom I have told you often, and now tell you even weeping, that they are the enemies of the cross of Christ: Whose end is destruction, whose God is their belly, and whose glory is in their shame, who mind earthly things.) Psalms 69:28; Let them be blotted out of the book of the living, and not be written with the righteous.

Revelation 13:9; If any man have an ear, let him hear.

We are constantly encouraged to heed God's Word, obey His commandments, and accept His offer and promise.

II Timothy 3:13-14; But evil men and seducers shall wax worse and worse, deceiving, and being deceived. But continue thou in the things which thou hast learned and hast been assured of, knowing of whom thou hast learned them;

Revelation 13:10; He that leadeth into captivity shall go into captivity: he that killeth with the sword must be killed with the sword. Here is the patience and the faith of the saints.

Your reward and fate is governed by the path that you have chosen to follow. The phrase "patience and the faith of the saints" indicates the ability of God's disciples to overcome the trials and tribulations thrust upon them, yet remain steadfast in their allegiance to God and Christ.

Isaiah 33:1;Woe to thee that spoilest, and thou wast not spoiled; and dealest treacherously, and they dealt not treacherously with thee! when thou shalt cease to spoil, thou shalt be spoiled; and when thou shalt make an end to deal treacherously, they shall deal treacherously with thee.

Habakkuk 2:8;Because thou hast spoiled many nations, all the remnant of the people shall spoil thee; because of men's blood, and for the violence of the land, of the city, and of all that dwell therein

Revelation 13:11; And I beheld another beast coming up out of the earth; and he had two horns like a lamb, and he spake as a dragon.

This earth beast represents false prophets or teachers leading people astray with doctrine that is contrary to God's Word. The word "earth" reflects earthly wisdom as opposed to wisdom from above. The word "beast" signifies that it is controlled by and promoting evil, anti-Christian doctrine from Satan. The phrase, "he had two horns", reveals that it's power is restricted to mankind and that it agrees and is in harmony with the sea-beast. The phrase "like a lamb" means that its power of control-

ling and deceiving others is by portraying itself as a teacher of God's Word while the phrase "spake as a dragon" reveals that it is actually promoting evil, false doctrines and is subservient to Satan.

Matthew 7:15; Beware of false prophets, which come to you in sheep's clothing, but inwardly they are ravening wolves.

II Corinthians 11:13-15; For such are false apostles, deceitful workers, transforming themselves into the apostles of Christ. And no marvel; for Satan himself is transformed into an angel of light. Therefore it is no great thing if his ministers also be transformed as the ministers of righteousness; whose end shall be according to their works.

James 3:14-17; But if ye have bitter envying and strife in your hearts, glory not, and lie not against the truth. This wisdom descendeth not from above, but is earthly, sensual, devilish. For where envying and strife is, there is confusion and every evil work. But the wisdom that is from above is first pure, then peaceable, gentle, and easy to be intreated, full of mercy and good fruits, without partiality, and without hypocrisy.

II Peter 2:1; But there were false prophets also among the people, even as there shall be false teachers among you, who privily shall bring in damnable heresies, even denying the Lord that bought them, and bring upon themselves swift destruction.

Revelation 13:12; And he exerciseth all the power of the first beast before him, and causeth the earth and them which dwell therein to worship the first beast, whose deadly wound was healed.

Just as Satan empowered the sea beast, he also has given power to the earth beast to promote anti-Christian activity and worship false religions. The false prophets/teachers encourage people through deceit and sorcery to worship these anti-Christian doctrines and their false gods.

Ezekiel 13:1-15; And the word of the LORD came unto me, saying, Son of man, prophesy against the prophets of Israel that prophesy, and say thou unto them that prophesy out of their own hearts, Hear ye the word of the LORD; Thus saith the Lord GOD; Woe unto the foolish prophets, that follow their own spirit, and have seen nothing!

O Israel, thy prophets are like the foxes in the deserts. Ye have not gone up into the gaps, neither made up the hedge for the house of Israel to stand in the battle in the day of the LORD. They have seen vanity and lying divination, saying, The LORD saith: and the LORD hath not sent them: and they have made others to hope that they would confirm the word. Have ye not seen a vain vision, and have ye not spoken a lying divination, whereas ye say, The LORD saith it; albeit I have not spoken? Therefore thus saith the Lord GOD; Because ye have spoken vanity, and seen lies, therefore, behold, I am against you, saith the Lord GOD. And mine hand shall be upon the prophets that see vanity, and that divine lies: they shall not be in the assembly of my people, neither shall they be written in the writing of the house of Israel, neither shall they enter into the land of Israel; and ye shall know that I am the Lord God. Because, even because they have seduced my people, saying, Peace; and there was no peace; and one built up a wall, and, lo, others daubed it with untempered morter: Say unto them which daub it with untempered morter, that it shall fall: there shall be an overflowing shower; and ye, O great hailstones, shall fall; and a stormy wind shall rend it. Lo, when the wall is fallen, shall it not be said unto you, Where is the daubing wherewith ye have daubed it? Therefore thus saith the Lord GOD; I will even rend it with a stormy wind in my fury; and there shall be an overflowing shower in mine anger, and great hailstones in my fury to consume it. So will I break down the wall that ye have daubed with untempered morter, and bring it down to the ground, so that the foundation thereof shall be discovered, and it shall fall, and ye shall be consumed in the midst thereof: and ye shall know that I am the LORD. Thus will I accomplish my wrath upon the wall, and upon them that have daubed it with untempered morter, and will say unto you, The wall is no more, neither they that daubed it;
Revelation 13:13; And he doeth great wonders, so that he maketh fire come down from heaven on the earth in the sight of men,

Many false teachers have perfected the art of deceit through sorcery, witchcraft, and a glib tongue thereby leading many people astray from God's Word.

Matthew 24:24; For there shall arise false Christs, and false prophets, and shall shew great signs and wonders; insomuch that, if it were possible, they shall deceive the very elect.

Deuteronomy 13:1-3; If there arise among you a prophet, or a dreamer of dreams, and giveth thee a sign or a wonder, And the sign or the wonder come to pass, whereof he spake unto thee, saying, Let us go after other gods, which thou hast not known, and let us serve them; Thou shalt not hearken unto the words of that prophet, or that dreamer of dreams: for the LORD your God proveth you, to know whether ye love the LORD your God with all your heart and with all your soul.

Revelation 13:14; And deceiveth them that dwell on the earth by the means of those miracles which he had power to do in the sight of the beast; saying to them that dwell on the earth, that they should make an image to the beast, which had the wound by a sword, and did live.

The death or destruction of evil nations and empires that opposed God's doctrine did not completely destroy many of their false religions and doctrines that were renewed by those who did not accept God's Word. Satan continued his dominion of evil through those that survived the fall of their nations and empires by the renewing of their worship of false gods, idols, and emperors which leads to their spiritual death.

II Colossians 2:8; Beware lest any man spoil you through philosophy and vain deceit, after the tradition of men, after the rudiments of the world, and not after Christ.

Micah 3:5-7; Thus saith the LORD concerning the prophets that make my people err, that bite with their teeth, and cry, Peace; and he that putteth not into their mouths, they even prepare war against him. Therefore night shall be unto you, that ye shall not have a vision; and it shall be dark unto you, that ye shall not divine; and the sun shall go down over the prophets, and the day shall be dark over them. Then shall the seers be ashamed, and the diviners confounded: yea, they shall all cover their lips; for there is no answer of God.

Daniel 7:11-12; I beheld then because of the voice of the great words which the horn spake: I beheld even till the beast was slain, and his body destroyed, and given to the burning flame. As concerning the rest of the beasts, they had their dominion taken away: yet their lives were prolonged for a season and time.

Revelation 13:15; And he had power to give life unto the image of the beast, that the image of the beast should both speak, and cause that as many as would not worship the image of the beast should be killed.

Satan empowered the leaders and governments of evil nations and empires to control the objects, doctrines, and methods of worship by their subjects under penalty of death to those who refused to comply with their vision of false worship.

II Thessalonians 2:9-12; Even him, whose coming is after the working of Satan with all power and signs and lying wonders, And with all deceivableness of unrighteousness in them that perish; because they received not the love of the truth, that they might be saved. And for this cause God shall send them strong delusion, that they should believe a lie: That they all might be damned who believed not the truth, but had pleasure in unrighteousness.

Revelation 13:16; And he causeth all, both small and great, rich and poor, free and bond, to receive a mark in their right hand, or in their foreheads:

The designation of political or physical status, economic condition, and birthright effectively encompasses all subjects under any given government. To "receive" means to accept or to worship as reflected in Revelation 14:9 while the word "mark" means the name of the false entity as revealed in Revelation 14:11 and all who bore this mark shows that they observe this false worship. Having a mark indicates belonging to someone as a slave or disciple of that person or entity. Having the mark "in their right hand" reveals that they follow this worship with all of their earthly ability as the right hand signifies their strength and power. With the mark being "in their foreheads" signifies their knowledge of belonging to this master or false deity and also their public profession of their worship of this beast.

Revelation 13:17; And that no man might buy or sell, save he that had the mark, or the name of the beast, or the number of his name.

This was one of the edicts of some governments that forced false worship upon their subjects causing economic hardship to

those who refused to worship a false religion as dictated by the government.

Revelation 13:18; Here is wisdom. Let him that hath understanding count the number of the beast: for it is the number of a man; and his number is Six hundred threescore and six.

The word "beast" in this instance symbolizes an evil entity in opposition to God and, as indicated, is the number of a man. As the numeral six indicates sinister deeds by mankind, therefore the numeral 666 would be evil deeds compounded by man.

Psalms 107:43; Whoso is wise, and will observe these things, even they shall understand the lovingkindness of the LORD.

James 3:15; This wisdom descendeth not from above, but is earthly, sensual, devilish.

The book of James, chapter three, reflects evil inclinations and deeds by mankind.

CHAPTER 14

T his chapter reflects Satan's seat of evil as that great city, "Babylon", which is promised punishment by the wrath of God for leading nations astray. Christ is then represented as coming upon a white cloud with his angels and gathering his elect from earth unto heaven under the analogy of harvesting a crop with a sickle. Christ then brings judgment and destruction upon Satan and his evil dominion under the symbol of a winepress.

Revelation 14:1; And I looked, and, lo, a Lamb stood on the mount Sion, and with him an hundred forty and four thousand, having his Father's name written in their foreheads.

John's vision reveals Christ standing on Mount Sion indicating the permanence of His everlasting Kingdom. The phrase "an hundred forty and four thousand" represents all of the disciples of His organized religion as this is the numeral twelve compounded with the word "thousand" signifying a complete number. This number is symbolic only as reflected in chapter seven, verse nine. The phrase "having his Father's name written in their foreheads" reveals not only that all of his disciples belong to God but also that they are proclaiming openly unto others their allegiance to God. These are referred to as the "redeemed from the earth" in verse three.

Psalms 125:1-2; They that trust in the LORD shall be as mount Zion, which cannot be removed, but abideth for ever. As the mountains are round about Jerusalem, so the LORD is round about his people from henceforth even for ever.

Mount Sion represents residence in heaven.

Hebrews 12:22-23; But ye are come unto mount Sion, and unto the city of the living God, the heavenly Jerusalem, and to an innumerable company of angels, To the general assembly and church of the firstborn, which are written in heaven, and to God the Judge of all, and to the spirits of just men made perfect,

John 14:2-3; In my Father's house are many mansions: if it were not so, I would have told you. I go to prepare a place for you. And if I go and prepare a place for you, I will come again, and receive you unto myself; that where I am, there ye may be also.

Revelation 14:2; And I heard a voice from heaven, as the voice of many waters, and as the voice of a great thunder: and I heard the voice of harpers harping with their harps:

John heard a voice from heaven and described it as "the voice of many waters" indicating that this was the voice of the Lord while the phrase "as the voice of a great thunder" denotes power and authority. This reflects a judgment being issued that requires obeisance. This judgment is reflected in verses seven and eight as the destruction of Babylon. With John also hearing "the voice of harpers harping with their harps" reveals that the harpers recognized the voice as belonging to the Lord as harps are used to recognize and honor royalty or those with authority.

Ezekiel 43:2; And, behold, the glory of the God of Israel came from the way of the east: and his voice was like a noise of many waters: and the earth shined with his glory.

Revelation 1:15; And his feet like unto fine brass, as if they burned in a furnace; and his voice as the sound of many waters.

Revelation 14:3; And they sung as it were a new song before the throne, and before the four beasts, and the elders: and no man could learn that song but the hundred and forty and four thousand, which were redeemed from the earth.

To sing a new song means to honor and recognize achievement. As this new song was sung before the throne, beasts, and elders implies that the Lord was the recipient of this honor. The "hundred forty and four thousand" now singing the new song in heaven indicates that judgment day has arrived and these redeemed are now in heaven.

Isaiah 42:10-12; Sing unto the LORD a new song, and his praise from the end of the earth, ye that go down to the sea, and all that is therein; the isles, and the inhabitants thereof. Let the wilderness and the cities thereof lift up their voice, the villages that Kedar doth inhabit: let the inhabitants of the rock sing, let them shout from the top of the mountains. Let them give glory unto the LORD, and declare his praise in the islands.

Revelation 14:4; These are they which were not defiled with women; for they are virgins. These are they which follow the Lamb whithersoever he goeth. These were redeemed from among men, being the first-fruits unto God and to the Lamb.

The phraseology, "not defiled with women" refers to those who did not worship false idols or were not led astray into false worship but remained true and steadfast to the worship of God. Fornication is used to indicate spiritual fornication which is the worship of false gods or idolatry. The phrase "These are they which follow the Lamb whithersoever he goeth" reflects the disciples of Christ.

Numbers 25:1-5; And Israel abode in Shittim, and the people began to commit whoredom with the daughters of Moab. And they called the people unto the sacrifices of their gods: and the people did eat, and bowed down to their gods. And Israel joined himself unto Baalpeor: and the anger of the LORD was kindled against Israel. And the LORD said unto Moses, Take all the heads of the people, and hang them up before the LORD against the sun, that the fierce anger of the LORD may be turned away from Israel. And Moses said unto the judges of Israel, Slay ye every one his men that were joined unto Baalpeor.

Through the sacrifice and teachings of Christ, His disciples "were redeemed from among men" and purchased away from the worship of false gods of this earth, hence they became first-fruits of the Lord. First-fruits of the annual harvest of crops were a requirement as part of the worship service in the Mosaic Law.

James 1:18; Of his own will begat he us with the word of truth, that we should be a kind of first-fruits of his creatures.

225

II Corinthians 11:2; For I am jealous over you with godly jealousy: for I have espoused you to one husband, that I may present you as a chaste virgin to Christ.

Numbers 18:12; All the best of the oil, and all the best of the wine, and of the wheat, the first-fruits of them which they shall offer unto the LORD, them have I given thee.

Deuteronomy 26:2; That thou shalt take of the first of all the fruit of the earth, which thou shalt bring of thy land that the LORD thy God giveth thee, and shalt put it in a basket, and shalt go unto the place which the LORD thy God shall choose to place his name there.

Nehemiah 10:35; And to bring the first-fruits of our ground, and the first-fruits of all fruit of all trees, year by year, unto the house of the LORD:

Revelation 14:5; And in their mouth was found no guile: for they are without fault before the throne of God.

As guile means deceit or treachery, the phrase "found no guile" means that those disciples were as perfect as they were pure, holy, "without fault", and acceptable before God. They had not worshiped false idols, but had remained true to the worship of God only.

Psalms 32:2; Blessed is the man unto whom the LORD imputeth not iniquity, and in whose spirit there is no guile.

Zephaniah 3:13; The remnant of Israel shall not do iniquity, nor speak lies; neither shall a deceitful tongue be found in their mouth: for they shall feed and lie down, and none shall make them afraid.

Matthew 5:48; Be ye therefore perfect, even as your Father which is in heaven is perfect.

I Peter 2:22; Who did no sin, neither was guile found in his mouth:

Exodus 12:5; Your lamb shall be without blemish, a male of the first year: ye shall take it out from the sheep, or from the goats:

Leviticus 1:3; If his offering be a burnt sacrifice of the herd, let him offer a male without blemish: he shall offer it of his own voluntary will at the door of the tabernacle of the congregation before the LORD.

Leviticus 19:2; Speak unto all the congregation of the children of Israel, and say unto them, Ye shall be holy: for I the LORD your God am holy.

Revelation 14:6; And I saw another angel fly in the midst of heaven, having the everlasting gospel to preach unto them that dwell on the earth, and to every nation, and kindred, and tongue, and people,

John's vision of the angel flying "in the midst of heaven having the everlasting gospel to preach unto them that dwell on the earth" is the Word of God that is currently being spread throughout all of the earth during this Christian Gospel Dispensation period which is the period of time that God designated for His Word to be taught and preached to all peoples upon the earth.

Ephesians 3:9-11; And to make all men see what is the fellowship of the mystery, which from the beginning of the world hath been hid in God, who created all things by Jesus Christ: To the intent that now unto the principalities and powers in heavenly places might be known by the church the manifold wisdom of God, According to the eternal purpose which he purposed in Christ Jesus our Lord:

Revelation 14:7; Saying with a loud voice, Fear God, and give glory to him; for the hour of his judgment is come: and worship him that made heaven, and earth, and the sea, and the fountains of waters.

John's vision of the angel also symbolically reveals the message that we must obey and honor God while there is still time to do so before the hour of His judgment falls upon earth and all therein. His Word offers us a plan of salvation but it requires that we worship only Him as the creator of all things.

Malachi 4:1; For, behold, the day cometh, that shall burn as an oven; and all the proud, yea, and all that do wickedly, shall be stubble: and the day that cometh shall burn them up, saith the LORD of hosts, that it shall leave them neither root nor branch.

Nehemiah 9:6; Thou, even thou, art LORD alone; thou hast made heaven, the heaven of heavens, with all their host, the earth, and all things that are therein, the seas, and all that is therein, and thou preservest them all; and the host of heaven worshippeth thee.

Revelation 14:8; And there followed another angel, saying, Babylon is fallen, is fallen, that great city, because she made all nations drink of the wine of the wrath of her fornication.

As Babylon is used to symbolically represent spiritual fornication, John's vision of another angel proclaiming "Babylon

is fallen, is fallen, that great city" reveals that Christ has defeated false religions with judgment day now upon us. The phrase "because she made all nations drink of the wine of the wrath of her fornication" means that false religions were spread throughout all nations as Babylon is symbolically recognized as the source or seat of Satan's evil doctrine.

Isaiah 21:9; And, behold, here cometh a chariot of men, with a couple of horsemen. And he answered and said, Babylon is fallen, is fallen; and all the graven images of her gods he hath broken unto the ground.

Revelation 14:9; And the third angel followed them, saying with a loud voice, If any man worship the beast and his image, and receive his mark in his forehead, or in his hand,

To speak "with a loud voice" is indicative that all will hear this message of the third angel. To "receive his mark in his forehead" is to proclaim openly unto others your allegiance and servitude unto this beast of evil opposition to God. To receive the mark of "the beast and his image" in your hand is indicative of worshiping the beast with all of your power as this mark was usually in the right hand which symbolically represented all of your strength.

Revelation 14:10; The same shall drink of the wine of the wrath of God, which is poured out without mixture into the cup of his indignation; and he shall be tormented with fire and brimstone in the presence of the holy angels, and in the presence of the Lamb:

This third angel is proclaiming loudly in order for all to hear that any worshiper of false religions or their idols will incur the full wrath of God with their punishment being eternal damnation before Christ and the holy angels. To "drink of the wine of the wrath of God" is to receive God's punishment. "Poured out without mixture" means that God's punishment will be full strength without being diluted. The phrase "he shall be tormented with fire and brimstone" reveals the punishment of condemnation to hell. The phrase "in the presence of the holy angels, and in the presence of the Lamb" indicates that the holy angels and Christ will be fully aware of this punishment being implemented.

Psalms 11:6; Upon the wicked he shall rain snares, fire and brimstone, and an horrible tempest: this shall be the portion of their cup.
Psalms 75:8; For in the hand of the LORD there is a cup, and the wine is red; it is full of mixture; and he poureth out of the same: but the dregs thereof, all the wicked of the earth shall wring them out, and drink them.
Jeremiah 25:15; For thus saith the LORD God of Israel unto me; Take the wine cup of this fury at my hand, and cause all the nations, to whom I send thee, to drink it.
Revelation 14:11; And the smoke of their torment ascendeth up for ever and ever: and they have no rest day nor night, who worship the beast and his image, and whosoever receiveth the mark of his name.

The phrase "the smoke of their torment ascendeth up for ever and ever" implies that their torment and punishment is everlasting with no relief day or night for those who choose to worship false gods or idols. The phrase "whosoever receiveth the mark of his name" refers to those people who are disciples of and proclaim openly their allegiance to these false gods.
Revelation 14:12; Here is the patience of the saints: here are they that keep the commandments of God, and the faith of Jesus.

The "patience of the saints" refers to those disciples that were subjected to persecution and tribulation, yet remained steadfast in the faith of Jesus and kept the commandments of God.
II Thessalonians 2:15; Therefore, brethren, stand fast, and hold the traditions which ye have been taught, whether by word, or our epistle.
Revelation 14:13; And I heard a voice from heaven saying unto me, Write, Blessed are the dead which die in the Lord from henceforth: Yea, saith the Spirit, that they may rest from their labours; and their works do follow them.

John heard a voice from heaven instructing him to write: "Blessed are the dead which die in the Lord from henceforth:" indicating the reward of heaven for those who had remained faithful to Christ primarily suggesting those Christians who gave their life as martyrs. The phrase "Yea, saith the Spirit, that they may rest from their labours;" reveals rest from their physical and spiritual struggle with the forces of Satan on earth. The

phrase "and their works do follow them" was proof that they had earned their reward.

Hebrews 4:9-10; There remaineth therefore a rest to the people of God. For he that is entered into his rest, he also hath ceased from his own works, as God did from his.

II Thessalonians 1:7; And to you who are troubled rest with us, when the Lord Jesus shall be revealed from heaven with his mighty angels,

Revelation 14:14; And I looked, and behold a white cloud, and upon the cloud one sat like unto the Son of man, having on his head a golden crown, and in his hand a sharp sickle.

This is Christ being represented as coming on a white cloud and described as "the Son of man". The color "white" symbolizes holiness and purity with the cloud indicating change. The change in this case is that Christ has come to redeem his disciples that are worthy of heaven. "Having on his head a golden crown" reveals his royal status as king over his church and one with authority to accomplish his mission with the adjective "golden" indicating great value to this cause. The sharp sickle in his hand shows that he is coming in judgment to harvest his kingdom and deliver it unto God using the analogy of harvesting a mature crop of grain.

The sickle was a tool used in farming to reap a crop of grain that was ripe and ready for harvest and with the sickle being described as "sharp" indicates readiness and the effectiveness of his mission.

Matthew 24:30; And then shall appear the sign of the Son of man in heaven: and then shall all the tribes of the earth mourn, and they shall see the Son of man coming in the clouds of heaven with power and great glory.

I Thessalonians 4:16; For the Lord himself shall descend from heaven with a shout, with the voice of the archangel, and with the trump of God: and the dead in Christ shall rise first:

Daniel 7:13; I saw in the night visions, and, behold, one like the Son of man came with the clouds of heaven, and came to the Ancient of days, and they brought him near before him.

Revelation 14:15; And another angel came out of the temple, crying with a loud voice to him that sat on the cloud, Thrust in thy sickle, and reap: for the time is come for thee to reap; for the harvest of the earth is ripe.

An angel is a messenger and servant of God and with the angel coming out of the temple shows that this message is from God and the message being delivered to Christ was that now was the time for gathering his disciples unto heaven. The phrase "crying with a loud voice" is to insure that the volume was loud enough for all people to hear and know that this is the final judgment day. The phrase "for the harvest of the earth is ripe" indicates that the Christian church is ready for deliverance unto heaven and that no other person is ready to accept Christ.

Jeremiah 51:33; For thus saith the LORD of hosts, the God of Israel; The daughter of Babylon is like a threshingfloor, it is time to thresh her: yet a little while, and the time of her harvest shall come.

John 4:35; Say not ye, There are yet four months, and then cometh harvest? behold, I say unto you, Lift up your eyes, and look on the fields; for they are white already to harvest.

Revelation 14:16; And he that sat on the cloud thrust in his sickle on the earth; and the earth was reaped.

This is Christ gathering his disciples to deliver them to God in heaven expressed with the analogy of a farmer harvesting his crop as a sickle was used by farmers to reap their mature crops. God and Christ always appear in, on, or with a cloud which indicates a change is to be made.

Matthew 3:12; Whose fan is in his hand, and he will throughly purge his floor, and gather his wheat into the garner; but he will burn up the chaff with unquenchable fire.

After the harvest, there was a need to separate the good grain from the undesirable chaff. To separate the chaff from the grain of a harvest a threshing floor was used to winnow the grain. To winnow the grain meant tossing it up into the air to allow the wind to blow the chaff away while letting the grain fall back down upon the threshing floor. When no wind was available, a fan was used to winnow the grain.

Amos 9:9; For, lo, I will command, and I will sift the house of Israel among all nations, like as corn is sifted in a sieve, yet shall not the least grain fall upon the earth.

Revelation 14:17; And another angel came out of the temple which is in heaven, he also having a sharp sickle.

This angel coming from the temple in heaven reveals that it was sent by God to aid Christ in the harvest of His followers. Christ foretold his disciples that he would return with his angels at his second coming to gather his elect.

Matthew 24:31; And he shall send his angels with a great sound of a trumpet, and they shall gather together his elect from the four winds, from one end of heaven to the other.

Matthew 25:31; When the Son of man shall come in his glory, and all the holy angels with him, then shall he sit upon the throne of his glory:

Revelation 14:18; And another angel came out from the altar, which had power over fire; and cried with a loud cry to him that had the sharp sickle, saying, Thrust in thy sharp sickle, and gather the clusters of the vine of the earth; for her grapes are fully ripe.

As this angel came out from the altar denotes that the instructions came from God. This angel is coming on judgment day with everlasting fire prepared for the enemies of Christ and issuing instructions from God unto Christ to gather His disciples. This analogy of harvesting grapes from the vineyard is the same as the analogy of harvesting a crop of grain, but, in this case, fire is being brought for the punishment of those being found unworthy as symbolized by the phrase "the vine of the earth". The vine was discarded and burnt after the grapes were removed.

Isaiah 66:15; For, behold, the LORD will come with fire, and with his chariots like a whirlwind, to render his anger with fury, and his rebuke with flames of fire.

Jeremiah 5:14; Wherefore thus saith the LORD God of hosts, Because ye speak this word, behold, I will make my words in thy mouth fire, and this people wood, and it shall devour them.

Matthew 13:30; Let both grow together until the harvest: and in the time of harvest I will say to the reapers, Gather ye together first the tares, and bind them in bundles to burn them: but gather the wheat into my barn.

Matthew 25:32-34,41; And before him shall be gathered all nations: and he shall separate them one from another, as a shepherd divideth his sheep from the goats: And he shall set the sheep on his right hand, but the goats on the left. Then shall the King say unto them on his right hand, Come, ye blessed of my Father, inherit the kingdom prepared for you from the foundation of the world: Then shall he say also unto them on the left hand, Depart from me, ye cursed, into everlasting fire, prepared for the devil and his angels:

Revelation 14:19; And the angel thrust in his sickle into the earth, and gathered the vine of the earth, and cast it into the great winepress of the wrath of God.

This reflects punishment of the wicked by the judgment of God using the analogy of a winepress which crushed the harvest of grapes to extract the juice for making wine. This angel is gathering the wicked foes of Christ and casting them "into the great winepress of the wrath of God" which reflects punishment and destruction unto the enemies of Christ.

Joel 3:13; Put ye in the sickle, for the harvest is ripe: come, get you down; for the press is full, the fats overflow; for their wickedness is great.

Revelation 19:15; And out of his mouth goeth a sharp sword, that with it he should smite the nations: and he shall rule them with a rod of iron: and he treadeth the winepress of the fierceness and wrath of Almighty God.

The evil of this earth will be destroyed by the Word of God which is represented as a sharp sword out of the mouth of Christ.

Revelation 14:20; And the winepress was trodden without the city, and blood came out of the winepress, even unto the horse bridles, by the space of a thousand and six hundred furlongs.

The mass destruction of the enemies of Christ is shown symbolically as being trodden by the winepress of God. Being trodden outside of the city implies keeping the city pure and undefiled as the city represents heaven. This will be massive punishment as the measurement of blood is given as to reach the horse bridles. The word "blood" indicates spiritual death and

used with the word "thousand" signifies a complete quantity of those people spiritually lost with the numeral "six" referring to evil, sinister opposition of God and Christ.

Isaiah 63:3-6; I have trodden the winepress alone; and of the people there was none with me: for I will tread them in mine anger, and trample them in my fury; and their blood shall be sprinkled upon my garments, and I will stain all my raiment. For the day of vengeance is in mine heart, and the year of my redeemed is come. And I looked, and there was none to help; and I wondered that there was none to uphold: therefore mine own arm brought salvation unto me; and my fury, it upheld me. And I will tread down the people in mine anger, and make them drunk in my fury, and I will bring down their strength to the earth.

CHAPTER 15

C hapters fifteen and sixteen reveal the final judgments of God as plagues symbolized by vials of wrath being dispensed upon the earth, sea, rivers, fountains of waters, sun, seat of the beast, Euphrates river, and the air thereby completing the destruction of Satan and his evil forces at a place called Armageddon.

Revelation 15:1; And I saw another sign in heaven, great and marvellous, seven angels having the seven last plagues; for in them is filled up the wrath of God.

John's vision of "another sign in heaven, great and marvellous" reveals the significance of the events that are about to take place which are the final judgments with the "seven angels having the seven last plagues" that symbolize the complete destruction of earth and the enemies of Christ and his kingdom.

John 3:36; He that believeth on the Son hath everlasting life: and he that believeth not the Son shall not see life; but the wrath of God abideth on him.

Romans 1:18; For the wrath of God is revealed from heaven against all ungodliness and unrighteousness of men, who hold the truth in unrighteousness;

Romans 2:5-6; But after thy hardness and impenitent heart treasurest up unto thyself wrath against the day of wrath and revelation of the righteous judgment of God; Who will render to every man according to his deeds:

Revelation 15:2; And I saw as it were a sea of glass mingled with fire: and them that had gotten the victory over the beast, and over his image, and over his mark, and over the number of his name, stand on the sea of glass, having the harps of God.

"Victory over the beast" was achieved by refusing to worship false gods or images nor become subservient unto them as indicated by not displaying their mark of servitude or ownership. The "sea of glass" indicates transparency or the ability to enter the temple of the tabernacle of testimony and approach God in prayer through Christ whereas under the Mosaic Law only the priests were allowed to approach God in the temple on behalf of the people. The phrase "mingled with fire" reveals that these disciples of the Lord had persevered in their tribulations on earth and had achieved victory over all anti-Christian doctrine by remaining steadfast in their faith of Christ and thus receiving their reward of salvation in heaven as indicated by their standing "on the sea of glass, having the harps of God". The phrase "having the harps of God" reveals that these disciples had been accepted in heaven as saints and were now honoring Him with harps. John the Baptist foretold of Christ baptizing with the Holy Ghost and with fire.

Matthew 3:11; I indeed baptize you with water unto repentance. but he that cometh after me is mightier than I, whose shoes I am not worthy to bear: he shall baptize you with the Holy Ghost, and with fire:

Ephesians 2:14; For he is our peace, who hath made both one, and hath broken down the middle wall of partition between us;

I Peter 5:8-9; Be sober, be vigilant; because your adversary the devil, as a roaring lion, walketh about, seeking whom he may devour: Whom resist stedfast in the faith, knowing that the same afflictions are accomplished in your brethren that are in the world.

Revelation 15:3; And they sing the song of Moses the servant of God, and the song of the Lamb, saying, Great and marvellous are thy works, Lord God Almighty; just and true are thy ways, thou King of saints.

The song of Moses and the Lamb was sang to honor the Lord as He had protected the children of Israel from the Pharaoh of Egypt and his army by delivering them safely through the Red Sea. The disciples of Christ have now been safely delivered unto

heaven and were singing the same song of Moses and the Lamb in recognition of this grand achievement. This is another indication of their being found worthy and accepted by God as they are now in heaven extolling the virtues of God and their pleasure in doing so.

Exodus 15:1; Then sang Moses and the children of Israel this song unto the LORD, and spake, saying, I will sing unto the LORD, for he hath triumphed gloriously: the horse and his rider hath he thrown into the sea.

Exodus 15:2; The LORD is my strength and song, and he is become my salvation: he is my God, and I will prepare him an habitation; my father's God, and I will exalt him.

Psalms 77:13-14; Thy way, O God, is in the sanctuary: who is so great a God as our God?

Thou art the God that doest wonders: thou hast declared thy strength among the people

Psalms 145:17; The LORD is righteous in all his ways, and holy in all his works.

Revelation 15:4; Who shall not fear thee, O Lord, and glorify thy name? for thou only art holy: for all nations shall come and worship before thee; for thy judgments are made manifest.

These disciples of the Lord are honoring, praising, and recognizing God as holy and all-powerful with all nations succumbing to Him as His judgments are being implemented for all to see.

Exodus 15:14-16; The people shall hear, and be afraid: sorrow shall take hold on the inhabitants of Palestina. Then the dukes of Edom shall be amazed; the mighty men of Moab, trembling shall take hold upon them; all the inhabitants of Canaan shall melt away. Fear and dread shall fall upon them; by the greatness of thine arm they shall be as still as a stone; till thy people pass over, O LORD, till the people pass over, which thou hast purchased.

Psalms 86:8-10;Among the gods there is none like unto thee, O Lord; neither are there any works like unto thy works. All nations whom thou hast made shall come and worship before thee, O Lord; and shall glorify thy name. For thou art great, and doest wondrous things: thou art God alone.

Revelation 15:5; And after that I looked, and, behold, the temple of the tabernacle of the testimony in heaven was opened:

With "the temple of the tabernacle of the testimony in heaven" being opened further indicates that those who had accepted God, kept His commandments, and found worthy were now able to enter and dwell in the house of the Lord after the seven angels had exited and accomplished their mission of dispensing the seven plagues. During the Mosaic Law the temple had replaced the tabernacle with the testimony requiring the use of the furnishings in the Levitical service. The furnishings consisted of lampstands, tables, the ark, and those items within such as Aaron's rod, a pot of manna, book of the law, etc.

Psalms 27:4-6; One thing have I desired of the LORD, that will I seek after; that I may dwell in the house of the LORD all the days of my life, to behold the beauty of the LORD, and to enquire in his temple. For in the time of trouble he shall hide me in his pavilion: in the secret of his tabernacle shall he hide me; he shall set me up upon a rock. And now shall mine head be lifted up above mine enemies round about me: therefore will I offer in his tabernacle sacrifices of joy; I will sing, yea, I will sing praises unto the LORD.

Revelation 15:6; And the seven angels came out of the temple, having the seven plagues, clothed in pure and white linen, and having their breasts girded with golden girdles.

The seven angels coming from the temple and having the seven plagues indicates that they were sent by God to fulfill His mission of the final battle accomplishing victory over Satan. Being "clothed in pure and white linen" indicates righteousness and reveals they are without sin and worthy of fulfilling the assigned tasks designated by God. The color "white" indicates purity and holiness while "linen" reflects the righteousness of the saints. "Having their breasts girded with golden girdles" reveals their great value to God as they were dressed and prepared to fulfill His mission just as the Levitical priests did in their assigned tasks under the Mosaic Law.

Exodus 28:2-8; And thou shalt make holy garments for Aaron thy brother for glory and for beauty. And thou shalt speak unto all that are wise hearted, whom I have filled with the spirit of wisdom, that they may make Aaron's garments to consecrate him, that he may minister unto me in the priest's office. And these are the garments which they shall make; a breastplate, and an ephod, and a robe, and a broidered coat, a mitre, and a girdle: and they shall make holy garments for Aaron thy brother, and his sons, that he may minister unto me in the priest's office. And they shall take gold, and blue, and purple, and scarlet, and fine linen. And they shall make the ephod of gold, of blue, and of purple, of scarlet, and fine twined linen, with cunning work. It shall have the two shoulderpieces thereof joined at the two edges thereof; and so it shall be joined together. And the curious girdle of the ephod, which is upon it, shall be of the same, according to the work thereof; even of gold, of blue, and purple, and scarlet, and fine twined linen.

Revelation 15:7; And one of the four beasts gave unto the seven angels seven golden vials full of the wrath of God, who liveth for ever and ever.

The seven angels were now given their assignments by one of the cherubims to dispense the wrath of God upon earth and mankind to accomplish victory over Satan and his evil dominion. Deut 28:20; The LORD shall send upon thee cursing, vexation, and rebuke, in all that thou settest thine hand unto for to do, until thou be destroyed, and until thou perish quickly; because of the wickedness of thy doings, whereby thou hast forsaken me.

II Thessalonians 1:8; In flaming fire taking vengeance on them that know not God, and that obey not the gospel of our Lord Jesus Christ: Revelation 15:8; And the temple was filled with smoke from the glory of God, and from his power; and no man was able to enter into the temple, till the seven plagues of the seven angels were fulfilled.

Smoke indicated God's presence in the temple with no one being allowed inside the temple until the seven plagues were finished upon earth and mankind. The presence of a cloud or smoke reveals the presence of the Lord with no one allowed to enter the temple or tabernacle until it was cleared of the cloud or smoke. Exodus 33:19-20; And he said, I will make all my goodness pass before thee, and I will proclaim the name of the LORD before thee; and will be gracious to whom I will be gracious, and will shew mercy on whom I will shew mercy. And he said, Thou canst not see my face: for there shall no man see me, and live.

Exodus 40:34-35; Then a cloud covered the tent of the congregation, and the glory of the LORD filled the tabernacle. And Moses was not able to enter into the tent of the congregation, because the cloud abode thereon, and the glory of the LORD filled the tabernacle.

I Kings 8:10-11; And it came to pass, when the priests were come out of the holy place, that the cloud filled the house of the LORD, So that the priests could not stand to minister because of the cloud: for the glory of the LORD had filled the house of the LORD.

II Chronicles 5:14; So that the priests could not stand to minister by reason of the cloud: for the glory of the LORD had filled the house of God. (Isaiah 6:4; 14:31.)

II Thessalonians 1:9; Who shall be punished with everlasting destruction from the presence of the Lord, and from the glory of his power;

CHAPTER 16

Revelation 16:1; And I heard a great voice out of the temple saying to the seven angels, Go your ways, and pour out the vials of the wrath of God upon the earth.

John heard and recorded the instructions of God speaking out of the temple in a great voice to the seven angels to begin the destruction upon the earth. The "great voice" reflects authority while the phrase "out of the temple" signifies that it is God speaking and "pouring out the vials of wrath" indicates the onset of the final judgment of God "upon the earth" and being seven angels indicates complete destruction of earth and all therein.

Deuteronomy 28:20; The LORD shall send upon thee cursing, vexation, and rebuke, in all that thou settest thine hand unto for to do, until thou be destroyed, and until thou perish quickly; because of the wickedness of thy doings, whereby thou hast forsaken me.

Revelation 16:2; And the first went, and poured out his vial upon the earth; and there fell a noisome and grievous sore upon the men which had the mark of the beast, and upon them which worshipped his image.

The first angel dispensed the first vial upon earth causing grievous sores like unto the plague by Moses upon the Egyptians. The phrase "which had the mark of the beast, and upon them which worshiped his image" indicates the plague affected all that deceived the Word of God and all that worshiped false gods and idolatry.

Exodus 9:8-9; And the LORD said unto Moses and unto Aaron, Take to you handfuls of ashes of the furnace, and let Moses sprinkle it toward the heaven in the sight of Pharaoh. And it shall become small dust in all the land of Egypt, and shall be a boil breaking forth with blains upon man, and upon beast, throughout all the land of Egypt. Deuteronomy 28:22,27; The LORD shall smite thee with a consumption, and with a fever, and with an inflammation, and with an extreme burning, and with the sword, and with blasting, and with mildew; and they shall pursue thee until thou perish. The LORD will smite thee with the botch of Egypt, and with the emerods, and with the scab, and with the itch, whereof thou canst not be healed.

Revelation 16:3; And the second angel poured out his vial upon the sea; and it became as the blood of a dead man: and every living soul died in the sea.

The "sea" represents a multitude of nations that followed false worship and the evil anti-Christian doctrines of Satan and is now receiving the wrath of the Lord on judgment day as "blood" indicates death. The phrase "every living soul" reveals that this is a final judgment encompassing all people while the phrase "died in the sea" reflects the loss of spiritual life in these nations.

Isaiah 17:12-13; Woe to the multitude of many people, which make a noise like the noise of the seas; and to the rushing of nations, that make a rushing like the rushing of mighty waters! The nations shall rush like the rushing of many waters: but God shall rebuke them, and they shall flee far off, and shall be chased as the chaff of the mountains before the wind, and like a rolling thing before the whirlwind.

Jeremiah 51:36; Therefore thus saith the LORD; Behold, I will plead thy cause, and take vengeance for thee; and I will dry up her sea, and make her springs dry.

Ezekiel 26:16; Then all the princes of the sea shall come down from their thrones, and lay away their robes, and put off their broidered garments: they shall clothe themselves with trembling; they shall sit upon the ground, and shall tremble at every moment, and be astonished at thee.

Revelation 16:4; And the third angel poured out his vial upon the rivers and fountains of waters; and they became blood.

The word "rivers" represents the flow of evil knowledge from "fountains of waters" which is the source of these evil doctrines. Becoming "blood" signifies the death and destruction of those entities. (Reference the explanation of Revelation 8:10 whereupon Satan came to earth and instilled his evil doctrines. Revelation 16:4 now shows the destruction of those evil doctrines symbolized as "rivers" and "fountains of waters")

Revelation 8:10; And the third angel sounded, and there fell a great star from heaven, burning as it were a lamp, and it fell upon the third part of the rivers, and upon the fountains of waters;

Habakkuk 3:8; Was the LORD displeased against the rivers? was thine anger against the rivers? was thy wrath against the sea, that thou didst ride upon thine horses and thy chariots of salvation?

This plague is likened unto the plague of Egypt by God through the hands of Moses and Aaron whereupon the waters were turned unto blood with nothing being able to live in them.

Exodus 7:17-21; Thus saith the LORD, In this thou shalt know that I am the LORD: behold, I will smite with the rod that is in mine hand upon the waters which are in the river, and they shall be turned to blood. And the fish that is in the river shall die, and the river shall stink; and the Egyptians shall lothe to drink of the water of the river. And the LORD spake unto Moses, Say unto Aaron, Take thy rod, and stretch out thine hand upon the waters of Egypt, upon their streams, upon their rivers, and upon their ponds, and upon all their pools of water, that they may become blood; and that there may be blood throughout all the land of Egypt, both in vessels of wood, and in vessels of stone. And Moses and Aaron did so, as the LORD commanded; and he lifted up the rod, and smote the waters that were in the river, in the sight of Pharaoh, and in the sight of his servants; and all the waters that were in the river were turned to blood. And the fish that was in the river died; and the river stank, and the Egyptians could not drink of the water of the river; and there was blood throughout all the land of Egypt.

Revelation 16:5; And I heard the angel of the waters say, Thou art righteous, O Lord, which art, and wast, and shalt be, because thou hast judged thus.

This angel has fulfilled the duty of casting the vial of wrath upon the waters and now is praising God as an eternal and righteous judge of mankind. The word "waters" implies Satan's evil doctrines and the people that promoted those doctrines.

Psalms 7:9; Oh let the wickedness of the wicked come to an end; but establish the just: for the righteous God trieth the hearts and reins.

Psalms 145:13; Thy kingdom is an everlasting kingdom, and thy dominion endureth throughout all generations.

Revelation 16:6; For they have shed the blood of saints and prophets, and thou hast given them blood to drink; for they are worthy.

The angel of the waters is giving John the reason that God has now dispensed His wrath upon Satan's dominion of evil which is the vindication of the blood of his servants, the saints and prophets. The phrase, "and thou hast given them blood to drink; for they are worthy" reveals spiritual death to those persecutors of God's servants as their evil actions had earned this retribution.

Matthew 23:34-35; Wherefore, behold, I send unto you prophets, and wise men, and scribes: and some of them ye shall kill and crucify; and some of them shall ye scourge in your synagogues, and persecute them from city to city: That upon you may come all the righteous blood shed upon the earth, from the blood of righteous Abel unto the blood of Zacharias son of Barachias, whom ye slew between the temple and the altar.

Deuteronomy 32:41; If I whet my glittering sword, and mine hand take hold on judgment; I will render vengeance to mine enemies, and will reward them that hate me.

Isaiah 63:4; For the day of vengeance is in mine heart, and the year of my redeemed is come.

Romans 12:19; Dearly beloved, avenge not yourselves, but rather give place unto wrath: for it is written, Vengeance is mine; I will repay, saith the Lord.

Revelation 16:7; And I heard another out of the altar say, Even so, Lord God Almighty, true and righteous are thy judgments.

John heard and recorded another voice out of the altar praising God as the Almighty Lord and for His true and righteous judgments. The second voice proclaiming this judgment of

God as true and righteous is confirmation by a second witness verifying it as being true.

Deuteronomy 19:15; One witness shall not rise up against a man for any iniquity, or for any sin, in any sin that he sinneth: at the mouth of two witnesses, or at the mouth of three witnesses, shall the matter be established.

II Corinthians 13:1; This is the third time I am coming to you. In the mouth of two or three witnesses shall every word be established.

Matthew 18:16; But if he will not hear thee, then take with thee one or two more, that in the mouth of two or three witnesses every word may be established.

I Kings 8:32; Then hear thou in heaven, and do, and judge thy servants, condemning the wicked, to bring his way upon his head; and justifying the righteous, to give him according to his righteousness.

Psalms 145:17; The LORD is righteous in all his ways, and holy in all his works.

Ecclesiastes 3:17; I said in mine heart, God shall judge the righteous and the wicked: for there is a time there for every purpose and for every work.

Revelation 16:8; And the fourth angel poured out his vial upon the sun; and power was given unto him to scorch men with fire.

As the sun represents light with the dispensing of God's Word upon earth and the establishment of the religious worship of Him then the angel pouring out the vial of wrath upon the sun indicates the halting of spiritual blessings representing the ceasing of the Christian dispensation period upon earth thereby creating much spiritual punishment as implied by the phrase "to scorch men with fire".

Isaiah 13:10; For the stars of heaven and the constellations thereof shall not give their light: the sun shall be darkened in his going forth, and the moon shall not cause her light to shine.

Isaiah 66:15; For, behold, the LORD will come with fire, and with his chariots like a whirlwind, to render his anger with fury, and his rebuke with flames of fire.

Joel 2:31; The sun shall be turned into darkness, and the moon into blood, before the great and terrible day of the LORD come.

Matthew 24:29-31; Immediately after the tribulation of those days shall the sun be darkened, and the moon shall not give her light, and the stars shall fall from heaven, and the powers of the heavens shall be shaken: And then shall appear the sign of the Son of man in heaven: and then shall all the tribes of the earth mourn, and they shall see the Son of man coming in the clouds of heaven with power and great glory. And he shall send his angels with a great sound of a trumpet, and they shall gather together his elect from the four winds, from one end of heaven to the other.

Revelation 16:9; And men were scorched with great heat, and blasphemed the name of God, which hath power over these plagues: and they repented not to give him glory.

The ceasing of spiritual blessings upon earth caused great anguish among many people and even though they suffered from this punishment brought upon them they still blasphemed and refused to recognize and give glory unto God who has displayed His power with the dispensing of these plagues. The phrase "scorched with great heat" signifies being without the protection of the religion of God.

Deuteronomy 28:15,20; But it shall come to pass, if thou wilt not hearken unto the voice of the LORD thy God, to observe to do all his commandments and his statutes which I command thee this day; that all these curses shall come upon thee, and overtake thee: The LORD shall send upon thee cursing, vexation, and rebuke, in all that thou settest thine hand unto for to do, until thou be destroyed, and until thou perish quickly; because of the wickedness of thy doings, whereby thou hast forsaken me.

Isaiah 4:6; And there shall be a tabernacle for a shadow in the day time from the heat, and for a place of refuge, and for a covert from storm and from rain.

Isaiah 25:4; For thou hast been a strength to the poor, a strength to the needy in his distress, a refuge from the storm, a shadow from the heat, when the blast of the terrible ones is as a storm against the wall.

Isaiah 49:10; They shall not hunger nor thirst; neither shall the heat nor sun smite them: for he that hath mercy on them shall lead them, even by the springs of water shall he guide them.

Ezekiel 20:27; Therefore, son of man, speak unto the house of Israel, and say unto them, Thus saith the Lord GOD; Yet in this your fathers have blasphemed me, in that they have committed a trespass against me.

Romans 2:24; For the name of God is blasphemed among the Gentiles through you, as it is written.

II Peter 3:12; Looking for and hasting unto the coming of the day of God, wherein the heavens being on fire shall be dissolved, and the elements shall melt with fervent heat?

Revelation 16:10; And the fifth angel poured out his vial upon the seat of the beast; and his kingdom was full of darkness; and they gnawed their tongues for pain,

This angel brought the wrath of God directly to "the seat of the beast" which is the throne of Satan obscuring and abolishing his false doctrines as indicated by the phrase "his kingdom was full of darkness" which meant that Satan's words will no longer be broadcast or promoted to the people of earth. The phrase "and they gnawed their tongues for pain" reflects the pain from the punishment that they were receiving.

Ezekiel 32:7; And when I shall put thee out, I will cover the heaven, and make the stars thereof dark; I will cover the sun with a cloud, and the moon shall not give her light.

Daniel 7:26; But the judgment shall sit, and they shall take away his dominion, to consume and to destroy it unto the end.

Revelation 16:11; And blasphemed the God of heaven because of their pains and their sores, and repented not of their deeds.

By refusing to recognize the true God, the disciples of Satan suffered their plagues instilled by the wrath of God, refused to repent, and blasphemed God because of the spiritual pain from their punishment.

Deuteronomy 28:20; The LORD shall send upon thee cursing, vexation, and rebuke, in all that thou settest thine hand unto for to do, until thou be destroyed, and until thou perish quickly; because of the wickedness of thy doings, whereby thou hast forsaken me.

Psalms 74:10; God, how long shall the adversary reproach? shall the enemy blaspheme thy name for ever?

Revelation 16:12; And the sixth angel poured out his vial upon the great river Euphrates; and the water thereof was dried up, that the way of the kings of the east might be prepared.

This angel brought the wrath of God upon the flowing and distribution of Satan's evil doctrine halting the furthering of this evil knowledge as indicated by the phrase "and the water thereof was dried up". As Babylon is symbolic for false worship along with the abominations of the earth and is considered to be the source of evil, therefore the river Euphrates flowing from Babylon symbolizes the flowing and distribution of this evil doctrine. The phrase "that the way of the kings of the east might be prepared" refers to the halting of this flowing of Satan's false doctrine as preparation being made in order for Christ to conquer the evil reign of Satan symbolized by the city Babylon. The phrase "the kings of the east" represent Christ being aided by the ten kings referred to in chapter seventeen, verse sixteen.

Isaiah 41:2; Who raised up the righteous man from the east, called him to his foot, gave the nations before him, and made him rule over kings? he gave them as the dust to his sword, and as driven stubble to his bow.

Jeremiah 50:38; A drought is upon her waters; and they shall be dried up: for it is the land of graven images, and they are mad upon their idols.

Jeremiah 51:55; Because the LORD hath spoiled Babylon, and destroyed out of her the great voice; when her waves do roar like great waters, a noise of their voice is uttered:

Revelation 16:13; And I saw three unclean spirits like frogs come out of the mouth of the dragon, and out of the mouth of the beast, and out of the mouth of the false prophet.

As frogs were deemed unclean, they are used symbolically to represent evil spirits emanating from Satan, the dragon, and the beast which is evil, anti-Christian doctrine and the false prophet which represents false teachers.

Leviticus 11:10-11; And all that have not fins and scales in the seas, and in the rivers, of all that move in the waters, and of any living thing which is in the waters, they shall be an abomination unto you:

They shall be even an abomination unto you; ye shall not eat of their flesh, but ye shall have their carcases in abomination.

Revelation 16:14: For they are the spirits of devils, working miracles, which go forth unto the kings of the earth and of the whole world, to gather them to the battle of that great day of God Almighty.

Frogs, being unclean, represent the spirits of devils working through all of Satan's followers, and reflects their on-going spiritual battle with the teachings of Christ during this Christian gospel dispensation period.

Matthew 24:24; For there shall arise false Christs, and false prophets, and shall shew great signs and wonders; insomuch that, if it were possible, they shall deceive the very elect.

Mark 13:22;For false Christs and false prophets shall rise, and shall shew signs and wonders, to seduce, if it were possible, even the elect.

II Peter 2:1;But there were false prophets also among the people, even as there shall be false teachers among you, who privily shall bring in damnable heresies, even denying the Lord that bought them, and bring upon themselves swift destruction.

Revelation 16:15; Behold, I come as a thief. Blessed is he that watcheth, and keepeth his garments, lest he walk naked, and they see his shame.

A thief comes with stealth and does not foretell when he comes on his mission so as to catch his prey unawares. The phrase "watcheth, and keepeth his garments" indicates being prepared whereas the phrase "walk naked" means being unprepared while the word "shame" shows regret for being unprepared.

Matthew 24:43; But know this, that if the goodman of the house had known in what watch the thief would come, he would have watched, and would not have suffered his house to be broken up.

I Thessalonians 5:2,4; For yourselves know perfectly that the day of the Lord so cometh as a thief in the night. But ye, brethren, are not in darkness, that that day should overtake you as a thief.

II Peter 3:10; But the day of the Lord will come as a thief in the night; in the which the heavens shall pass away with a great noise, and the elements shall melt with fervent heat, the earth also and the works that are therein shall be burned up.

Revelation 16:16; And he gathered them together into a place called in the Hebrew tongue Armageddon.

The word "Armageddon" has been translated as "harmegiddon" which means "the mount of the assembly" and also as "harmegiddo" which means "Mount Megiddo" where two great battles have been fought. II Kings 23:29 relates one battle by the Israelites and Judges 4:6 and 5:19 relates another battle by Canaanites. This is symbolic of all spiritual battles when God's people become discouraged and God reveals His power in order to revitalize them.

Judges 4:5-7; And she dwelt under the palm tree of Deborah between Ramah and Bethel in mount Ephraim: and the children of Israel came up to her for judgment. And she sent and called Barak the son of Abinoam out of Kedeshnaphtali, and said unto him, Hath not the LORD God of Israel commanded, saying, Go and draw toward mount Tabor, and take with thee ten thousand men of the children of Naphtali and of the children of Zebulun? And I will draw unto thee to the river Kishon Sisera, the captain of Jabin's army, with his chariots and his multitude; and I will deliver him into thine hand.

Judges 5:19; The kings came and fought, then fought the kings of Canaan in Taanach by the waters of Megiddo; they took no gain of money.

II Kings 23:29; In his days Pharaohnechoh king of Egypt went up against the king of Assyria to the river Euphrates: and king Josiah went against him; and he slew him at Megiddo, when he had seen him.

Revelation 16:17; And the seventh angel poured out his vial into the air; and there came a great voice out of the temple of heaven, from the throne, saying, It is done.

Satan is considered as the prince of the air, so pouring out the vial of wrath in the air is symbolical of completely defeating Satan's reign of evil and covering everything over earth with God's judgment. John recorded "a great voice out of the temple of heaven, from the throne", proclaiming "It is done" indicating that the task of victory over Satan has been completed with this final judgment. The term "great voice" reveals that the message

is from God and implies an announcement loud enough for all to hear.

Ephesians 2:2; Wherein in time past ye walked according to the course of this world, according to the prince of the power of the air, the spirit that now worketh in the children of disobedience:

Revelation 10:7; But in the days of the voice of the seventh angel, when he shall begin to sound, the mystery of God should be finished, as he hath declared to his servants the prophets.

Revelation 11:15; And the seventh angel sounded; and there were great voices in heaven, saying, The kingdoms of this world are become the kingdoms of our Lord, and of his Christ; and he shall reign for ever and ever.

This final victory by Christ was prophesied by many Scriptures.

Daniel 2:44; And in the days of these kings shall the God of heaven set up a kingdom, which shall never be destroyed: and the kingdom shall not be left to other people, but it shall break in pieces and consume all these kingdoms, and it shall stand for ever.

Daniel 7:14,18,27; And there was given him dominion, and glory, and a kingdom, that all people, nations, and languages, should serve him: his dominion is an everlasting dominion, which shall not pass away, and his kingdom that which shall not be destroyed. But the saints of the most High shall take the kingdom, and possess the kingdom for ever, even for ever and ever. And the kingdom and dominion, and the greatness of the kingdom under the whole heaven, shall be given to the people of the saints of the most High, whose kingdom is an everlasting kingdom, and all dominions shall serve and obey him.

Revelation 16:18; And there were voices, and thunders, and lightnings; and there was a great earthquake, such as was not since men were upon the earth, so mighty an earthquake, and so great.

Voices signify edicts of God with thunders, lightnings, and a great earthquake being symbols of the imposing judgments with the phrase "such as was not since men were upon the earth, so mighty an earthquake, and so great" indicating that these judgments were far greater than any previous judgments of God as these were the judgments providing final victory over Satan.

Being four entities (voices, thunders, lightnings, and great earthquake) reflects that these judgments were fostered upon those on earth.

Isaiah 24:21; And it shall come to pass in that day, that the LORD shall punish the host of the high ones that are on high, and the kings of the earth upon the earth.

Isaiah 66:6; A voice of noise from the city, a voice from the temple, a voice of the LORD that rendereth recompence to his enemies.

Daniel 12:1; And at that time shall Michael stand up, the great prince which standeth for the children of thy people: and there shall be a time of trouble, such as never was since there was a nation even to that same time: and at that time thy people shall be delivered, every one that shall be found written in the book.

Revelation 16:19; And the great city was divided into three parts, and the cities of the nations fell: and great Babylon came in remembrance before God, to give unto her the cup of the wine of the fierceness of his wrath.

Babylon is symbolic as the source of all enemies of Christ and the source of all evil knowledge emanating from Satan. The division into three parts is identified in verse thirteen as the dragon, which is Satan; the beast, symbolizing anti-Christian doctrine; and the false prophet, meaning false teachers.

The phrase "the cities of the nations fell" reveals that God's final judgment was carried out with the destruction of all of the governments, kings, leaders, and people who were followers of Satan's evil doctrines.

The phrase "great Babylon came in remembrance before God" proves that God had not forgotten the persecution of His disciples and that Babylon was the source of evil combating the teachings of Christ.

The phrase "to give unto her the cup of the wine of the fierceness of his wrath" represents the punishment of God being carried out on the final judgment day.

Jeremiah 51:24,29,36,43; And I will render unto Babylon and to all the inhabitants of Chaldea all their evil that they have done in Zion in your sight, saith the LORD. And the land shall tremble and sorrow: for every purpose of the LORD shall be performed against

Babylon, to make the land of Babylon a desolation without an inhabitant. Therefore thus saith the LORD; Behold, I will plead thy cause,
and take vengeance for thee; and I will dry up her sea, and make her
springs dry. Her cities are a desolation, a dry land, and a wilderness,
a land wherein no man dwelleth, neither doth any son of man pass
thereby.

Isaiah 51:17,22; Awake, awake, stand up, O Jerusalem, which hast
drunk at the hand of the LORD the cup of his fury; thou hast drunken
the dregs of the cup of trembling, and wrung them out. Thus saith thy
Lord the LORD, and thy God that pleadeth the cause of his people,
Behold, I have taken out of thine hand the cup of trembling, even
the dregs of the cup of my fury; thou shalt no more drink it again:

Ezekiel 26:19; For thus saith the Lord GOD; When I shall make thee
a desolate city, like the cities that are not inhabited; when I shall
bring up the deep upon thee, and great waters shall cover thee;

Revelation 16:20; And every island fled away, and the mountains
were not found.

**The phrase "And every island fled away" represents that all
far away places would be affected by this final judgment of God.
The phrase "and the mountains were not found" indicates that
all of the evil kingdoms and nations were also destroyed.**

Isaiah 24:4; The earth mourneth and fadeth away, the world lan-
guisheth and fadeth away, the haughty people of the earth do
languish.

Ezekiel 26:15,18; Thus saith the Lord GOD to Tyrus; Shall not the
isles shake at the sound of thy fall, when the wounded cry, when the
slaughter is made in the midst of thee? Now shall the isles tremble in
the day of thy fall; yea, the isles that are in the sea shall be troubled
at thy departure.

Jeremiah 51:25; Behold, I am against thee, O destroying mountain,
saith the LORD, which destroyest all the earth: and I will stretch out
mine hand upon thee, and roll thee down from the rocks, and will
make thee a burnt mountain.

Revelation 16:21; And there fell upon men a great hail out of heaven,
every stone about the weight of a talent: and men blasphemed
God because of the plague of the hail; for the plague thereof was
exceeding great.

The term "great hail" represents a judgment of God indicating another symbolic description of the great destruction of earth and mankind on judgment day with many people still refusing to accept Christ while cursing God for the plagues being thrust upon them. The use of the word "great" in describing the earthquake in verse eighteen, and also as the description of hail and plague in verse twenty-one, indicates that this is the final judgment.

Psalms 18:13; The LORD also thundered in the heavens, and the Highest gave his voice; hail stones and coals of fire.

Isaiah 28:2; Behold, the Lord hath a mighty and strong one, which as a tempest of hail and a destroying storm, as a flood of mighty waters overflowing, shall cast down to the earth with the hand.

CHAPTER 17

T his chapter details the judgment brought upon Satan's evil forces symbolized as "the great whore that sitteth upon many waters" and a "woman upon a scarlet coloured beast" whose loyalty was to "Babylon" as written upon her forehead. This woman is described as responsible for the death of many saints and martyrs. The city "Babylon" is symbolic of Satan's dominion of evil and is depicted in this chapter as a progression through a succession of evil empires from one generation unto another generation and from one kingdom unto another kingdom eventually going into perdition.

Revelation 17:1; And there came one of the seven angels which had the seven vials, and talked with me, saying unto me, Come hither; I will shew unto thee the judgment of the great whore that sitteth upon many waters:

This angel instructed John to come and be shown the judgment of God regarding the destruction of the "great whore" which is also symbolically called "Babylon" as it represents all of the false idol worship as reflected by the word "whore" and the seat of evil opposition of God. The phrase "that sitteth upon many waters" means a multitude of many peoples and nations that had been affected by this evil entity.

Jeremiah 51:13; O thou that dwellest upon many waters, abundant in treasures, thine end is come, and the measure of thy covetousness.

Revelation 17:2; With whom the kings of the earth have committed fornication, and the inhabitants of the earth have been made drunk with the wine of her fornication.

Committing "fornication" is an adulterous term implying the worship of false gods and/or idolatry instead of the one true Lord God. The phrase "kings of the earth" reveals that this worship of false gods and idolatry encompassed many nations as reflected by the plurality of the word "kings". Being "made drunk with the wine of her fornication" reveals that the people that were subject to the rule of these kings were being led astray into false worship by this evil entity identified as "the great whore".

Jeremiah 51:7; Babylon hath been a golden cup in the LORD's hand, that made all the earth drunken: the nations have drunken of her wine; therefore the nations are mad.

Revelation 17:3; So he carried me away in the spirit into the wilderness: and I saw a woman sit upon a scarlet coloured beast, full of names of blasphemy, having seven heads and ten horns.

The angel spiritually carried John away to a point where he was able to observe this evil entity. The phrase "into the wilderness" signifies unconquered territory and the battleground for wherever the spiritual war between Christ and Satan is being waged which is all of earth. The term "woman" signifies the mother or birth of this entity. The phrase "sit upon a scarlet coloured beast" implies the evil intent of this entity as the word "scarlet" reflects a multitude of sins and the word "beast" is a term that describes all evil Anti-Christian doctrine. The phrase "having seven heads" reveals Satan's complete authority over this evil entity with the term "ten horns" representing a succession of earthly kings among mankind empowered by Satan to implement his evil Anti-Christian doctrine.

Daniel 7:20-21,24; And of the ten horns that were in his head, and of the other which came up, and before whom three fell; even of that horn that had eyes, and a mouth that spake very great things, whose look was more stout than his fellows. I beheld, and the same horn made war with the saints, and prevailed against them; And the ten horns out of this kingdom are ten kings that shall arise: and another shall rise after them; and he shall be diverse from the first, and he shall subdue three kings.

Revelation 17:4; And the woman was arrayed in purple and scarlet colour, and decked with gold and precious stones and pearls, having a golden cup in her hand full of abominations and filthiness of her fornication:

Being arrayed in "purple" indicates the royal status of a ruler with the color "scarlet" revealing an evil, sinful nature composed of a multitude of sins. The phrase "decked with gold and precious stones and pearls" shows the wealth of evil riches and the value of this ruler in regard to their evil cause. The phrase "having a golden cup in her hand" shows that this entity is currently in control of the content of this container. With the golden cup "full of abominations and filthiness of her fornication" reveals the intent of this entity which is the spreading of evil abominations to God and the worship of false gods or idolatry throughout the world.

Jeremiah 51:7-9; Babylon hath been a golden cup in the LORD's hand, that made all the earth drunken: the nations have drunken of her wine; therefore the nations are mad. Babylon is suddenly fallen and destroyed: howl for her; take balm for her pain, if so be she may be healed. We would have healed Babylon, but she is not healed: forsake her, and let us go every one into his own country: for her judgment reacheth unto heaven, and is lifted up even to the skies.

These verses reveal that God is always in control of Babylon.

Revelation 17:5; And upon her forehead was a name written, MYSTERY, BABYLON THE GREAT, THE MOTHER OF HARLOTS AND ABOMINATIONS OF THE EARTH.

To wear or to write upon the forehead was to declare openly for all to see your allegiance or worship of a particular god, cause or entity and your mindful intent for doing so. This declaration of Babylon as the great and the mother of harlots and abominations of the earth reveals that this city is recognized as the seat of Satan and the source of all evil Anti-Christian doctrine.

Revelation 14:8; And there followed another angel, saying, Babylon is fallen, is fallen, that great city, because she made all nations drink of the wine of the wrath of her fornication.

I John 2:16; For all that is in the world, the lust of the flesh, and the lust of the eyes, and the pride of life, is not of the Father, but is of the world.

Revelation 17:6; And I saw the woman drunken with the blood of the saints, and with the blood of the martyrs of Jesus: and when I saw her, I wondered with great admiration.

The term "woman" indicates the source of the opposition to Christ and is also symbolically called Babylon reflecting the responsibility for the persecution and deaths of the disciples of our Lord implied by the word "drunken" many of whom freely gave their lives for the cause of Christianity. The phrase "blood of the saints" reflects the loss of spiritual life by being led astray from the worship of the Lord God while the phrase "blood of the martyrs of Jesus" reflects those who lost their physical life for the testimony of Christ and held steadfast to the faith becoming martyrs thereby earning their reward of heaven. The phrase, "I wondered with great admiration" reveals John's astonishment at the great power wielded by Satan's evil opposition to Christ.

Jeremiah 51:34-35; Nebuchadnezzar the king of Babylon hath devoured me, he hath crushed me, he hath made me an empty vessel, he hath swallowed me up like a dragon, he hath filled his belly with my delicates, he hath cast me out. The violence done to me and to my flesh be upon Babylon, shall the inhabitant of Zion say; and my blood upon the inhabitants of Chaldea, shall Jerusalem say.

Revelation 17:7; And the angel said unto me, Wherefore didst thou marvel? I will tell thee the mystery of the woman, and of the beast that carrieth her, which hath the seven heads and ten horns.

John is being asked by the angel why he was astonished about the "woman" and the "beast that carried her" described as having "seven heads and ten horns". John was also told that he would be informed of this mystery.

Revelation 17:8; The beast that thou sawest was, and is not; and shall ascend out of the bottomless pit, and go into perdition: and they that dwell on the earth shall wonder, whose names were not written in the book of life from the foundation of the world, when they behold the beast that was, and is not, and yet is.

The "beast" is all anti-Christian doctrine and the phrase "was, and is not" means that this particular evil entity had been, but is no longer active. The phrase "shall ascend out of the bottomless pit" indicates that it was originating from the evil abode of Satan while the phrase "go into perdition" signifies eternal destruction. The phrase "and they that dwell on the earth shall wonder" implies perplexity at the power of God that caused the destruction of the beast. The phrase "whose names were not written in the book of life from the foundation of the world" reveals that this perplexity is restricted to those who are not disciples of our Lord God and were unaware of His supreme power while the phrase "when they behold the beast that was, and is not, and yet is" shows that these forces of evil progress from one generation unto another generation and from one evil empire unto another evil empire. For instance, the phrase "was, and is not" refers to evil empires that no longer exist such as the Chaldean empire, the Medo-Persian empire, the Macedonian empire, and the Roman empire while the phrase "and yet is" defines current evil empires that are anti-Christian such as the nations of Islam and also principles that are currently being employed that are abominations to God such as our own government in its promotion of homosexuality and the removal of references to God and Christianity from public places. Each of these entities eventually goes "into perdition".

Psalms 69:28; Let them be blotted out of the book of the living, and not be written with the righteous.

Revelation 9:1;And the fifth angel sounded, and I saw a star fall from heaven unto the earth: and to him was given the key of the bottomless pit.

This is Satan establishing his evil dominion upon earth with the "beast" being anti-Christian doctrine and the agenda of Satan. While the "beast" is being defeated by Christian doctrine, it will not completely perish until the death of Satan.

Revelation 17:9; And here is the mind which hath wisdom. The seven heads are seven mountains, on which the woman sitteth.

Mountains symbolically represent nations or kingdoms with the numeral seven indicating a complete number of kingdoms under God's plan. The phrase "on which the woman sitteth" indicates that these kingdoms accept, endorse, and promote the evil doctrine of the "woman" which is symbolically considered as the source or beginning of Satan's dominion of evil.

Isaiah 2:2,14; And it shall come to pass in the last days, that the mountain of the LORD's house shall be established in the top of the mountains, and shall be exalted above the hills; and all nations shall flow unto it. And upon all the high mountains, and upon all the hills that are lifted up,

Jeremiah 51:25; Behold, I am against thee, O destroying mountain, saith the LORD, which destroyest all the earth: and I will stretch out mine hand upon thee, and roll thee down from the rocks, and will make thee a burnt mountain.

Daniel 2:35; Then was the iron, the clay, the brass, the silver, and the gold, broken to pieces together, and became like the chaff of the summer threshingfloors; and the wind carried them away, that no place was found for them: and the stone that smote the image became a great mountain, and filled the whole earth.

The metals that composed the metallic image of Nebuchadnezzar's dream were kingdoms that were interpreted by Daniel who credited God for this prophecy.

Revelation 17:10; And there are seven kings: five are fallen, and one is, and the other is not yet come; and when he cometh, he must continue a short space.

The term "seven kings" implies that this is a complete number of kings during this time period of Gospel Dispensation and not an actual numerical value. This verse indicates that the "woman's" evil doctrine was prevalent in a past period of mankind as indicated by the phrase "five are fallen", is in existence in the present by the phrase "and one is" and will continue in the future by the phrase "and the other is not yet come", and will continue to exist for a short period of time as denoted by the phrase "he must continue a short space".

Revelation 17:11; And the beast that was, and is not, even he is the eighth, and is of the seven, and goeth into perdition.

The "beast", which is evil, anti-Christian doctrine is considered as ruling in the "seven" evil kingdoms as indicated by the phrase "even he is the eighth, and is of the seven" while the phrase "goeth into perdition" reveals final eternal destruction. The numeral "seven" does not indicate an actual mathematical value, but rather, a complete number of kingdoms as determined by God which implies that the "beast" which is anti-Christian doctrine will continue to exist in these kingdoms and progress from one kingdom unto another until its final destruction by God.

II Thessalonians 2:3; Let no man deceive you by any means: for that day shall not come, except there come a falling away first, and that man of sin be revealed, the son of perdition;

Revelation 17:12; And the ten horns which thou sawest are ten kings, which have received no kingdom as yet; but receive power as kings one hour with the beast.

The numeral "ten" used to describe the horns and kings indicates that this power is restricted to mankind with their "power" coming from Satan while the "beast" is Satan's evil anti-Christian doctrine. The phrase "have received no kingdom yet" implies that these kings are coming in the future from the time of the writing of John. This "power as kings" is also limited to a short period of time as revealed by the phrase "one hour with the beast".

Daniel 7:20,24; And of the ten horns that were in his head, and of the other which came up, and before whom three fell; even of that horn that had eyes, and a mouth that spake very great things, whose look was more stout than his fellows. And the ten horns out of this kingdom are ten kings that shall arise: and another shall rise after them; and he shall be diverse from the first, and he shall subdue three kings.

Daniel 12:7; And I heard the man clothed in linen, which was upon the waters of the river, when he held up his right hand and his left hand unto heaven, and sware by him that liveth for ever that it shall be for a time, times, and an half; and when he shall have accomplished to scatter the power of the holy people, all these things shall be finished.

Revelation 17:13; These have one mind, and shall give their power and strength unto the beast.

The phrase "These have one mind" reveals a common goal
and united purpose of this succession of earthly kings which is
dedication to serving Satan's evil purposes through anti-Christian
doctrine.

Revelation 17:14; These shall make war with the Lamb, and the
Lamb shall overcome them: for he is Lord of lords, and King of
kings: and they that are with him are called, and chosen, and faithful.

These kingdoms that are making war with the "Lamb",
which is Christ, are under the control and influence of Satan
with the goal of promoting evil, anti-Christian doctrine, but
Christ will prevail and conquer these dominions of Satan. The
disciples of Christ are referred to as the "called, and chosen, and
faithful".

Jeremiah 51:1; Thus saith the LORD; Behold, I will raise up against
Babylon, and against them that dwell in the midst of them that rise
up against me, a destroying wind;

Daniel 7:26-27; But the judgment shall sit, and they shall take away
his dominion, to consume and to destroy it unto the end. And the
kingdom and dominion, and the greatness of the kingdom under the
whole heaven, shall be given to the people of the saints of the most
High, whose kingdom is an everlasting kingdom, and all dominions
shall serve and obey him.

Revelation 17:15; And he saith unto me, The waters which thou
sawest, where the whore sitteth, are peoples, and multitudes, and
nations, and tongues.

The angel speaking unto John explained and described the
term "waters" as peoples, multitudes, nations, and tongues. The
phrase "where the whore sitteth" implies the worship of false
gods and/or idolatry by these people as opposed to the worship
of the one true God as the word "whore" signifies spiritual fornication. Being described as four entities, "peoples, and multitudes, and nations, and tongues", confirms them as residents
over all of earth.

Isaiah 8:7-8; Now therefore, behold, the Lord bringeth up upon them
the waters of the river, strong and many, even the king of Assyria,
and all his glory: and he shall come up over all his channels, and go
over all his banks: And he shall pass through Judah; he shall over-

flow and go over, he shall reach even to the neck; and the stretching out of his wings shall fill the breadth of thy land, O Immanuel.

Jeremiah 51:13; O thou that dwellest upon many waters, abundant in treasures, thine end is come, and the measure of thy covetousness. Revelation 17:16; And the ten horns which thou sawest upon the beast, these shall hate the whore, and shall make her desolate and naked, and shall eat her flesh, and burn her with fire.

The "ten horns" represent a succession of earthly kings while the phrase "these shall hate the whore" indicates they have learned of the Christian Doctrine, accepted Christ, and have now turned against the "beast" which is evil, anti-Christian doctrine with the "whore" being worship of false gods or idolatry. These earthly kingdoms accepting Christ reveals the progress being made by the spreading of God's Word. The term "Babylon" is symbolic as the source of all evil, false worship, and abominations to God. To make "her desolate and naked" is to remove these evil entities from "Babylon" while to "eat her flesh" is to strip her of all earthly power and the phrase to "burn her with fire" symbolizes complete destruction.

Ezekiel 27:36; The merchants among the people shall hiss at thee; thou shalt be a terror, and never shalt be any more.

Jeremiah 50:9,41-43; For, lo, I will raise and cause to come up against Babylon an assembly of great nations from the north country: and they shall set themselves in array against her; from thence she shall be taken: their arrows shall be as of a mighty expert man; none shall return in vain. Behold, a people shall come from the north, and a great nation, and many kings shall be raised up from the coasts of the earth. They shall hold the bow and the lance: they are cruel, and will not shew mercy: their voice shall roar like the sea, and they shall ride upon horses, every one put in array, like a man to the battle, against thee, O daughter of Babylon. The king of Babylon hath heard the report of them, and his hands waxed feeble: anguish took hold of him, and pangs as of a woman in travail.

Jeremiah 51:27-28,55; Set ye up a standard in the land, blow the trumpet among the nations, prepare the nations against her, call together against her the kingdoms of Ararat, Minni, and Ashchenaz; appoint a captain against her; cause the horses to come up as the rough caterpillers. Prepare against her the nations with the kings of the Medes, the captains thereof, and all the rulers thereof, and all the land of his dominion. Because the LORD hath spoiled Babylon, and destroyed out of her the great voice; when her waves do roar like great waters, a noise of their voice is uttered:

Jeremiah 5:14; Wherefore thus saith the LORD God of hosts, Because ye speak this word, behold, I will make my words in thy mouth fire, and this people wood, and it shall devour them.

Revelation 17:17; For God hath put in their hearts to fulfil his will, and to agree, and give their kingdom unto the beast, until the words of God shall be fulfilled.

God is in control and it was His will to have this succession of kingdoms support the dominion of Satan allowing his evil to flourish for a period of time until His words were fulfilled. Allowing evil to flourish for a period of time exposes the corrupt nature of Satan's dominion influencing many people to turn to Christianity.

Jeremiah 51:7; Babylon hath been a golden cup in the LORD's hand, that made all the earth drunken: the nations have drunken of her wine; therefore the nations are mad.

Daniel 7:25; And he shall speak great words against the most High, and shall wear out the saints of the most High, and think to change times and laws: and they shall be given into his hand until a time and times and the dividing of time.

II Thessalonians 2:11; And for this cause God shall send them strong delusion, that they should believe a lie:

II Thessalonians 2:8; And then shall that Wicked be revealed, whom the Lord shall consume with the spirit of his mouth, and shall destroy with the brightness of his coming:

Revelation 17:18; And the woman which thou sawest is that great city, which reigneth over the kings of the earth.

The angel is explaining unto John the interpretation of the vision of the "woman" as the great city of "Babylon" which represents the throne of Satan and the source of all evil that is in opposition to Christ. Sitting upon the "scarlet coloured beast" demonstrates the sinful nature of this entity and its goal of corrupting the various nations. To "reigneth over the kings of the

earth" is to control and export Satan's dominion of evil unto other kingdoms.

Isaiah 13:19; And Babylon, the glory of kingdoms, the beauty of the Chaldees' excellency, shall be as when God overthrew Sodom and Gomorrah.

CHAPTER 18

This chapter describes the death of Babylon, the seat of Satan, the source of all evil, because her evil had spiritually destroyed many people. Many of her companions in this promotion of evil lamented her death and the fact that it came very quickly. Verses seven through nineteen dramatize spiritual loss in physical terms with a dual meaning of exposing the fallacy of placing your faith in temporary material wealth as opposed to spiritual wealth which is everlasting and brings true happiness. Revelation 18:1; And after these things I saw another angel come down from heaven, having great power; and the earth was lightened with his glory.

The phrase "after these things" refers to the establishment of Satan's dominion of evil upon earth as detailed in chapter seventeen and expressed symbolically as John saw "a woman sit upon a scarlet coloured beast, full of names of blasphemy, having seven heads and ten horns".

The angel that John saw coming down from heaven with great power is Christ coming to render the judgment of God upon this establishment of evil symbolically referred to as "Babylon". The phrase "and the earth was lightened with his glory" reflects the regal status of Christ bringing God's Word unto earth with which to combat Satan.

Numbers 14:21; But as truly as I live, all the earth shall be filled with the glory of the LORD.

Psalms 72:19; And blessed be his glorious name for ever: and let the whole earth be filled with his glory; Amen, and Amen.

Isaiah 6:3; And one cried unto another, and said, Holy, holy, holy, is the LORD of hosts: the whole earth is full of his glory.

Ezekiel 43:2; And, behold, the glory of the God of Israel came from the way of the east: and his voice was like a noise of many waters: and the earth shined with his glory.

Matthew 17:2; And was transfigured before them: and his face did shine as the sun, and his raiment was white as the light.

Mark 9:3; And his raiment became shining, exceeding white as snow; so as no fuller on earth can white them.

Revelation 18:2; And he cried mightily with a strong voice, saying, Babylon the great is fallen, is fallen, and is become the habitation of devils, and the hold of every foul spirit, and a cage of every unclean and hateful bird.

Christ crying "mightily with a strong voice" reflects His immense power with the ability to accomplish God's mission of destroying Satan's dominion of evil. As "Babylon" is symbolically considered the source of all evil that is in opposition to God, therefore this pronouncement of "Babylon the great is fallen" indicates that God has recognized that "Babylon" is the seat of Satan's reign and has sent Christ to combat this source of evil. The phrase "and is become the habitation of devils, and the hold of every foul spirit, and a cage of every unclean and hateful bird" reflects the degenerative state of all types of evil into which "Babylon" has fallen.

Isaiah 13:19,21-22; And Babylon, the glory of kingdoms, the beauty of the Chaldees' excellency, shall be as when God overthrew Sodom and Gomorrah. But wild beasts of the desert shall lie there; and their houses shall be full of doleful creatures; and owls shall dwell there, and satyrs shall dance there. And the wild beasts of the islands shall cry in their desolate houses, and dragons in their pleasant palaces: and her time is near to come, and her days shall not be prolonged.

Isaiah 21:9; And, behold, here cometh a chariot of men, with a couple of horsemen. And he answered and said, Babylon is fallen, is fallen; and all the graven images of her gods he hath broken unto the ground.

Jeremiah 50:39; Therefore the wild beasts of the desert with the wild beasts of the islands shall dwell there, and the owls shall dwell therein: and it shall be no more inhabited for ever; neither shall it be dwelt in from generation to generation.

Jeremiah 51:24,29,37; And I will render unto Babylon and to all the inhabitants of Chaldea all their evil that they have done in Zion in your sight, saith the LORD. And the land shall tremble and sorrow: for every purpose of the LORD shall be performed against Babylon, to make the land of Babylon a desolation without an inhabitant. And Babylon shall become heaps, a dwelling place for dragons, an astonishment, and an hissing, without an inhabitant.

Revelation 18:3; For all nations have drunk of the wine of the wrath of her fornication, and the kings of the earth have committed fornication with her, and the merchants of the earth are waxed rich through the abundance of her delicacies.

This pronouncement of "For all nations have drunk of the wine of the wrath of her fornication" indicates that "Babylon" has promoted the worship of false gods and idolatry unto other nations while the phrase "and the kings of the earth have committed fornication with her" reveals that other nations have participated in this furthering of evil, false worship. The phrase "and the merchants of the earth are waxed rich through the abundance of her delicacies" suggests that other nations pursuit of this false worship, abominations to God, and anti-Christian doctrine along with the pursuit of material wealth over spiritual wealth has become deeply ingrained into their societies.

Jeremiah 51:7; Babylon hath been a golden cup in the LORD's hand, that made all the earth drunken: the nations have drunken of her wine; therefore the nations are mad.

Ezekiel 28:4-5; With thy wisdom and with thine understanding thou hast gotten thee riches, and hast gotten gold and silver into thy treasures: By thy great wisdom and by thy traffick hast thou increased thy riches, and thine heart is lifted up because of thy riches:

Revelation 18:4; And I heard another voice from heaven, saying, Come out of her, my people, that ye be not partakers of her sins, and that ye receive not of her plagues.

This is a plea from God instructing His people to not be led astray by the evil examples and leadership of "Babylon" into abominations, blasphemy, immoral acts, and false worship as

indicated by the phrase "that ye be not partakers of her sins" in order that they also will not be punished along with the destruction of "Babylon" as revealed by the phrase "that ye receive not of her plagues".

Isaiah 48:20; Go ye forth of Babylon, flee ye from the Chaldeans, with a voice of singing declare ye, tell this, utter it even to the end of the earth; say ye, The LORD hath redeemed his servant Jacob.

Jeremiah 51:6,45; Flee out of the midst of Babylon, and deliver every man his soul: be not cut off in her iniquity; for this is the time of the LORD's vengeance; he will render unto her a recompence. My people, go ye out of the midst of her, and deliver ye every man his soul from the fierce anger of the LORD.

Revelation 18:5; For her sins have reached unto heaven, and God hath remembered her iniquities.

God is ever aware of all sins on earth and has reserved judgment for them. The sinful nature and iniquities of "Babylon" has reached the point of God's judgment being inflicted upon them.

Isaiah 66:17-18; They that sanctify themselves, and purify themselves in the gardens behind one tree in the midst, eating swine's flesh, and the abomination, and the mouse, shall be consumed together, saith the LORD. For I know their works and their thoughts: it shall come, that I will gather all nations and tongues; and they shall come, and see my glory.

Jeremiah 51:9; We would have healed Babylon, but she is not healed: forsake her, and let us go every one into his own country: for her judgment reacheth unto heaven, and is lifted up even to the skies.

God's awareness of all activities upon earth is reflected by the "Seven Spirits of God" as recorded in Revelation chapter four, verse five and chapter five, verse six.

Zechariah 4:10; For who hath despised the day of small things? for they shall rejoice, and shall see the plummet in the hand of Zerubbabel with those seven; they are the eyes of the LORD, which run to and fro through the whole earth.

Revelation 18:6; Reward her even as she rewarded you, and double unto her double according to her works: in the cup which she hath filled fill to her double.

God has promised to properly reward those that have sewn the seeds of evil and unrighteousness and to repay and punish two-fold for the persecution suffered by His disciples at the hand of "Babylon".

Exodus 22:7,9; If a man shall deliver unto his neighbour money or stuff to keep, and it be stolen out of the man's house; if the thief be found, let him pay double. For all manner of trespass, whether it be for ox, for ass, for sheep, for raiment, or for any manner of lost thing which another challengeth to be his, the cause of both parties shall come before the judges; and whom the judges shall condemn, he shall pay double unto his neighbour.

Jeremiah 51:35,44,49,57; The violence done to me and to my flesh be upon Babylon, shall the inhabitant of Zion say; and my blood upon the inhabitants of Chaldea, shall Jerusalem say. And I will punish Bel in Babylon, and I will bring forth out of his mouth that which he hath swallowed up: and the nations shall not flow together any more unto him: yea, the wall of Babylon shall fall. As Babylon hath caused the slain of Israel to fall, so at Babylon shall fall the slain of all the earth. And I will make drunk her princes, and her wise men, her captains, and her rulers, and her mighty men: and they shall sleep a perpetual sleep, and not wake, saith the King, whose name is the LORD of hosts. (Jeremiah 50:15,29; 51:24,25.)

Verses seven through nineteen dramatize spiritual loss in symbolic, physical terms that will be suffered by pursuing the path of false worship and/or material gain with the dual meaning of exposing the fallacy of placing your faith in temporary material wealth as opposed to spiritual wealth which is everlasting and brings true happiness.

Revelation 18:7; How much she hath glorified herself, and lived deliciously, so much torment and sorrow give her: for she saith in her heart, I sit a queen, and am no widow, and shall see no sorrow.

God recognizes the prideful nature of those that take delight in false worship along with earthly gain and place themselves above others to be acknowledged as superior while failing to acknowledge Him as the source of all benevolence. The term "lived deliciously" implies deriving temporary happiness from

the earthly pleasures of false worship, abominations, immoral pleasures, and material gain.

Proverbs 16:18; Pride goeth before destruction, and an haughty spirit before a fall.

Isaiah 5:14-15; Therefore hell hath enlarged herself, and opened her mouth without measure: and their glory, and their multitude, and their pomp, and he that rejoiceth, shall descend into it. And the mean man shall be brought down, and the mighty man shall be humbled, and the eyes of the lofty shall be humbled:

Jeremiah 50:32; And the most proud shall stumble and fall, and none shall raise him up: and I will kindle a fire in his cities, and it shall devour all round about him.

Ezekiel 28:2; Son of man, say unto the prince of Tyrus, Thus saith the Lord GOD; Because thine heart is lifted up, and thou hast said, I am a God, I sit in the seat of God, in the midst of the seas; yet thou art a man, and not God, though thou set thine heart as the heart of God:

Revelation 18:8; Therefore shall her plagues come in one day, death, and mourning, and famine; and she shall be utterly burned with fire: for strong is the Lord God who judgeth her.

The punishment of the Lord will come swiftly unto those who fail to recognize God as our Lord and the creator of all things. The words "plagues, death, mourning, and famine" represent the punishment and remorse for following the path of opposition to our Lord. The term "one day" reflects the swiftness of that punishment while the word "death" implies spiritual loss of life. The phrase "utterly burned with fire" reveals complete destruction while the phrase "for strong is the Lord God who judgeth her" indicates the power, authority, and ability of God to invoke and deliver this punishment.

Isaiah 5:26; And he will lift up an ensign to the nations from far, and will hiss unto them from the end of the earth: and, behold, they shall come with speed swiftly:

Isaiah 47:9; But these two things shall come to thee in a moment in one day, the loss of children, and widowhood: they shall come upon thee in their perfection for the multitude of thy sorceries, and for the great abundance of thine enchantments.

Isaiah 66:15-16; For, behold, the LORD will come with fire, and with his chariots like a whirlwind, to render his anger with fury, and his rebuke with flames of fire. For by fire and by his sword will the LORD plead with all flesh: and the slain of the LORD shall be many. Jeremiah 50:31; Behold, I am against thee, O thou most proud, saith the Lord GOD of hosts: for thy day is come, the time that I will visit thee.

Jeremiah 51:58; Thus saith the LORD of hosts; The broad walls of Babylon shall be utterly broken, and her high gates shall be burned with fire; and the people shall labour in vain, and the folk in the fire, and they shall be weary. (Jeremiah 5:14.)

Revelation 18:9; And the kings of the earth, who have committed fornication and lived deliciously with her, shall bewail her, and lament for her, when they shall see the smoke of her burning,

All of the kings who had been influenced by and joined with "Babylon" in the worshiping of various false gods were now lamenting the death of "Babylon" as they view her destruction. The term "committed fornication" represents the worshiping of false gods as opposed to worshiping the one true God. The phrase "lived deliciously with her" implies eager complicity regarding this false worship along with the pursuit and promotion of evil abominations expressed as material wealth. The phrase "when they shall see the smoke of her burning" means observing the death and destruction of "Babylon".

Proverbs 16:19; Better it is to be of an humble spirit with the lowly, than to divide the spoil with the proud.

Jeremiah 50:46; At the noise of the taking of Babylon the earth is moved, and the cry is heard among the nations.

Ezekiel 27:33; When thy wares went forth out of the seas, thou filledst many people; thou didst enrich the kings of the earth with the multitude of thy riches and of thy merchandise.

Ezekiel 28:17; Thine heart was lifted up because of thy beauty, thou hast corrupted thy wisdom by reason of thy brightness: I will cast thee to the ground, I will lay thee before kings, that they may behold thee.

Revelation 18:10; Standing afar off for the fear of her torment, saying, Alas, alas, that great city Babylon, that mighty city! for in one hour is thy judgment come.

The phrase "Standing afar off for the fear of her torment" implies those kings trying to hide for fear of suffering the same fate and also attempting to disguise their complicity. The lamenting of "Alas, alas that great city Babylon, that mighty city!" expresses astonishment at the destruction of an entity that had become so great and powerful in the pursuit and promotion of evil. The phrase "for in one hour is thy judgment come" suggests that the destruction of Babylon will occur quickly in a short period of time.

Isaiah 21:9; And, behold, here cometh a chariot of men, with a couple of horsemen. And he answered and said, Babylon is fallen, is fallen; and all the graven images of her gods he hath broken unto the ground.

Ezekiel 27:35; All the inhabitants of the isles shall be astonished at thee, and their kings shall be sore afraid, they shall be troubled in their countenance.

Revelation 18:11; And the merchants of the earth shall weep and mourn over her; for no man buyeth their merchandise any more:

The phrase "merchants of the earth" means other nations and peoples that are complicit with "Babylon" in the pursuit of false worship and earthly pleasures.

With the death of Babylon, the promotion of false worship along with the trafficking of the various abominations to God will cease as expressed in the phrase "no man buyeth their merchandise any more". The word "merchandise" implies all types of evil acts and abominations.

Jeremiah 51:13; O thou that dwellest upon many waters, abundant in treasures, thine end is come, and the measure of thy covetousness.

Ezekiel 27:13,15,27,36; Javan, Tubal, and Meshech, they were thy merchants: they traded the persons of men and vessels of brass in thy market. The men of Dedan were thy merchants; many isles were the merchandise of thine hand: they brought thee for a present horns of ivory and ebony. Thy riches, and thy fairs, thy merchandise, thy mariners, and thy pilots, thy calkers, and the occupiers of thy merchandise, and all thy men of war, that are in thee, and in all thy company which is in the midst of thee, shall fall into the midst of the seas in the day of thy ruin. The merchants among the people shall hiss at thee; thou shalt be a terror, and never shalt be any more.

Revelation 18:12; The merchandise of gold, and silver, and precious stones, and of pearls, and fine linen, and purple, and silk, and scarlet, and all thyine wood, and all manner vessels of ivory, and all manner vessels of most precious wood, and of brass, and iron, and marble,

All of these items of material value reflect the pursuit of material gain and evil, earthly pleasures as opposed to the pursuit of true wealth which is spiritual. The varied items listed as "merchandise" reflect not only material wealth but also are symbols for the spiritual wealth that will be lost on the final judgment day of God because of this pursuit of earthly pleasures and false worship.

Luke 16:9,11,13; And I say unto you, Make to yourselves friends of the mammon of unrighteousness; that, when ye fail, they may receive you into everlasting habitations. If therefore ye have not been faithful in the unrighteous mammon, who will commit to your trust the true riches? No servant can serve two masters: for either he will hate the one, and love the other; or else he will hold to the one, and despise the other. Ye cannot serve God and mammon.

Ezekiel 27:6-7,12,16,24; Of the oaks of Bashan have they made thine oars; the company of the Ashurites have made thy benches of ivory, brought out of the isles of Chittim. Fine linen with broidered work from Egypt was that which thou spreadest forth to be thy sail; blue and purple from the isles of Elishah was that which covered thee. Tarshish was thy merchant by reason of the multitude of all kind of riches; with silver, iron, tin, and lead, they traded in thy fairs. Syria was thy merchant by reason of the multitude of the wares of thy making: they occupied in thy fairs with emeralds, purple, and broidered work, and fine linen, and coral, and agate. These were thy merchants in all sorts of things, in blue clothes, and broidered work, and in chests of rich apparel, bound with cords, and made of cedar, among thy merchandise.

Revelation 18:13; And cinnamon, and odours, and ointments, and frankincense, and wine, and oil, and fine flour, and wheat, and beasts, and sheep, and horses, and chariots, and slaves, and souls of men.

This is a listing of more "merchandise" expressed as material wealth. The pursuit of actual material wealth could lessen your desire of obtaining spiritual salvation which brings true happiness.

Matthew 6:24; No man can serve two masters: for either he will hate the one, and love the other; or else he will hold to the one, and despise the other. Ye cannot serve God and mammon.

Ezekiel 27:14,17,20-22; They of the house of Togarmah traded in thy fairs with horses and horsemen and mules. Judah, and the land of Israel, they were thy merchants: they traded in thy market wheat of Minnith, and Pannag, and honey, and oil, and balm. Dedan was thy merchant in precious clothes for chariots. Arabia, and all the princes of Kedar, they occupied with thee in lambs, and rams, and goats: in these were they thy merchants. The merchants of Sheba and Raamah, they were thy merchants: they occupied in thy fairs with chief of all spices, and with all precious stones, and gold.

Exekiel 28:4; With thy wisdom and with thine understanding thou hast gotten thee riches, and hast gotten gold and silver into thy treasures:

Revelation 18:14; And the fruits that thy soul lusted after are departed from thee, and all things which were dainty and goodly are departed from thee, and thou shalt find them no more at all.

The vision given to John by Christ reveals that false worship along with material gain will not be ever-lasting, but will vanish with the second coming of Christ.

Jeremiah 51:13; O thou that dwellest upon many waters, abundant in treasures, thine end is come, and the measure of thy covetousness.

Ezekiel 27:27; Thy riches, and thy fairs, thy merchandise, thy mariners, and thy pilots, thy calkers, and the occupiers of thy merchandise, and all thy men of war, that are in thee, and in all thy company which is in the midst of thee, shall fall into the midst of the seas in the day of thy ruin.

Revelation 18:15; The merchants of these things, which were made rich by her, shall stand afar off for the fear of her torment, weeping and wailing,

The phrase "The merchants of these things" implies those peoples and nations that were complicit with "Babylon" in the pursuit of false worship, evil abominations, and material gain while the phrase "which were made rich by her" indicates the depth of this evil pursuit. The phrase "shall stand afar off for the fear of her torment, weeping and wailing" would convey the thought of attempting to hide from the wrath of God while lamenting the loss of their life-style.

Jeremiah 50:46; At the noise of the taking of Babylon the earth is moved, and the cry is heard among the nations.

Ezekiel 26:16-17; Then all the princes of the sea shall come down from their thrones, and lay away their robes, and put off their broidered garments: they shall clothe themselves with trembling; they shall sit upon the ground, and shall tremble at every moment, and be astonished at thee. And they shall take up a lamentation for thee, and say to thee, How art thou destroyed, that wast inhabited of seafaring men, the renowned city, which wast strong in the sea, she and her inhabitants, which cause their terror to be on all that haunt it!

Revelation 18:16; And saying, Alas, alas, that great city, that was clothed in fine linen, and purple, and scarlet, and decked with gold, and precious stones, and pearls!

Those people and nations that participated with "Babylon" in idolatry and placed their faith in material gain are now lamenting the fall of their evil practices. Being expressed as various items indicating great wealth and status reflects the immense depth of this evil.

Ezekiel 27:22,29, The merchants of Sheba and Raamah, they were thy merchants: they occupied in thy fairs with chief of all spices, and with all precious stones, and gold. And all that handle the oar, the mariners, and all the pilots of the sea, shall come down from their ships, they shall stand upon the land;

Revelation 18:17; For in one hour so great riches is come to nought. And every shipmaster, and all the company in ships, and sailors, and as many as trade by sea, stood afar off,

The phrase "For in one hour so great riches is come to nought" means that this accumulation of earthly, great riches will be destroyed in a short period of time. Those trading partners that were involved with this wicked city, "Babylon", observed this destruction. This is spiritual destruction expressed in physical terminology. The term "great riches" reveals the depth of their descent into their evil practices. A dual meaning is that all material wealth is temporary and perishable as opposed to spiritual wealth that is everlasting. The phrase "stood afar off" reveals that those peoples and nations that had joined with "Babylon" in the pursuit and promotion of evil practices were trying to hide from the wrath of God.

Ezekiel 27:26-29; Thy rowers have brought thee into great waters: the east wind hath broken thee in the midst of the seas. Thy riches, and thy fairs, thy merchandise, thy mariners, and thy pilots, thy calkers, and the occupiers of thy merchandise, and all thy men of war, that are in thee, and in all thy company which is in the midst of thee, shall fall into the midst of the seas in the day of thy ruin. The suburbs shall shake at the sound of the cry of thy pilots And all that handle the oar, the mariners, and all the pilots of the sea, shall come down from their ships, they shall stand upon the land;

Revelation 18:18; And cried when they saw the smoke of her burning, saying, What city is like unto this great city!

The "smoke of her burning" implies the fall and destruction of "Babylon". The phrase "What city is like unto this great city!" reflects astonishment that so great an entity could be so completely destroyed in a short period of time. The term "great city" implies the notion that this evil power was so great that it affected and influenced many nations and peoples to be led astray into condemnation.

Jeremiah 51:58; Thus saith the LORD of hosts; The broad walls of Babylon shall be utterly broken, and her high gates shall be burned with fire; and the people shall labour in vain, and the folk in the fire, and they shall be weary.

Ezekiel 27:31; And they shall make themselves utterly bald for thee, and gird them with sackcloth, and they shall weep for thee with bitterness of heart and bitter wailing.

Ezekiel 28:19; All they that know thee among the people shall be astonished at thee: thou shalt be a terror, and never shalt thou be any more.

Revelation 18:19; And they cast dust on their heads, and cried, weeping and wailing, saying, Alas, alas, that great city, wherein were made rich all that had ships in the sea by reason of her costliness! for in one hour is she made desolate.

Casting dust upon the head along with weeping and wailing was an outward expression of immense grief. Part of the lamenting was induced by the realization that their false religion along with their opposition to God and their material pursuit of wealth brought about this destruction. The phrase "wherein were made rich all that had ships in the sea" implies other nations that were complicit with Babylon in this pursuit and promotion of evil practices and abominations to God. The phrase "for in one hour is she made desolate" reveals that this destruction by the judgment of God occurred in a short period of time.

Ezekiel 26:19; For thus saith the Lord GOD; When I shall make thee a desolate city, like the cities that are not inhabited; when I shall bring up the deep upon thee, and great waters shall cover thee;

Ezekiel 27:30; And shall cause their voice to be heard against thee, and shall cry bitterly, and shall cast up dust upon their heads, they shall wallow themselves in the ashes:

Jeremiah 50:46; At the noise of the taking of Babylon the earth is moved, and the cry is heard among the nations.

Jeremiah 51:26,29; And they shall not take of thee a stone for a corner, nor a stone for foundations; but thou shalt be desolate for ever, saith the LORD. And the land shall tremble and sorrow: for every purpose of the LORD shall be performed against Babylon, to make the land of Babylon a desolation without an inhabitant.

Revelation 18:20; Rejoice over her, thou heaven, and ye holy apostles and prophets; for God hath avenged you on her.

Rejoicing will occur in heaven when God delivers vengeance upon His enemies who persecuted His apostles, prophets, and saints as that will indicate victory over Satan and his dominion

of evil halting the promotion of evil and vindicating the deaths of His servants.

Deuteronomy 32:41; If I whet my glittering sword, and mine hand take hold on judgment; I will render vengeance to mine enemies, and will reward them that hate me.

Psalms 58:10-11; The righteous shall rejoice when he seeth the vengeance: he shall wash his feet in the blood of the wicked. So that a man shall say, Verily there is a reward for the righteous: verily he is a God that judgeth in the earth.

Isaiah 44:23; Sing, O ye heavens; for the LORD hath done it: shout, ye lower parts of the earth: break forth into singing, ye mountains, O forest, and every tree therein: for the LORD hath redeemed Jacob, and glorified himself in Israel.

Isaiah 63:4; For the day of vengeance is in mine heart, and the year of my redeemed is come.

Jeremiah 50:33-34; Thus saith the LORD of hosts; The children of Israel and the children of Judah were oppressed together: and all that took them captives held them fast; they refused to let them go. Their Redeemer is strong; the LORD of hosts is his name: he shall throughly plead their cause, that he may give rest to the land, and disquiet the inhabitants of Babylon.

Jeremiah 51:48; Then the heaven and the earth, and all that is therein, shall sing for Babylon: for the spoilers shall come unto her from the north, saith the LORD.

Romans 12:19; Dearly beloved, avenge not yourselves, but rather give place unto wrath: for it is written, Vengeance is mine; I will repay, saith the Lord.

Revelation 18:21; And a mighty angel took up a stone like a great millstone, and cast it into the sea, saying, Thus with violence shall that great city Babylon be thrown down, and shall be found no more at all.

The "mighty angel" casting a stone like unto a great millstone into the sea represents violent death to a person or entity. The phrase "shall be found no more at all" means complete and final destruction by the judgment of God.

Judges 9:53; And a certain woman cast a piece of a millstone upon Abimelech's head, and all to brake his skull.

II Samuel 11:21; Who smote Abimelech the son of Jerubbesheth? did not a woman cast a piece of a millstone upon him from the wall, that he died in Thebez? why went ye nigh the wall? then say thou, Thy servant Uriah the Hittite is dead also.

Jeremiah 51:63-64; And it shall be, when thou hast made an end of reading this book, that thou shalt bind a stone to it, and cast it into the midst of Euphrates: And thou shalt say, Thus shall Babylon sink, and shall not rise from the evil that I will bring upon her: and they shall be weary. Thus far are the words of Jeremiah.

Mark 9:42; And whosoever shall offend one of these little ones that believe in me, it is better for him that a millstone were hanged about his neck, and he were cast into the sea.

Revelation 18:22; And the voice of harpers, and musicians, and of pipers, and trumpeters, shall be heard no more at all in thee; and no craftsman, of whatsoever craft he be, shall be found any more in thee; and the sound of a millstone shall be heard no more at all in thee;

As there are no sounds of activity from various musicians and craftsmen implies that there was no person left alive to play a musical instrument or practice a trade which would indicate the complete destruction of Babylon.

Isaiah 24:8; The mirth of tabrets ceaseth, the noise of them that rejoice endeth, the joy of the harp ceaseth.

Ezekiel 26:13; And I will cause the noise of thy songs to cease; and the sound of thy harps shall be no more heard.

Revelation 18:23; And the light of a candle shall shine no more at all in thee; and the voice of the bridegroom and of the bride shall be heard no more at all in thee: for thy merchants were the great men of the earth; for by thy sorceries were all nations deceived.

As the word "light" signifies the imparting of knowledge, the phrase "the light of a candle shall shine no more at all in thee" indicates complete destruction and death preventing this entity from the further spreading of evil knowledge. The phrase "the voice of the bridegroom and of the bride shall be heard no more at all in thee" also indicates the ceasing of all human activity. The phrase "for thy merchants were the great men of the earth" shows their previous status among mankind reflecting

their great loss while the phrase "for by thy sorceries were all nations deceived" reveals the reason they were destroyed which was their promotion of false worship by deceit, abominations to God, and anti-Christian doctrine.

Job 18:5-6; Yea, the light of the wicked shall be put out, and the spark of his fire shall not shine. The light shall be dark in his tabernacle, and his candle shall be put out with him.

Jeremiah 7:34; Then will I cause to cease from the cities of Judah, and from the streets of Jerusalem, the voice of mirth, and the voice of gladness, the voice of the bridegroom, and the voice of the bride: for the land shall be desolate.

Jeremiah 25:10; Moreover I will take from them the voice of mirth, and the voice of gladness, the voice of the bridegroom, and the voice of the bride, the sound of the millstones, and the light of the candle.

Revelation 18:24; And in her was found the blood of prophets, and of saints, and of all that were slain upon the earth.

The word "her" implies "Babylon" which represents the seat of Satan's dominion of evil with the word "blood" implying spiritual death of those prophets, saints, and all others that were slain upon the earth by being led astray into false worship by this evil entity.

Psalms 79:2-3; The dead bodies of thy servants have they given to be meat unto the fowls of the heaven, the flesh of thy saints unto the beasts of the earth. Their blood have they shed like water round about Jerusalem; and there was none to bury them.

Jeremiah 51:49; As Babylon hath caused the slain of Israel to fall, so at Babylon shall fall the slain of all the earth.

Lamentations 4:13; For the sins of her prophets, and the iniquities of her priests, that have shed the blood of the just in the midst of her,

Luke 11:49-50; Therefore also said the wisdom of God, I will send them prophets and apostles, and some of them they shall slay and persecute: That the blood of all the prophets, which was shed from the foundation of the world, may be required of this generation;

CHAPTER 19

his chapter reveals Christ gathering unto heaven his disciples symbolized as his wife and represented as the marriage supper of the Lamb. The bride is described as dressed in fine linen, clean and white, indicating righteousness and purity. Christ is pictured as sitting upon a white horse with the color "white" signifying his holiness and purity while the symbol of a "horse" suggests warfare. The sharp sword proceeding out of his mouth indicates that Christ is waging his spiritual war with Satan through God's Word. Being called faithful and true reflects his dependability and value to God in regards to this mission of combating evil and fulfilling of the prophecies. The beast and the false prophet represent the entities and the method by which Satan is waging war and deceiving many people are now being cast into the lake of fire representing victory by Christ.

Revelation 19:1; And after these things I heard a great voice of much people in heaven, saying, Alleluia; Salvation, and glory, and honour, and power, unto the Lord our God:

The phrase "And after these things" refers to the judgments of God as implemented and detailed in chapter eighteen destroying "Babylon" which is considered as the seat or source of Satan's evil empire. The phrase "I heard a great voice of much people in heaven" reveals that John heard the voice of God's people offering praise unto God. With the five words, "Alleluia; Salvation, and glory, and honour, and power," descriptive of these praises suggests that they came from God's disciples among mankind.

Revelation 4:11; Thou art worthy, O Lord, to receive glory and honour and power: for thou hast created all things, and for thy pleasure they are and were created.

Revelation 5:13; And every creature which is in heaven, and on the earth, and under the earth, and such as are in the sea, and all that are in them, heard I saying, Blessing, and honour, and glory, and power, be unto him that sitteth upon the throne, and unto the Lamb for ever and ever.

Revelation 19:2; For true and righteous are his judgments: for he hath judged the great whore, which did corrupt the earth with her fornication, and hath avenged the blood of his servants at her hand.

God's judgments against the great whore "Babylon" are described as "true and righteous" signifying His perfect nature with the word "true" reflecting the fulfilling of the prophecies and the word "righteous" indicating justice. "Babylon" was the evil, corrupting influence of false worship upon the various peoples of earth as indicated by the phrase "which did corrupt the earth with her fornication" while the phrase "and hath avenged the blood of his servants at her hand" describes God's judgments as being victorious upon "Babylon" as vengeance for the persecution of His disciples.

Deuteronomy 32:43; Rejoice, O ye nations, with his people: for he will avenge the blood of his servants, and will render vengeance to his adversaries, and will be merciful unto his land, and to his people.

Psalms 19:9; The fear of the LORD is clean, enduring for ever: the judgments of the LORD are true and righteous altogether.

Psalms 119:137,160; Righteous art thou, O LORD, and upright are thy judgments. Thy word is true from the beginning: and every one of thy righteous judgments endureth for ever.

Isaiah 63:4; For the day of vengeance is in mine heart, and the year of my redeemed is come.

Revelation 19:3; And again they said, Alleluia. And her smoke rose up for ever and ever.

This praise unto God that relates "And her smoke rose up for ever and ever" reveals that the death of "Babylon" is everlasting death.

Isaiah 34:10; It shall not be quenched night nor day; the smoke thereof shall go up for ever: from generation to generation it shall lie waste; none shall pass through it for ever and ever.

Revelation 19:4; And the four and twenty elders and the four beasts fell down and worshipped God that sat on the throne, saying, Amen; Alleluia.

The "four and twenty elders" are the twelve tribes of Israel coupled with the twelve apostles of Christ that represent the leaders of the established religions of God while the "four beasts" reflect God's disciples all of whom fell down and worshiped God on His throne. (For the definition of the four beasts, reference chapter four, verses six and seven.) The phrase "that sat on the throne" reveals God's royal status as supreme ruler over everything.

Psalms 66:4; All the earth shall worship thee, and shall sing unto thee; they shall sing to thy name. Selah.

Revelation 19:5; And a voice came out of the throne, saying, Praise our God, all ye his servants, and ye that fear him, both small and great.

The voice that John heard coming out of the throne was the voice of all of God's disciples praising Him. The four living creatures are described in chapter four, verse six as being "in the midst of the throne, and round about the throne" and along with the twenty-four elders represent all of the saints in heaven.

Psalms 135:1-3; Praise ye the LORD. Praise ye the name of the LORD; praise him, O ye servants of the LORD. Ye that stand in the house of the LORD, in the courts of the house of our God. Praise the LORD; for the LORD is good: sing praises unto his name; for it is pleasant.

Revelation 19:6; And I heard as it were the voice of a great multitude, and as the voice of many waters, and as the voice of mighty thunderings, saying, Alleluia: for the Lord God omnipotent reigneth.

John's description of the voice as "the voice of a great multitude, and as the voice of many waters" implies a large number of people while the phrase "and as the voice of mighty thunderings" suggests that the people were speaking in unison creating a large rumbling. These saints were honoring God with praise

and recognizing Him as being everywhere and the supreme ruler over everything.

Revelation 19:7; Let us be glad and rejoice, and give honour to him: for the marriage of the Lamb is come, and his wife hath made herself ready.

Satan was now defeated and the heavenly host were rejoicing and honoring God as the phrase "for the marriage of the Lamb is come" suggests that Christ is gathering all of His disciples unto Him in heaven while the phrase "and his wife hath made herself ready" refers to those Christians that had accepted Christ as the Son of God, kept his commandments, and had remained steadfast in the faith were ready to join Christ in the new heaven. Christ used a parable to explain the kingdom of heaven in:

Matthew 22:1-2; And Jesus answered and spake unto them again by parables, and said, *The kingdom of heaven is like unto a certain king, which made a marriage for his son,*

Matthew 25:10; And while they went to buy, the bridegroom came; and they that were ready went in with him to the marriage: and the door was shut.

John 3:29; He that hath the bride is the bridegroom: but the friend of the bridegroom, which standeth and heareth him, rejoiceth greatly because of the bridegroom's voice: this my joy therefore is fulfilled.

Isaiah 54:5; For thy Maker is thine husband; the LORD of hosts is his name; and thy Redeemer the Holy One of Israel; The God of the whole earth shall he be called.

II Corinthians 11:2; For I am jealous over you with godly jealousy: for I have espoused you to one husband, that I may present you as a chaste virgin to Christ.

Revelation 19:8; And to her was granted that she should be arrayed in fine linen, clean and white: for the fine linen is the righteousness of saints.

To be dressed in fine linen, clean, and white reflects righteousness of saints and purity as in freedom from sin, and along with the acceptance of Christ makes one holy and worthy of the honor of joining Christ in heaven as His bride.

Isaiah 61:10; I will greatly rejoice in the LORD, my soul shall be joyful in my God; for he hath clothed me with the garments of salvation, he hath covered me with the robe of righteousness, as a bridegroom decketh himself with ornaments, and as a bride adorneth herself with her jewels.

Matthew 22:11-14; And when the king came in to see the guests, he saw there a man which had not on a wedding garment: And he saith unto him, Friend, how camest thou in hither not having a wedding garment? And he was speechless. Then said the king to the servants, Bind him hand and foot, and take him away, and cast him into outer darkness, there shall be weeping and gnashing of teeth. For many are called, but few are chosen.

Revelation 19:9; And he saith unto me, Write, Blessed are they which are called unto the marriage supper of the Lamb. And he saith unto me, These are the true sayings of God.

Christ explained to John that those disciples who had kept the commandments of God were blessed and rewarded by being called unto the marriage supper of the Lamb. To be invited to a marriage supper was a great honor reserved for special guests.

II Timothy 4:8; Henceforth there is laid up for me a crown of righteousness, which the Lord, the righteous judge, shall give me at that day: and not to me only, but unto all them also that love his appearing.

Revelation 19:10; And I fell at his feet to worship him. And he said unto me, See thou do it not: I am thy fellow-servant, and of thy brethren that have the testimony of Jesus: worship God: for the testimony of Jesus is the spirit of prophecy.

John fell at the feet of this angel to worship him but was instructed to not do so as the angel explained to him that he also was a fellow-servant of God along with other disciples that had accepted the testimony of Jesus Christ and further explained that this testimony is the "spirit of prophecy" which is the preaching and teaching of God's Word. This was the angel that instructed him to write in verse nine regarding those that were called unto the marriage supper of the Lamb as being blessed.

John 13:16; Verily, verily, I say unto you, The servant is not greater than his lord; neither he that is sent greater than he that sent him.

Revelation 19:11; And I saw heaven opened, and behold a white horse; and he that sat upon him was called Faithful and True, and in righteousness he doth judge and make war.

Through an opening in heaven John witnessed Christ sitting on a white horse. The color white signifies holiness and purity while the horse represents war or a battle which is the battle between Christ and Satan of good versus evil. John further describes Christ as "Faithful and True, and in righteousness" because he is implementing God's plan of judgment and waging a spiritual war with Satan. The term "Faithful" reflects his reliability in executing God's plan and the keeping of the promises made by the prophecies while the word "True" proves all of the predictions by the fulfillment of those prophecies. The term "righteousness" defines justification for this war with Satan.

Psalms 45:3-4; Gird thy sword upon thy thigh, O most mighty, with thy glory and thy majesty. And in thy majesty ride prosperously because of truth and meekness and righteousness; and thy right hand shall teach thee terrible things.

Isaiah 11:4; But with righteousness shall he judge the poor, and reprove with equity for the meek of the earth: and he shall smite the earth: with the rod of his mouth, and with the breath of his lips shall he slay the wicked.

Revelation 19:12; His eyes were as a flame of fire, and on his head were many crowns; and he had a name written, that no man knew, but he himself.

The phrase "His eyes were as a flame of fire" denotes the ability of Christ to penetrate the innermost thoughts of mankind and comprehend all knowledge while the phrase "and on his head were many crowns" portrays his status as king and ruler over all peoples and nations. The phrase "and he had a name written, that no man knew, but he himself" reveals that his mission came directly from God. Also, the children of Israel believed that no one could properly pronounce the name of God which they referred to in their writings as Jehovah, therefore, they used the phrase "he had a name written, that no man knew, but he himself".

Revelation 2:17; He that hath an ear, let him hear what the Spirit saith unto the churches; To him that overcometh will I give to eat of the hidden manna, and will give him a white stone, and in the stone a new name written, which no man knoweth saving he that receiveth it.

Revelation 19:13; And he was clothed with a vesture dipped in blood: and his name is called The Word of God.

John further describes Christ as being "clothed with a vesture dipped in blood" which indicates that He has been engaged in the spiritual battle with Satan and returned victorious as indicated in verse two.

Isaiah 63:2-3; Wherefore art thou red in thine apparel, and thy garments like him that treadeth in the winefat? I have trodden the winepress alone; and of the people there was none with me: for I will tread them in mine anger, and trample them in my fury; and their blood shall be sprinkled upon my garments, and I will stain all my raiment.

The phrase "and his name is called The Word of God" reveals the purpose of his mission was to teach the Word of God, establish His Kingdom upon earth, and at the proper time deliver this kingdom to God. The phrase "Word of God" is actually regarded as the Lord God.

John 1:1; In the beginning was the Word, and the Word was with God, and the Word was God.

Revelation 19:14; And the armies which were in heaven followed him upon white horses, clothed in fine linen, white and clean.

"The armies which were in heaven" are angels in heaven provided by God to aid Christ in his battle with Satan. The phrase "followed him upon white horses" reveals their readiness for battle while the phrase "clothed in fine linen, white and clean" reflects their righteousness, holiness and purity as angels of God.

Daniel 12:1; And at that time shall Michael stand up, the great prince which standeth for the children of thy people: and there shall be a time of trouble, such as never was since there was a nation even to that same time: and at that time thy people shall be delivered, every one that shall be found written in the book.

Isaiah 26:20-21; Come, my people, enter thou into thy chambers, and shut thy doors about thee: hide thyself as it were for a little moment, until the indignation be overpast. For, behold, the LORD cometh out of his place to punish the inhabitants of the earth for their iniquity: the earth also shall disclose her blood, and shall no more cover her slain.

Revelation 19:15; And out of his mouth goeth a sharp sword, that with it he should smite the nations: and he shall rule them with a rod of iron: and he treadeth the winepress of the fierceness and wrath of Almighty God.

The phrase "out of his mouth goeth a sharp sword" suggests that the battle with Satan is being fought with the preaching and teaching of the Word of God by which he will "smite the nations" and "rule them with a rod of iron" which indicates victory over all evil and implies complete sovereignty over all nations with spiritual punishment. The phrase "treadeth the winepress of the fierceness and wrath of Almighty God" signifies punishment by the judgment of God.

II Thessalonians 2:8; And then shall that Wicked be revealed, whom the Lord shall consume with the spirit of his mouth, and shall destroy with the brightness of his coming:

Isaiah 63:3; I have trodden the winepress alone; and of the people there was none with me: for I will tread them in mine anger, and trample them in my fury; and their blood shall be sprinkled upon my garments, and I will stain all my raiment.

Revelation 19:16; And he hath on his vesture and on his thigh a name written, KING OF KINGS, AND LORD OF LORDS.

With the name being written on his clothing and his thigh is a public profession intended for everyone to see that his mission is from God and the name itself being "KING OF KINGS, AND LORD OF LORDS" describes his status and capability to perform this mission. It was a common practice in John's day to place an inscription upon the clothing of images of deities usually over their thigh to honor them and reveal their name.

Deuteronomy 10:17; For the LORD your God is God of gods, and Lord of lords, a great God, a mighty, and a terrible, which regardeth not persons, nor taketh reward:

Daniel 2:47; The king answered unto Daniel, and said, Of a truth it is, that your God is a God of gods, and a Lord of kings, and a revealer of secrets, seeing thou couldest reveal this secret.

Revelation 19:17; And I saw an angel standing in the sun; and he cried with a loud voice, saying to all the fowls that fly in the midst of heaven, Come and gather yourselves together unto the supper of the great God;

The "angel" is Christ and "standing in the sun" implies that his power is derived from God and His establishment of religion. Speaking in a loud voice is insuring that everyone hears the message. To invite "the fowls that fly in the midst of heaven" to "Come and gather yourselves together unto the supper of the great God" suggests that much death has occurred by the judgment of God providing a feast for birds who consume carrion. This is spiritual death reflected in physical terminology.

Isaiah 13:6; Howl ye; for the day of the LORD is at hand; it shall come as a destruction from the Almighty.

Ezekiel 39:17; And, thou son of man, thus saith the Lord GOD; Speak unto every feathered fowl, and to every beast of the field, Assemble yourselves, and come; gather yourselves on every side to my sacrifice that I do sacrifice for you, even a great sacrifice upon the mountains of Israel, that ye may eat flesh, and drink blood.

Revelation 19:18; That ye may eat the flesh of kings, and the flesh of captains, and the flesh of mighty men, and the flesh of horses, and of them that sit on them, and the flesh of all men, both free and bond, both small and great.

To "eat the flesh of" references the birds who feast on carrion which implies victory by the death of all listed opponents.

Ezekiel 39:18,20; Ye shall eat the flesh of the mighty, and drink the blood of the princes of the earth, of rams, of lambs, and of goats, of bullocks, all of them fatlings of Bashan. Thus ye shall be filled at my table with horses and chariots, with mighty men, and with all men of war, saith the Lord GOD.

Revelation 19:19; And I saw the beast, and the kings of the earth, and their armies, gathered together to make war against him that sat on the horse, and against his army.

The "beast" is a term representing all evil opposition to Christ while "the kings of the earth, and their armies" signifies all of the followers of this evil opposition. The phrase "gathered together to make war against him that sat on the horse, and against his army" represents the assembling of all evil forces to engage in the spiritual battle between Christ and his disciples versus Satan and his followers. The "horse" is an emblem of war or a battle.

Revelation 19:20; And the beast was taken, and with him the false prophet that wrought miracles before him, with which he deceived them that had received the mark of the beast, and them that worshipped his image. These both were cast alive into a lake of fire burning with brimstone.

The phrase "And the beast was taken" reflects victory by Christ over his evil opposition while the phrase "and with him the false prophet" also refers to victory over false teachers who used false testimony and sorcery to "wrought miracles" deceiving any who listened or observed. The phrase "them that had received the mark of the beast, and them that worshipped his image" indicates those people who openly pledged allegiance to false gods, heeded Satan's evil doctrine by the deceit of false prophets and worshiped idolatry.

Matthew 24:24; For there shall arise false Christs, and false prophets, and shall shew great signs and wonders; insomuch that, if it were possible, they shall deceive the very elect.

Revelation 16:13-14; And I saw three unclean spirits like frogs come out of the mouth of the dragon, and out of the mouth of the beast, and out of the mouth of the false prophet. For they are the spirits of devils, working miracles, which go forth unto the kings of the earth and of the whole world, to gather them to the battle of that great day of God Almighty.

Revelation 19:21; And the remnant were slain with the sword of him that sat upon the horse, which sword proceeded out of his mouth: and all the fowls were filled with their flesh.

The phrase "And the remnant were slain" indicates the death of those people who still had not accepted Christ as their savior by the final judgment day of God. The phrases "with the sword" and "which sword proceeded out of his mouth" indicates that their spiritual death was by the Word of God through Christ while the phrase "of him that sat upon the horse" describes Christ in his role of doing battle with Satan and his dominion of evil as the horse is symbolic of battle or war.

Psalms 57:4; My soul is among lions: and I lie even among them that are set on fire, even the sons of men, whose teeth are spears and arrows, and their tongue a sharp sword.

CHAPTER 20

T his chapter repeats the same theme of Satan being cast out of heaven and Christ being sent by God to combat Satan's dominion of evil. The binding of Satan is by the Word of God symbolized as a great chain. The thousand years of Satan being restricted is the period of time established by God for His Word to be preached and taught upon earth. The final judgment and destruction of Satan and his forces of evil is depicted as their being cast into the lake of fire and brimstone.

The "book of life" indicates that judgment was made for all people according to their deeds during their physical lifetime upon earth with whosoever not being written in this book also being cast into the lake of fire.

Revelation 20:1; And I saw an angel come down from heaven, having the key of the bottomless pit and a great chain in his hand.

This angel in John's vision is Christ sent by God from heaven with the necessary power and authority to establish His kingdom upon earth and to control and defeat Satan along with his dominion of evil. Having the key of the bottomless pit is proof of his power and authority to accomplish this mission of God. Christ proclaims this power in:

Revelation 1:18; I am he that liveth, and was dead; and, behold, I am alive for evermore, Amen; and have the keys of hell and of death.

The "bottomless pit" is Satan's dominion of evil and the great chain in the hand of Christ is the Word of God with which Satan is bound. The chain being described as "great" signifies the power and authority of God's Word. Christ being given full

authority for this mission by God is indicated by the chain being in his hand.

Jude 1:6; And the angels which kept not their first estate, but left their own habitation, he hath reserved in everlasting chains under darkness unto the judgment of the great day.

Revelation 20:2; And he laid hold on the dragon, that old serpent, which is the Devil, and Satan, and bound him a thousand years,

Satan and his forces had a free reign to spread evil before God established His Word on earth through His two witnesses, the Mosaic Law and Christ. With the establishment of firstly; the Mosaic Law, and later with the teachings of Christ; Satan and his dominion of evil became bound or restricted. This "thousand years" is symbolic for the complete period of time established by God for mankind to preach and teach His Word upon earth under the Christian Dispensation period.

Matthew 12:28-29; But if I cast out devils by the Spirit of God, then the kingdom of God is come unto you. Or else how can one enter into a strong man's house, and spoil his goods, except he first bind the strong man? and then he will spoil his house.

Romans 8:37; Nay, in all these things we are more than conquerors through him that loved us.

I Corinthians 15:57; But thanks be to God, which giveth us the victory through our Lord Jesus Christ.

Revelation 12:11; And they overcame him by the blood of the Lamb, and by the word of their testimony; and they loved not their lives unto the death.

Revelation 20:3; And cast him into the bottomless pit, and shut him up, and set a seal upon him, that he should deceive the nations no more, till the thousand years should be fulfilled: and after that he must be loosed a little season.

Satan was restricted to the "bottomless pit" of never-ending evil. The seal placed upon him was the Word of God that enlightened people to the fallacy of following Satan unto their doom as reflected by the phrase "he should deceive the nations no more". The Word of God also offers salvation to those who choose to accept Christ as their savior.

Jude 1:6; And the angels which kept not their first estate, but left their own habitation, he hath reserved in everlasting chains under darkness unto the judgment of the great day.

Revelation 9:1-3; And the fifth angel sounded, and I saw a star fall from heaven unto the earth: and to him was given the key of the bottomless pit. And he opened the bottomless pit; and there arose a smoke out of the pit, as the smoke of a great furnace; and the sun and the air were darkened by reason of the smoke of the pit. And there came out of the smoke locusts upon the earth: and unto them was given power, as the scorpions of the earth have power.

The phrase "till the thousand years should be fulfilled" refers to the period of time established by God for His Word to be preached and taught upon earth by the Christian Dispensation while the phrase "and after that he must be loosed a little season" references a shorter period of time that begins with the fulfillment of the "thousand years" upon earth and ends with the final judgment day. This phrase "loosed a little season" also indicates that evil will reign during this period of time which will bring about the final judgment of God.

Mark 13:20; And except that the Lord had shortened those days, no flesh should be saved: but for the elect's sake, whom he hath chosen, he hath shortened the days.

This shorter period of time between the "thousand years" and the final judgment day is symbolized as "three and one-half days" as referenced in chapter eleven, verses seven, eight, and nine.

Revelation 11:7-9; And when they shall have finished their testimony, the beast that ascendeth out of the bottomless pit shall make war against them, and shall overcome them, and kill them. And their dead bodies shall lie in the street of the great city, which spiritually is called Sodom and Egypt, where also our Lord was crucified. And they of the people and kindreds and tongues and nations shall see their dead bodies three days and an half, and shall not suffer their dead bodies to be put in graves.

Revelation 20:4; And I saw thrones, and they sat upon them, and judgment was given unto them: and I saw the souls of them that were beheaded for the witness of Jesus, and for the word of God, and which had not worshipped the beast, neither his image, neither had received his mark upon their foreheads, or in their hands; and they lived and reigned with Christ a thousand years.

John describes his vision into heaven as "I saw thrones, and they sat upon them, and judgment was given unto them" implies royalty and refers to those in authority. The authority or power given to those sitting upon the thrones appears to be the judgment that granted acceptance into heaven for the martyrs revealed by the phrase "and I saw the souls of them" describing those saints which had lost their temporal lives because they were disciples of Christ as indicated by the phrase "that were beheaded for the witness of Jesus". These martyrs for Christ that had remained faithful, even under heavy persecution, denoted by the phrases "and for the word of God, and which had not worshipped the beast", and had not succumbed to the evils of Satan nor worshiped false idols implied by the phrase "neither his image"; nor professed their allegiance to any anti-Christian entity as suggested by the phrase "neither had received his mark upon their foreheads, or in their hands" were with Christ in heaven during this "thousand years" while his Word was being preached and taught upon earth. These martyrs appear to have been given this privilege of early resurrection because of the following prayer to the Lord God as recorded in the book of Psalms.

Psalms 90:4,14-17; For a thousand years in thy sight are but as yesterday when it is past, and as a watch in the night. O satisfy us early with thy mercy; that we may rejoice and be glad all our days. Make us glad according to the days wherein thou hast afflicted us, and the years wherein we have seen evil. Let thy work appear unto thy servants, and thy glory unto their children. And let the beauty of the LORD our God be upon us: and establish thou the work of our hands upon us; yea, the work of our hands establish thou it.

John 5:21-23; For as the Father raiseth up the dead, and quickeneth them; even so the Son quickeneth whom he will. For the Father judgeth no man, but hath committed all judgment unto the Son: That all men should honour the Son, even as they honour the Father. He that honoureth not the Son honoureth not the Father which hath sent him.

Revelation 20:5; But the rest of the dead lived not again until the thousand years were finished. This is the first resurrection.

The "first resurrection" is reserved for those who lost their lives for the witness of Jesus Christ. The later resurrection is reserved for all other disciples of God and Christ who are found worthy at the second coming of Christ.

John 5:37-39; And the Father himself, which hath sent me, hath borne witness of me. Ye have neither heard his voice at any time, nor seen his shape. And ye have not his word abiding in you: for whom he hath sent, him ye believe not. Search the scriptures; for in them ye think ye have eternal life: and they are they which testify of me.

Revelation 20:6; Blessed and holy is he that hath part in the first resurrection: on such the second death hath no power, but they shall be priests of God and of Christ, and shall reign with him a thousand years.

These are the martyrs who gave their lives for the testimony of Christ, obeyed and kept his commandments, remained steadfast in their faith, been found worthy, and were rewarded in the first resurrection for their effort. They will reign with Christ in heaven as priests of God and Christ during this "thousand years" period of time. The other disciples found worthy will be raised upon the second coming of Christ.

I Thessalonians 4:15-17; For this we say unto you by the word of the Lord, that we which are alive and remain unto the coming of the Lord shall not prevent them which are asleep. For the Lord himself shall descend from heaven with a shout, with the voice of the archangel, and with the trump of God: and the dead in Christ shall rise first: Then we which are alive and remain shall be caught up together with them in the clouds, to meet the Lord in the air: and so shall we ever be with the Lord.

John 5:24; Verily, verily, I say unto you, He that heareth my word, and believeth on him that sent me, hath everlasting life, and shall not come into condemnation; but is passed from death unto life.

Romans 8:17; And if children, then heirs; heirs of God, and joint-heirs with Christ; if so be that we suffer with him, that we may be also glorified together.

Revelation 1:5-6; And from Jesus Christ, who is the faithful witness, and the first begotten of the dead, and the prince of the kings of the earth. Unto him that loved us, and washed us from our sins in his own blood, And hath made us kings and priests unto God and his Father; to him be glory and dominion for ever and ever. Amen.

Revelation 20:7; And when the thousand years are expired, Satan shall be loosed out of his prison,

After the period of time that God's Word was spread throughout earth by His two witnesses; the Mosaic Law and Christ, Satan will again rule for a short period of time, designated by the symbol of three and one-half days, as put forth in chapter eleven, verses seven, eight, and nine.

II Peter 3:8; But, beloved, be not ignorant of this one thing, that one day is with the Lord as a thousand years, and a thousand years as one day.

Revelation 11:7-9; And when they shall have finished their testimony, the beast that ascendeth out of the bottomless pit shall make war against them, and shall overcome them, and kill them. And their dead bodies shall lie in the street of the great city, which spiritually is called Sodom and Egypt, where also our Lord was crucified. And they of the people and kindreds and tongues and nations shall see their dead bodies three days and an half, and shall not suffer their dead bodies to be put in graves.

Revelation 20:8; And shall go out to deceive the nations which are in the four quarters of the earth, Gog and Magog, to gather them together to battle: the number of whom is as the sand of the sea.

With Satan now having free reign for a short period of time, his evil dominion grows and spreads to the "four quarters of the earth" encompassing a great number of enemies of Christ as reflected by the phrase "Gog and Magog" with the number being designated as "the number of whom is as the sand of the sea."

The symbolism of the phrase "Gog and Magog" is appropriate for this short period of time that Satan and his evil dominion will reign as it reflects the immense number of enemies brought into battle in the latter days of the kingdom of Israel and was of short duration. Ezekiel was forewarned by

God of this large accumulation of enemies being brought into battle along with its outcome.

Ezekiel 38:2-8; Son of man, set thy face against Gog, the land of Magog, the chief prince of Meshech and Tubal, and prophesy against him, And say, Thus saith the Lord GOD; Behold, I am against thee, O Gog, the chief prince of Meshech and Tubal: And I will turn thee back, and put hooks into thy jaws, and I will bring thee forth, and all thine army, horses and horsemen, all of them clothed with all sorts of armour, even a great company with bucklers and shields, all of them handling swords: Persia, Ethiopia, and Libya with them; all of them with shield and helmet: Gomer, and all his bands; the house of Togarmah of the north quarters, and all his bands: and many people with thee. Be thou prepared, and prepare for thyself, thou, and all thy company that are assembled unto thee, and be thou a guard unto them. After many days thou shalt be visited: in the latter years thou shalt come into the land that is brought back from the sword, and is gathered out of many people, against the mountains of Israel, which have been always waste: but it is brought forth out of the nations, and they shall dwell safely all of them.

Revelation 20:9; And they went up on the breadth of the earth, and compassed the camp of the saints about, and the beloved city: and fire came down from God out of heaven, and devoured them.

The term "breadth of the earth" indicates that Satan spread his evil over all of earth during this period of time symbolized as three and one-half days and attacked all of the saints upon earth as indicated by the phrase "and compassed the camp of the saints about". The Kingdom of Christ or the Church of Christ is symbolically considered as the "camp of the saints" and "the beloved city". Other terms descriptive of this kingdom established by Christ are "New Jerusalem", "Bride of Christ", and "the Holy City". In retaliation for the attack upon His disciples, God brought His final judgment and destroyed Satan and his evil dominion as indicated by the phrase "and fire came down from God out of heaven, and devoured them."

Mark 13:19-20; For in those days shall be affliction, such as was not from the beginning of the creation which God created unto this time, neither shall be. And except that the Lord had shortened those days, no flesh should be saved: but for the elect's sake, whom he hath chosen, he hath shortened the days.

Daniel 12:1; And at that time shall Michael stand up, the great prince which standeth for the children of thy people: and there shall be a time of trouble, such as never was since there was a nation even to that same time: and at that time thy people shall be delivered, every one that shall be found written in the book.

II Peter 3:7,10; But the heavens and the earth, which are now, by the same word are kept in store, reserved unto fire against the day of judgment and perdition of ungodly men. But the day of the Lord will come as a thief in the night; in the which the heavens shall pass away with a great noise, and the elements shall melt with fervent heat, the earth also and the works that are therein shall be burned up.

Revelation 20:10; And the devil that deceived them was cast into the lake of fire and brimstone, where the beast and the false prophet are, and shall be tormented day and night for ever and ever.

One of the main instruments used by Satan in his promotion of evil is deception as confirmed by the phrase "And the devil that deceived them". The final judgment of God relegates Satan to "the lake of fire and brimstone" suggesting severe punishment while the phrase "where the beast and the false prophet are" reveals that Satan's evil forces were subjected to the same fate. The phrase "shall be tormented day and night for ever and ever" represents eternal punishment.

Revelation 14:10-11; The same shall drink of the wine of the wrath of God, which is poured out without mixture into the cup of his indignation; and he shall be tormented with fire and brimstone in the presence of the holy angels, and in the presence of the Lamb: And the smoke of their torment ascendeth up for ever and ever: and they have no rest day nor night, who worship the beast and his image, and whosoever receiveth the mark of his name.

Revelation 20:11; And I saw a great white throne, and him that sat on it, from whose face the earth and the heaven fled away; and there was found no place for them.

John next observed "a great white throne" suggesting a majestic presence by the adjective "great" with the color "white" representing purity and holiness while the word "throne"

reveals royalty. The phrase "him that sat on it" is the Lord God described by the phrase "from whose face the earth and the heaven fled away" which reveals His complete control and authority over everything in heaven and earth. The phrase "and there was found no place for them" reflects God's judgment as to the fate of Satan and his evil forces.

Daniel 7:10; I beheld till the thrones were cast down, and the Ancient of days did sit, whose garment was white as snow, and the hair of his head like the pure wool: his throne was like the fiery flame, and his wheels as burning fire.

Revelation 20:12; And I saw the dead, small and great, stand before God; and the books were opened: and another book was opened, which is the book of life: and the dead were judged out of those things which were written in the books, according to their works.

This vision of John reveals the final judgment day when everyone, regardless of their political status or station in life as described by the phrase "small and great", must give an account for their deeds upon earth. The phrase "and the books were opened" indicates that their judgment will be based upon the recordings of everyone's deeds during their physical life upon earth while the phrase "and another book was opened, which is the book of life" reveals those that are found worthy of heaven. The dead are now to be judged based on their works as recorded in the books.

John 5:25,28; Verily, verily, I say unto you, The hour is coming, and now is, when the dead shall hear the voice of the Son of God: and they that hear shall live. Marvel not at this: for the hour is coming, in the which all that are in the graves shall hear his voice,

Acts 24:15; And have hope toward God, which they themselves also allow, that there shall be a resurrection of the dead, both of the just and unjust.

Revelation 20:13; And the sea gave up the dead which were in it; and death and hell delivered up the dead which were in them: and they were judged every man according to their works.

John recorded that all of the dead everywhere on earth, as indicated by the phrases "And the sea gave up the dead" and "death and hell delivered up the dead", will now stand before the judgment of God to face their earthly deeds as revealed by the phrase "and they were judged every man according to their works."

Daniel 12:2; And many of them that sleep in the dust of the earth shall awake, some to everlasting life, and some to shame and everlasting contempt.

John 5:29; And shall come forth; they that have done good, unto the resurrection of life; and they that have done evil, unto the resurrection of damnation.

I Thessalonians 4:15; For this we say unto you by the word of the Lord, that we which are alive and remain unto the coming of the Lord shall not prevent them which are asleep.

Revelation 20:14; And death and hell were cast into the lake of fire. This is the second death.

John records the fate of death and hell as being cast into "the lake of fire". The first death is the physical death while the "second death" is spiritual loss of life reflecting the loss of eternal salvation in heaven with God and Christ.

I Corinthians 15:26; The last enemy that shall be destroyed is death.

Revelation 20:15; And whosoever was not found written in the book of life was cast into the lake of fire.

The "book of life" represents those found worthy of joining Christ in heaven with God. Those not found in the "book of life" are relegated to the same fate as Satan which is being cast into the "lake of fire".

Psalms 69:28; Let them be blotted out of the book of the living, and not be written with the righteous.

Revelation 17:8; The beast that thou sawest was, and is not; and shall ascend out of the bottomless pit, and go into perdition: and they that dwell on the earth shall wonder, whose names were not written in the book of life from the foundation of the world, when they behold the beast that was, and is not, and yet is.

CHAPTER 21

For those that are found worthy, this chapter reveals the reward of heaven under the symbols of a new heaven and a new earth also called the holy city, and new Jerusalem. For those found unworthy shall have their part of the lake of fire and brimstone. This great city is described as lying foursquare measuring twelve thousand furlongs each in length, breadth, and height. It is also described as having twelve gates with twelve angels with the names of the twelve tribes of Israel and each gate is of one pearl. This holy city also has twelve foundations garnished with all manner of precious stones with the names of the twelve apostles.

Revelation 21:1; And I saw a new heaven and a new earth: for the first heaven and the first earth were passed away; and there was no more sea.

The vision given to John allows him to see the final judgment day that completely destroys this earth and heaven with our Lord God providing a new home as promised for His disciples that are found worthy of salvation. The phrase "a new heaven and a new earth" is descriptive of the heavenly paradise with Christ as promised to all saints that are found worthy. The phrase "and there was no more sea" reveals the complete destruction of all life on this earth as the word "sea" represents a multitude of people.

Isaiah 66:22; For as the new heavens and the new earth, which I will make, shall remain before me, saith the LORD, so shall your seed and your name remain.

John 14:2-3; In my Father's house are many mansions: if it were not so, I would have told you. I go to prepare a place for you. And if I go and prepare a place for you, I will come again, and receive you unto myself; that where I am, there ye may be also.

II Peter 3:10,13; But the day of the Lord will come as a thief in the night; in the which the heavens shall pass away with a great noise, and the elements shall melt with fervent heat, the earth also and the works that are therein shall be burned up. Nevertheless we, according to his promise, look for new heavens and a new earth, wherein dwelleth righteousness.

Revelation 21:2; And I John saw the holy city, new Jerusalem, coming down from God out of heaven, prepared as a bride adorned for her husband.

The phrase, "the holy city, new Jerusalem", identifies the destiny for the followers of Christ and the Lord God with the phrase "coming down from God out of heaven" revealing that this new home was provided by the Lord God. The phrase "prepared as a bride adorned for her husband" suggests that all qualifications for becoming members of the kingdom of Christ have been met.

Isaiah 52:1; Awake, awake; put on thy strength, O Zion; put on thy beautiful garments, O Jerusalem, the holy city: for henceforth there shall no more come into thee the uncircumcised and the unclean.

Ephesians 5:26-27; That he might sanctify and cleanse it with the washing of water by the word, That he might present it to himself a glorious church, not having spot, or wrinkle, or any such thing; but that it should be holy and without blemish.

Revelation 21:3; And I heard a great voice out of heaven saying, Behold, the tabernacle of God is with men, and he will dwell with them, and they shall be his people, and God himself shall be with them, and be their God.

John hearing "a great voice out of heaven" reveals that this message is from God stating that His religious communication is with men and that He will dwell with them as their God and that they will be His people.

Leviticus 26:11-12; And I set my tabernacle among you: and my soul shall not abhor you.

And I will walk among you, and will be your God, and ye shall be my people.

Jeremiah 3:17; At that time they shall call Jerusalem the throne of the LORD; and all the nations shall be gathered unto it, to the name of the LORD, to Jerusalem: neither shall they walk any more after the imagination of their evil heart.

Revelation 21:4; And God shall wipe away all tears from their eyes; and there shall be no more death, neither sorrow, nor crying, neither shall there be any more pain: for the former things are passed away.

John's vision further reveals that God will take away all unhappiness including tears, death, sorrow, crying, and pain leaving only happiness and joy amidst His people. All of the unpleasant episodes and entities of this physical life will be replaced with only pleasant and enjoyable qualities at the destruction of this heaven and earth. With the complete destruction of mankind, there will no longer be a physical death and with the division of the righteous saints into heaven and the unrighteous into eternal damnation, there will no longer be a spiritual death.

Isaiah 25:8; He will swallow up death in victory; and the Lord GOD will wipe away tears from off all faces; and the rebuke of his people shall he take away from off all the earth: for the LORD hath spoken it.

Revelation 7:17; For the Lamb which is in the midst of the throne shall feed them, and shall lead them unto living fountains of waters: and God shall wipe away all tears from their eyes.

Revelation 21:5; And he that sat upon the throne said, Behold, I make all things new. And he said unto me, Write: for these words are true and faithful.

The phrase "And he that sat upon the throne said" identifies God as the one delivering the message making the statement "Behold, I make all things new" which indicates a complete change from our current physical life into a new realm of an enjoyable and beautiful existence of spiritual life. God further instructs John to record this message as it is a "true and faithful" promise. This is the culmination of God's promise through His servant, Jeremiah as recorded in:

Jeremiah 31:31-34; Behold, the days come, saith the LORD, that I will make a new covenant with the house of Israel, and with the house of Judah: Not according to the covenant that I made with their fathers in the day that I took them by the hand to bring them out of the land of Egypt; which my covenant they brake, although I was an husband unto them, saith the LORD: But this shall be the covenant that I will make with the house of Israel; After those days, saith the LORD, I will put my law in their inward parts, and write it in their hearts; and will be their God, and they shall be my people. And they shall teach no more every man his neighbour, and every man his brother, saying, Know the LORD: for they shall all know me, from the least of them unto the greatest of them, saith the LORD: for I will forgive their iniquity, and I will remember their sin no more.

Ezekiel 18:31; Cast away from you all your transgressions, whereby ye have transgressed; and make you a new heart and a new spirit: for why will ye die, O house of Israel?

Ephesians 2:15; Having abolished in his flesh the enmity, even the law of commandments contained in ordinances; for to make in himself of twain one new man, so making peace;

Revelation 21:6; And he said unto me, It is done. I am Alpha and Omega, the beginning and the end. I will give unto him that is athirst of the fountain of the water of life freely.

John was told by God, "It is done", indicating that His judgments had destroyed the current heavens and earth to eliminate the evil dominion of Satan while also establishing a new heavens and earth as an abode for His people. God next informed John of His eternal existence as expressed by the phrase "I am Alpha and Omega, the beginning and the end." These terms, Alpha and Omega, are the first and last letters of the Greek alphabet signifying the beginning and the end thus portraying eternity. John was then told that the offer of Christian salvation to those seeking it would be freely given as indicated by the phrase "I will give unto him that is athirst of the fountain of the water of life freely" with the word "athirst" representing a person's desire to participate of this offer of eternal salvation in heaven. The word "freely" also implies a bountiful, benevolent gift.

Isaiah 12:3; Therefore with joy shall ye draw water out of the wells of salvation.

Isaiah 55:1; Ho, every one that thirsteth, come ye to the waters, and he that hath no money; come ye, buy, and eat; yea, come, buy wine and milk without money and without price.

Jeremiah 17:13; O LORD, the hope of Israel, all that forsake thee shall be ashamed, and they that depart from me shall be written in the earth, because they have forsaken the LORD, the fountain of living waters.

Revelation 1:8; I am Alpha and Omega, the beginning and the ending, saith the Lord, which is, and which was, and which is to come, the Almighty. (Revelation 1:11.)

Revelation 14:7; Saying with a loud voice, Fear God, and give glory to him; for the hour of his judgment is come: and worship him that made heaven, and earth, and the sea, and the fountains of waters.

Revelation 21:7; He that overcometh shall inherit all things; and I will be his God, and he shall be my son.

John recorded this promise of God to accept those saints into heaven who had remained faithful while resisting all of the temptations and held steadfast in their faith amidst all of the persecutions of Satan. The apostle John also recorded our ability to remain steadfast in other writings.

John 5:4; For whatsoever is born of God overcometh the world: and this is the victory that overcometh the world, even our faith.

The apostle Paul, who endured many hardships and persecutions in his mission of bringing the Gospel message to the gentiles, also confirmed that he had remained faithful in his letter to Timothy.

II Timothy 4:7; I have fought a good fight, I have finished my course, I have kept the faith:

Jesus Christ indicates this same promise of God through many different analogies as reflected in the letters to the various churches recorded in Revelation, chapters two and three.

Revelation 2:7; He that hath an ear, let him hear what the Spirit saith unto the churches; To him that overcometh will I give to eat of the tree of life, which is in the midst of the paradise of God.

Revelation 2:11; He that hath an ear, let him hear what the Spirit saith unto the churches; He that overcometh shall not be hurt of the second death.

Revelation 2:17; He that hath an ear, let him hear what the Spirit saith unto the churches; To him that overcometh will I give to eat of the hidden manna, and will give him a white stone, and in the stone a new name written, which no man knoweth saving he that receiveth it.

Revelation 2:26; And he that overcometh, and keepeth my works unto the end, to him will I give power over the nations:

Revelation 3:5; He that overcometh, the same shall be clothed in white raiment; and I will not blot out his name out of the book of life, but I will confess his name before my Father, and before his angels.

Revelation 3:12; Him that overcometh will I make a pillar in the temple of my God, and he shall go no more out: and I will write upon him the name of my God, and the name of the city of my God, which is new Jerusalem, which cometh down out of heaven from my God: and I will write upon him my new name.

Revelation 3:21; To him that overcometh will I grant to sit with me in my throne, even as I also overcame, and am set down with my Father in his throne.

Revelation 21:8; But the fearful, and unbelieving, and the abominable, and murderers, and whoremongers, and sorcerers, and idolaters, and all liars, shall have their part in the lake which burneth with fire and brimstone: which is the second death.

John next records the various abominations to God along with the fate of those who choose this path in life that is adverse to God and His commandments. These descriptive terms effectively encompass all evil doers upon earth. The "second death" is spiritual death with the fate of these evil doers being relegated to the lake of fire and brimstone.

I Corinthians 5:10; Yet not altogether with the fornicators of this world, or with the covetous, or extortioners, or with idolaters; for then must ye needs go out of the world.

I Corinthians 6:9-10; Know ye not that the unrighteous shall not inherit the kingdom of God? Be not deceived: neither fornicators, nor idolaters, nor adulterers, nor effeminate, nor abusers of themselves with mankind, Nor thieves, nor covetous, nor drunkards, nor revilers, nor extortioners, shall inherit the kingdom of God.

Revelation 21:9; And there came unto me one of the seven angels which had the seven vials full of the seven last plagues, and talked with me, saying, Come hither, I will shew thee the bride, the Lamb's wife.

The bride of the Lamb are those people who have obeyed the Gospel message, accepted Christ as the emissary of God, repented of their sins, kept his commandments, remained faithful by avoiding the temptations of Satan, and are now found worthy to join him in the new heavens and earth under the symbol of his wife. Christ taught about the kingdom of heaven with a parable using the analogy of a marriage of the son of a king.

Matthew 22:2-14,30; The kingdom of heaven is like unto a certain king, which made a marriage for his son, And sent forth his servants to call them that were bidden to the wedding: and they would not come. Again, he sent forth other servants, saying, Tell them which are bidden, Behold, I have prepared my dinner: my oxen and my fatlings are killed, and all things are ready: come unto the marriage. But they made light of it, and went their ways, one to his farm, another to his merchandise: And the remnant took his servants, and entreated them spitefully, and slew them. But when the king heard thereof, he was wroth: and he sent forth his armies, and destroyed those murderers, and burned up their city. Then saith he to his servants, The wedding is ready, but they which were bidden were not worthy. Go ye therefore into the highways, and as many as ye shall find, bid to the marriage. So those servants went out into the highways, and gathered together all as many as they found, both bad and good: and the wedding was furnished with guests. And when the king came in to see the guests, he saw there a man which had not on a wedding garment: And he saith unto him, Friend, how camest thou in hither not having a wedding garment? And he was speechless. Then said the king to the servants, Bind him hand and foot, and take him away, and cast him into outer darkness, there shall be weeping and gnashing of teeth. For many are called, but few are chosen. For in the resurrection they neither marry, nor are given in marriage, but are as the angels of God in heaven.

This analogy by Christ in Matthew, chapter twenty-two, describes the events of the establishment of the Mosaic Law and Christianity upon earth leading up to resurrection day. The King is God who sent His Son, Christ, unto earth to garner disciples and combat evil. The servants were prophets sent by God describing the blessings of the reward of heaven for those under the Mosaic Law. Many rejected this offer while others persecuted these prophets invoking the wrath of God bringing about their destruction and the offer of salvation being extended unto the Gentiles with some of the people not making proper preparations of the requirements set forth of obeying the commandments of God and Christ resulting in their rejection on the final judgment day.

Revelation 19:7; Let us be glad and rejoice, and give honour to him: for the marriage of the Lamb is come, and his wife hath made herself ready.

Revelation 21:10; And he carried me away in the spirit to a great and high mountain, and shewed me that great city, the holy Jerusalem, descending out of heaven from God,

The terms; great and high mountain, holy mountain, mountain of the Lord, great city, holy city, holy Jerusalem, and new Jerusalem are all indicative of the religion of the worship of our Lord God and also represent heaven as the abode of the saints. Each of these terms represents the Kingdom or the Church of Christ. When John was carried away in the spirit, his vision was that of these disciples of God in their new abode of the new heavens and earth described as "descending out of heaven from God".

Isaiah 52:1; Awake, awake; put on thy strength, O Zion; put on thy beautiful garments, O Jerusalem, the holy city: for henceforth there shall no more come into thee the uncircumcised and the unclean.

Isaiah 66:20; And they shall bring all your brethren for an offering unto the LORD out of all nations upon horses, and in chariots, and in litters, and upon mules, and upon swift beasts, to my holy mountain Jerusalem, saith the LORD, as the children of Israel bring an offering in a clean vessel into the house of the LORD.

Daniel 9:16; O LORD, according to all thy righteousness, I beseech thee, let thine anger and thy fury be turned away from thy city Jerusalem, thy holy mountain: because for our sins, and for the iniquities of our fathers, Jerusalem and thy people are become a reproach to all that are about us.

Joel 3:17; So shall ye know that I am the LORD your God dwelling in Zion, my holy mountain: then shall Jerusalem be holy, and there shall no strangers pass through her any more.

Zechariah 8:3; Thus saith the LORD; I am returned unto Zion, and will dwell in the midst of Jerusalem: and Jerusalem shall be called a city of truth; and the mountain of the LORD of hosts the holy mountain. (Nehemiah 11:1; Ezekiel 48:1-35.)

Revelation 21:11; Having the glory of God: and her light was like unto a stone most precious, even like a jasper stone, clear as crystal;

The Church/Kingdom of Christ being described by the phrase "Having the glory of God" implies having the pure and holy qualities of God and the knowledge of His Word while the phrase "and her light was like unto a stone most precious" reveals the great value of this heavenly kingdom to God as "light" reflects glory and knowledge of God's Word. The description "even like a jasper stone" indicates a new entity as a jasper stone is of varied shades of green suggesting a rebirth or new beginning and is also very hard representing durability and longevity while the phrase "clear as crystal" signifies all impurities having been removed.

Exodus 28:20; And the fourth row a beryl, and an onyx, and a jasper: they shall be set in gold in their inclosings.

II Corinthians 3:18; But we all, with open face beholding as in a glass the glory of the Lord, are changed into the same image from glory to glory, even as by the Spirit of the Lord.

II Corinthians 4:6; For God, who commanded the light to shine out of darkness, hath shined in our hearts, to give the light of the knowledge of the glory of God in the face of Jesus Christ.

Revelation 4:3; And he that sat was to look upon like a jasper and a sardine stone: and there was a rainbow round about the throne, in sight like unto an emerald.

An emerald is also green reflecting a rebirth or new beginning.

Revelation 21:12; And had a wall great and high, and had twelve gates, and at the gates twelve angels, and names written thereon, which are the names of the twelve tribes of the children of Israel:

The wall being great and high signifies protection and safety from any persecution or oppression by outside forces thereby ensuring a peaceful and blissful environment. The wall having twelve gates with each gate having the name of one the twelve tribes of the children of Israel reflects the way or method of entrance into this religion of God that was built and organized through the twelve tribes of Israel. With each of the twelve gates having an angel further ensures the protection and safety from any evil entities.

The precious stones that are reflective of the twelve tribes of Israel are:

Exodus 39:10-14; And they set in it four rows of stones: the first row was a sardius, a topaz, and a carbuncle: this was the first row. And the second row, an emerald, a sapphire, and a diamond. And the third row, a ligure, an agate, and an amethyst. And the fourth row, a beryl, an onyx, and a jasper: they were inclosed in ouches of gold in their inclosings. And the stones were according to the names of the children of Israel, twelve, according to their names, like the engravings of a signet, every one with his name, according to the twelve tribes.

Revelation 21:13; On the east three gates; on the north three gates; on the south three gates; and on the west three gates.

The dispersing of twelve gates reflects easy accessibility and readily available entrance into the sanctuary of heaven. Having three gates on each of the four sides is reflective of the method of encampment by the twelve tribes during their forty years in the wilderness. This twelve tribes listed differ from the original pattern of encampment as these tribes reflect the twelve sons of Jacob (Israel) which includes Levi and Joseph whereas the pattern of encampment in the wilderness did not have the tribe of Joseph but had the Levites in the middle around about the tabernacle and also included the two sons of Joseph: Ephraim and Manasseh.

Ezekiel 48:31-34; And the gates of the city shall be after the names of the tribes of Israel: three gates northward; one gate of Reuben, one gate of Judah, one gate of Levi. And at the east side four thousand and five hundred: and three gates; and one gate of Joseph, one gate of Benjamin, one gate of Dan. And at the south side four thousand and five hundred measures: and three gates; one gate of Simeon, one gate of Issachar, one gate of Zebulun. At the west side four thousand and five hundred, with their three gates; one gate of Gad, one gate of Asher, one gate of Naphtali.

Revelation 21:14; And the wall of the city had twelve foundations, and in them the names of the twelve apostles of the Lamb.

Organized religion is again indicated by the wall of the city having twelve foundations reflecting the names of each of the twelve apostles of Christ. Upon these twelve apostles Christ built his church. The foundation is the necessary first major part of any building supporting and securing that structure.

Matthew 16:18; And I say also unto thee, That thou art Peter, and upon this rock I will build my church; and the gates of hell shall not prevail against it.

Matthew 10:1-4; And when he had called unto him his twelve disciples, he gave them power against unclean spirits, to cast them out, and to heal all manner of sickness and all manner of disease. Now the names of the twelve apostles are these; The first, Simon, who is called Peter, and Andrew his brother; James the son of Zebedee, and John his brother; Philip, and Bartholomew; Thomas, and Matthew the publican; James the son of Alphaeus, and Lebbaeus, whose surname was Thaddaeus; Simon the Canaanite, and Judas Iscariot, who also betrayed him.

Revelation 21:15; And he that talked with me had a golden reed to measure the city, and the gates thereof, and the wall thereof.

The phrase "And he that talked with me" implies one of the angels that had a vial of one of the last plagues as reflected in verses nine and ten of this chapter. This vision of the city being shown to John represents the bride of Christ. A reed is an instrument of measure and with the reed being "golden" reflects the great value to God of this "city", the bride of Christ. To measure

something is to calculate or demonstrate the ability of that entity to withstand persecution, oppression, and opposition.

Ezekiel 40:2-3; In the visions of God brought he me into the land of Israel, and set me upon a very high mountain, by which was as the frame of a city on the south. And he brought me thither, and, behold, there was a man, whose appearance was like the appearance of brass, with a line of flax in his hand, and a measuring reed; and he stood in the gate.

Revelation 11:1; And there was given me a reed like unto a rod: and the angel stood, saying, Rise, and measure the temple of God, and the altar, and them that worship therein.

Revelation 21:16; And the city lieth foursquare, and the length is as large as the breadth: and he measured the city with the reed, twelve thousand furlongs. The length and the breadth and the height of it are equal.

The term "foursquare" implies perfection through equality while the measurement of twelve thousand furlongs reveals organized religion through the numeral "twelve" and completeness through the number "thousand". Eight furlongs equals approximately one mile in our standard of measurement.

Exodus 27:1; And thou shalt make an altar of shittim wood, five cubits long, and five cubits broad; the altar shall be foursquare: and the height thereof shall be three cubits.

Exodus 28:16; Foursquare it shall be being doubled; a span shall be the length thereof, and a span shall be the breadth thereof.

Exodus 38:1; And he made the altar of burnt offering of shittim wood: five cubits was the length thereof, and five cubits the breadth thereof; it was foursquare; and three cubits the height thereof.

Exodus 39:9; It was foursquare; they made the breastplate double: a span was the length thereof, and a span the breadth thereof, being doubled.

Ezekiel 40:47; So he measured the court, an hundred cubits long, and an hundred cubits broad, foursquare; and the altar that was before the house.

Revelation 21:17; And he measured the wall thereof, an hundred and forty and four cubits, according to the measure of a man, that is, of the angel.

Having a wall implies protection from adversity. The measurement of the wall by one of the angels holding a vial of one of the last plagues measured "an hundred and forty and four cubits" reflecting organized religion as the numeral twelve is the square root of one hundred forty-four.

A cubit is considered to be the measurement from the tip of the elbow to the tip of the middle finger. This determination of measurement is generally thought to have come from measurements taken from royalty thus creating variances in length from approximately eighteen to twenty-one inches.

Revelation 21:18; And the building of the wall of it was of jasper: and the city was pure gold, like unto clear glass.

Jasper is a precious stone that is of various shades of green suggesting a rebirth or new beginning and is also very hard indicating durability and longevity. The city being described as "pure gold" reflects the great value of heaven while the phrase "like unto clear glass" denotes all impurities being removed and also transparency revealing the ability to approach God through prayer.

II Corinthians 3:16,18; Nevertheless when it shall turn to the Lord, the vail shall be taken away. But we all, with open face beholding as in a glass the glory of the Lord, are changed into the same image from glory to glory, even as by the Spirit of the Lord.

Gold was considered a very precious and beautiful commodity as its usage in their worship services is reflected and detailed in the following scriptures.

(Exodus 25:11,17,24,29,31,36,38,39; Exodus 28:13,22,36; Exodus 30:3; Exodus 37:2,6,11,16,17,22,23,24,26,28; Exodus 39:15,25,30; I Kings 6:20,21; I Kings 7:48,49,50; II Chronicles 3:4; II Chronicles 4:20; II Chronicles 9:17; Psalms 21:3.)

Revelation 21:19; And the foundations of the wall of the city were garnished with all manner of precious stones. The first foundation was jasper; the second, sapphire; the third, a chalcedony; the fourth, an emerald;

The phrase "And the foundations of the wall of the city" indicates that the precious stones are reflective of the twelve apostles of Christ as revealed in verse fourteen. The foundations being "garnished with all manner of precious stones" reflects the immense beauty and value of this heavenly "city".

Isaiah 54:11-12; O thou afflicted, tossed with tempest, and not comforted, behold, I will lay thy stones with fair colours, and lay thy foundations with sapphires. And I will make thy windows of agates, and thy gates of carbuncles, and all thy borders of pleasant stones.

Revelation 21:20; The fifth, sardonyx; the sixth, sardius; the seventh, chrysolite; the eighth, beryl; the ninth, a topaz; the tenth, a chrysoprasus; the eleventh, a jacinth; the twelfth, an amethyst.

The precious stones listed in verses nineteen and twenty represent the twelve apostles of Jesus Christ and the foundation upon which he built his church.

Ezekiel 28:13; Thou hast been in Eden the garden of God; every precious stone was thy covering, the sardius, topaz, and the diamond, the beryl, the onyx, and the jasper, the sapphire, the emerald, and the carbuncle, and gold: the workmanship of thy tabrets and of thy pipes was prepared in thee in the day that thou wast created.

Revelation 21:21; And the twelve gates were twelve pearls; every several gate was of one pearl: and the street of the city was pure gold, as it were transparent glass.

As the pearl is indicative of such a great value that a person will surrender all of his worldly possessions to obtain it, then the symbolism of the pearl as the gate allowing entrance to heaven is appropriate as we leave all worldly possessions behind upon our entrance into heaven. The phrase "and the street of the city was pure gold" reflects the value of our path to spiritual salvation while the phrase "as it were transparent glass" reveals our access to God.

Matthew 13:45-46; Again, the kingdom of heaven is like unto a merchant man, seeking goodly pearls: Who, when he had found one pearl of great price, went and sold all that he had, and bought it.

Revelation 21:22; And I saw no temple therein: for the Lord God Almighty and the Lamb are the temple of it.

John observed no physical building as a spiritual existence will not require a physical dwelling, but rather, a spiritual dwelling as provided by the Lord God and the Lamb, Jesus Christ.

John 2:19-22; Jesus answered and said unto them, *Destroy this temple, and in three days I will raise it up*. Then said the Jews, Forty and six years was this temple in building, and wilt thou rear it up in three days? But he spake of the temple of his body. When therefore he was risen from the dead, his disciples remembered that he had said this unto them; and they believed the scripture, and the word which Jesus had said.

I Corinthians 3:16-17; Know ye not that ye are the temple of God, and that the Spirit of God dwelleth in you? If any man defile the temple of God, him shall God destroy; for the temple of God is holy, which temple ye are.

I Corinthians 6:19-20; What? know ye not that your body is the temple of the Holy Ghost which is in you, which ye have of God, and ye are not your own? For ye are bought with a price: therefore glorify God in your body, and in your spirit, which are God's.

II Corinthians 6:16; And what agreement hath the temple of God with idols? for ye are the temple of the living God; as God hath said, I will dwell in them, and walk in them; and I will be their God, and they shall be my people. (Revelation 3:12; Revelation 7:15.)

Revelation 21:23; And the city had no need of the sun, neither of the moon, to shine in it: for the glory of God did lighten it, and the Lamb is the light thereof.

Physical elements, such as light, that we are accustomed to on earth will no longer be required as heaven will be a spiritual existence enlightened by the glory and Word of our Lord God and Christ. There will also no longer be a need for an earthly religion as the sun indicates the Christian Church under Christ and the moon is indicative of the Mosaic Law. The sun and moon represent the light of God's Word on earth respectively to the Christian Church and the Mosaic Law.

Isaiah 24:23; Then the moon shall be confounded, and the sun ashamed, when the LORD of hosts shall reign in mount Zion, and in Jerusalem, and before his ancients gloriously.

Isaiah 60:19; The sun shall be no more thy light by day; neither for brightness shall the moon give light unto thee: but the LORD shall be unto thee an everlasting light, and thy God thy glory.

Jeremiah 31:35; Thus saith the LORD, which giveth the sun for a light by day, and the ordinances of the moon and of the stars for a light by night, which divideth the sea when the waves thereof roar; The LORD of hosts is his name:

II Corinthians 4:6; For God, who commanded the light to shine out of darkness, hath shined in our hearts, to give the light of the knowledge of the glory of God in the face of Jesus Christ.

Revelation 21:24; And the nations of them which are saved shall walk in the light of it: and the kings of the earth do bring their glory and honour into it.

The phrase "And the nations of them which are saved" refers to those people who have chosen to be disciples of God and Christ, obeyed their commandments, and remained steadfast in their faith have now been rewarded by their acceptance into heaven as reflected by the phrase "shall walk in the light of it". The phrase "and the kings of the earth do bring their glory and honour into it" reveals that those of royal status on earth who remained steadfast in the faith are now enhancing the number of those in heaven and bringing "glory and honour" unto the Lord by their presence. Each saint that has chosen the worship of God and Christ brings honor and glory unto them by that very act.

Isaiah 60:3,5; And the Gentiles shall come to thy light, and kings to the brightness of thy rising. Then thou shalt see, and flow together, and thine heart shall fear, and be enlarged; because the abundance of the sea shall be converted unto thee, the forces of the Gentiles shall come unto thee.

Revelation 21:25; And the gates of it shall not be shut at all by day: for there shall be no night there.

The phrase "And the gates of it shall not be shut at all by day" reveals that the offer of salvation from God was freely extended to all who would choose to accept it. As the terms darkness and night reflect the absence of God's Word, the phrase "for there shall be no night there" indicates the eternal presence of God and Christ.

Isaiah 60:11; Therefore thy gates shall be open continually; they shall not be shut day nor night; that men may bring unto thee the forces of the Gentiles, and that their kings may be brought.

Revelation 21:26; And they shall bring the glory and honour of the nations into it.

This statement suggests that the nations that hold fast to the faith while under persecution and temptations on earth brings honor and glory to the Lord God in heaven by their honorable and respectable life-style upon earth and their decision to worship God and Christ.

I Chronicles 16:27; Glory and honour are in his presence; strength and gladness are in his place.

Romans 2:7,10; To them who by patient continuance in well doing seek for glory and honour and immortality, eternal life: But glory, honour, and peace, to every man that worketh good, to the Jew first, and also to the Gentile:

I Peter 1:7; That the trial of your faith, being much more precious than of gold that perisheth, though it be tried with fire, might be found unto praise and honour and glory at the appearing of Jesus Christ:

II Peter 1:16-17; For we have not followed cunningly devised fables, when we made known unto you the power and coming of our Lord Jesus Christ, but were eyewitnesses of his majesty. For he received from God the Father honour and glory, when there came such a voice to him from the excellent glory, This is my beloved Son, in whom I am well pleased. (Revelation 4:9,11; 5:12-13; 7:12; 19:1.)

Revelation 21:27; And there shall in no wise enter into it any thing that defileth, neither whatsoever worketh abomination, or maketh a lie: but they which are written in the Lamb's book of life.

To ensure that heaven remains pure and holy with glory and honor unto the Lord God, nothing evil nor impure must ever be allowed to enter or defile it.

Isaiah 35:8; And an highway shall be there, and a way, and it shall be called The way of holiness; the unclean shall not pass over it; but it shall be for those: the wayfaring men, though fools, shall not err therein.

Isaiah 52:1; Awake, awake; put on thy strength, O Zion; put on thy beautiful garments, O Jerusalem, the holy city: for henceforth there shall no more come into thee the uncircumcised and the unclean.
Joel 3:17; So shall ye know that I am the LORD your God dwelling in Zion, my holy mountain: then shall Jerusalem be holy, and there shall no strangers pass through her any more.
Mark 7:20-23; And he said, That which cometh out of the man, that defileth the man. For from within, out of the heart of men, proceed evil thoughts, adulteries, fornications, murders, Thefts, covetousness, wickedness, deceit, lasciviousness, an evil eye, blasphemy, pride, foolishness: All these evil things come from within, and defile the man.

CHAPTER 22

The description of heaven is given in this chapter as having a pure river of water of life proceeding out of the throne of God and the Lamb with the tree of life on either side of the river bearing twelve manner of fruits each month. There will be no night there as the Lord God will give light.

Revelation 22:1; And he shewed me a pure river of water of life, clear as crystal, proceeding out of the throne of God and of the Lamb.

The phrase "water of life" reflects spiritual salvation in heaven with the word "pure" describing holiness without sin of the word "river" which indicates an immense volume of salvation freely flowing with the phrase "proceeding out of the throne of God and of the Lamb" revealing the source of this benevolence. The phrase "clear as crystal" denotes purity and the free access unto God as reflected by the removal of the "veil of separation" through the sacrifice of Christ.

Isaiah 12:3; Therefore with joy shall ye draw water out of the wells of salvation.

This promise of salvation implies true and everlasting happiness freely given.

John 4:14; But whosoever drinketh of the water that I shall give him shall never thirst; but the water that I shall give him shall be in him a well of water springing up into everlasting life.

Revelation 22:2; In the midst of the street of it, and on either side of the river, was there the tree of life, which bare twelve manner of fruits, and yielded her fruit every month: and the leaves of the tree were for the healing of the nations.

The phrase "tree of life" denotes eternal salvation with the numeral "twelve" suggesting organized religion of God and the word "fruits" revealing the sustenance of that religion. The phrase "and yielded her fruit every month" indicates continuing and everlasting sustenance by God to His disciples. The word "street" suggests accessibility of this religion throughout heaven while the phrase "In the midst of the street of it, and on either side of the river" reveals availability of this sustenance everywhere in heaven. The phrase "and the leaves of the tree were for the healing of the nations" indicates that there will be no more contention or strife between good and evil thereby eliminating all physical pain and suffering.

Psalms 147:3; He healeth the broken in heart, and bindeth up their wounds.

Proverbs 13:12; Hope deferred maketh the heart sick: but when the desire cometh, it is a tree of life.

Isaiah 49:10; They shall not hunger nor thirst; neither shall the heat nor sun smite them: for he that hath mercy on them shall lead them, even by the springs of water shall he guide them.

Jeremiah 17:14; Heal me, O LORD, and I shall be healed; save me, and I shall be saved: for thou art my praise.

Ezekiel 47:12; And by the river upon the bank thereof, on this side and on that side, shall grow all trees for meat, whose leaf shall not fade, neither shall the fruit thereof be consumed: it shall bring forth new fruit according to his months, because their waters they issued out of the sanctuary: and the fruit thereof shall be for meat, and the leaf thereof for medicine.

Revelation 2:7; He that hath an ear, let him hear what the Spirit saith unto the churches; To him that overcometh will I give to eat of the tree of life, which is in the midst of the paradise of God.

Revelation 22:3; And there shall be no more curse: but the throne of God and of the Lamb shall be in it; and his servants shall serve him:

The phrase "And there shall be no more curse" reflects the complete destruction of Satan and his evil dominion while the phrase "but the throne of God and of the Lamb shall be in it" reveals complete control by God and Christ. The phrase "and his servants shall serve him" indicates the recognition by their disciples of the authority and royal status of God and Christ as kings over their domain. Some versions of the Scriptures have the phrase "cursed person" rather than the word "curse" which simply means that after God's final judgment no evil person will be left to continue Satan's evil doctrine.

I Corinthians 3:16-17; Know ye not that ye are the temple of God, and that the Spirit of God dwelleth in you? If any man defile the temple of God, him shall God destroy; for the temple of God is holy, which temple ye are.

Revelation 22:4; And they shall see his face; and his name shall be in their foreheads.

The phrase "And they shall see his face" reflects the disciples accessibility unto God while the phrase "and his name shall be in their foreheads" denotes God's ownership of His disciples and their open proclamation unto everyone of their worship and servitude of the Lord God.

Matthew 5:8; Blessed are the pure in heart: for they shall see God.

I John 3:2; Beloved, now are we the sons of God, and it doth not yet appear what we shall be: but we know that, when he shall appear, we shall be like him; for we shall see him as he is.

Revelation 22:5; And there shall be no night there; and they need no candle, neither light of the sun; for the Lord God giveth them light: and they shall reign for ever and ever.

There will no longer be a need for physical or natural conveniences to bring light into our lives as God's presence will furnish the only light needed or wanted.

Isaiah 60:19-20; The sun shall be no more thy light by day; neither for brightness shall the moon give light unto thee: but the LORD shall be unto thee an everlasting light, and thy God thy glory. Thy sun shall no more go down; neither shall thy moon withdraw itself: for the LORD shall be thine everlasting light, and the days of thy mourning shall be ended.

Revelation 22:6; And he said unto me, These sayings are faithful and true: and the Lord God of the holy prophets sent his angel to shew unto his servants the things which must shortly be done.

The angel that was holding one of the vials of the last plagues that was informing and revealing to John these visions in heaven now confirmed that everything that John had witnessed was "faithful and true" and that this angel was sent by the "Lord God of the holy prophets" to reveal these things that "must shortly be done". The word "faithful" implies trustworthiness and dependability while the word "true" indicates verification and confirmation. The phrase "the things which must shortly be done" reflects the construction of heaven as the dwelling place of the saints.

John 14:2; In my Father's house are many mansions: if it were not so, I would have told you. I go to prepare a place for you.

Jeremiah 42:5; Then they said to Jeremiah, The LORD be a true and faithful witness between us, if we do not even according to all things for the which the LORD thy God shall send thee to us.

Revelation 3:14; And unto the angel of the church of the Laodiceans write; These things saith the Amen, the faithful and true witness, the beginning of the creation of God;

Revelation 21:5; And he that sat upon the throne said, Behold, I make all things new. And he said unto me, Write: for these words are true and faithful. (Revelation 19:11.)

Revelation 22:7; Behold, I come quickly: blessed is he that keepeth the sayings of the prophecy of this book.

Christ is confirming the speed of his return unto judgment and reminding his disciples of the necessity to keep and obey the things written therein in this book of prophecy as revealed unto his servant, John. The person that keeps the commandments of Christ will be blessed with eternal salvation in heaven.

Revelation 1:3; Blessed is he that readeth, and they that hear the words of this prophecy, and keep those things which are written therein: for the time is at hand.

Revelation 22:8; And I John saw these things, and heard them. And when I had heard and seen, I fell down to worship before the feet of the angel which shewed me these things.

John confirms that he saw and heard the visions revealed unto him which prompted him to fall down "to worship before the feet of the angel which shewed me these things".

Revelation 22:9; Then saith he unto me, See thou do it not: for I am thy fellowservant, and of thy brethren the prophets, and of them which keep the sayings of this book: worship God.

The angel instructed John to not worship him as he was also a fellowservant like unto the prophets and faithful disciples that also worship God.

John13:16; Verily, verily, I say unto you, The servant is not greater than his lord; neither he that is sent greater than he that sent him.

Revelation 22:10; And he saith unto me, Seal not the sayings of the prophecy of this book: for the time is at hand.

John was now instructed to reveal unto others the prophecies of what he had seen, heard, and recorded of the visions and sayings given unto him as there was a need for the urgency of this message.

Revelation 1:3; Blessed is he that readeth, and they that hear the words of this prophecy, and keep those things which are written therein: for the time is at hand.

Revelation 22:11; He that is unjust, let him be unjust still: and he which is filthy, let him be filthy still: and he that is righteous, let him be righteous still: and he that is holy, let him be holy still.

This instruction to John reveals that there will no longer be time for people to accept Christ as the final judgment day has arrived and those that are still unworthy will remain unworthy and those that are holy and righteous will now receive their reward.

Ezekiel 3:27; But when I speak with thee, I will open thy mouth, and thou shalt say unto them, Thus saith the Lord GOD; He that heareth, let him hear; and he that forbeareth, let him forbear: for they are a rebellious house.

Revelation 22:12; And, behold, I come quickly; and my reward is with me, to give every man according as his work shall be.

Christ is now instructing John that he will come quickly to righteously judge everyone according to their deeds.

Matthew 24:30-31; And then shall appear the sign of the Son of man in heaven: and then shall all the tribes of the earth mourn, and they shall see the Son of man coming in the clouds of heaven with power and great glory. And he shall send his angels with a great sound of a trumpet, and they shall gather together his elect from the four winds, from one end of heaven to the other.

I Thessalonians 4:16-17; For the Lord himself shall descend from heaven with a shout, with the voice of the archangel, and with the trump of God: and the dead in Christ shall rise first: Then we which are alive and remain shall be caught up together with them in the clouds, to meet the Lord in the air: and so shall we ever be with the Lord.

Romans 2:6-7; Who will render to every man according to his deeds: To them who by patient continuance in well doing seek for glory and honour and immortality, eternal life:

Romans 14:12; So then every one of us shall give account of himself to God.

Revelation 22:13; I am Alpha and Omega, the beginning and the end, the first and the last.

The Lord is proclaiming His status as which was, and which is, and which is to come indicating an eternal existence.

Isaiah 41:4; Who hath wrought and done it, calling the generations from the beginning? I the LORD, the first, and with the last; I am he.

Isaiah 44:6; Thus saith the LORD the King of Israel, and his redeemer the LORD of hosts; I am the first, and I am the last; and beside me there is no God.

Revelation 1:8; I am Alpha and Omega, the beginning and the ending, saith the Lord, which is, and which was, and which is to come, the Almighty.

Revelation 22:14; Blessed are they that do his commandments, that they may have right to the tree of life, and may enter in through the gates into the city.

This proclamation by the Lord of the benevolent gift of eternal salvation in heaven is directed to His faithful disciples under the symbolism of the "right to the tree of life" and the privilege of entering "through the gates into the city".

Psalms 111:10; The fear of the LORD is the beginning of wisdom: a good understanding have all they that do his commandments: his praise endureth for ever.

Psalms 112:1; Praise ye the LORD. Blessed is the man that feareth the LORD, that delighteth greatly in his commandments.

Revelation 14:12; Here is the patience of the saints: here are they that keep the commandments of God, and the faith of Jesus.

Revelation 22:15; For without are dogs, and sorcerers, and whoremongers, and murderers, and idolaters, and whosoever loveth and maketh a lie.

This statement reveals that those people who practiced and pursued the various abominations to God will not be allowed to enter heaven.

Galatians 5:19-21; Now the works of the flesh are manifest, which are these; Adultery, fornication, uncleanness, lasciviousness, Idolatry, witchcraft, hatred, variance, emulations, wrath, strife, seditions, heresies, Envyings, murders, drunkenness, revellings, and such like: of the which I tell you before, as I have also told you in time past, that they which do such things shall not inherit the kingdom of God.

Revelation 22:16; I Jesus have sent mine angel to testify unto you these things in the churches. I am the root and the offspring of David, and the bright and morning star.

Jesus confirms that he sent his angel unto his servant John with the instructions that he was to record the Word of God, the testimony of Christ, and all things that he saw. Jesus also confirms that he was sent by God to come through the offspring of David as the savior of mankind.

Numbers 24:17; I shall see him, but not now: I shall behold him, but not nigh: there shall come a Star out of Jacob, and a Sceptre shall rise out of Israel, and shall smite the corners of Moab, and destroy all the children of Sheth.

Matthew 2:2; Saying, Where is he that is born King of the Jews? for we have seen his star in the east, and are come to worship him.

Matthew 24:27; For as the lightning cometh out of the east, and shineth even unto the west; so shall also the coming of the Son of man be.

II Peter 1:19; We have also a more sure word of prophecy; whereunto ye do well that ye take heed, as unto a light that shineth in a dark place, until the day dawn, and the day star arise in your hearts:

Revelation 2:28; And I will give him the morning star.

Revelation 22:17; And the Spirit and the bride say, Come. And let him that heareth say, Come. And let him that is athirst come. And whosoever will, let him take the water of life freely.

This statement reflects the invitation of God to accept His offer of eternal salvation in heaven by acknowledging Him, obeying, and keeping His commandments. This offer is extended through the urging of the Holy Spirit, and the various avenues of the members of the Kingdom/Church of Christ, all who hear His Word, and all those who desire the offer of salvation. The phrase "whosoever will" indicates that this offer is extended to all people and the phrase "water of life" reflects eternal salvation in heaven.

Isaiah 55:1; Ho, every one that thirsteth, come ye to the waters, and he that hath no money; come ye, buy, and eat; yea, come, buy wine and milk without money and without price.

John 4:14; But whosoever drinketh of the water that I shall give him shall never thirst; but the water that I shall give him shall be in him a well of water springing up into everlasting life.

Revelation 22:18; For I testify unto every man that heareth the words of the prophecy of this book, If any man shall add unto these things, God shall add unto him the plagues that are written in this book:

The Lord states that no other meaning shall be added unto the words of this book with the penalty of doing so would be to suffer the plagues that are written in this book.

Revelation 22:19; And if any man shall take away from the words of the book of this prophecy, God shall take away his part out of the book of life, and out of the holy city, and from the things which are written in this book.

The Lord also states that removal of any of the words of this book that would obscure or lessen the meaning thereof would subject that person to forfeit their right to enter heaven and enjoy the privileges therein granted.

Exodus 32:33; And the LORD said unto Moses, Whosoever hath sinned against me, him will I blot out of my book.

Revelation 22:20; He which testifieth these things saith, *Surely I come quickly.* Amen. Even so, come, Lord Jesus.

The Lord has reaffirmed his intent to bring judgment quickly. The phrase "Even so, come, Lord Jesus" is the desire of his disciples who are ready for the second coming of Christ unto judgment.

II Timothy 4:8; Henceforth there is laid up for me a crown of righteousness, which the Lord, the righteous judge, shall give me at that day: and not to me only, but unto all them also that love his appearing.

Revelation 3:11; Behold, I come quickly: hold that fast which thou hast, that no man take thy crown.

Revelation 22:12; And, behold, I come quickly; and my reward is with me, to give every man according as his work shall be. (Revelation 2:5,16; 3:11; 22:7.)

Christ is stating that, upon his return, judgment will be made swiftly.

Revelation 22:21; The grace of our Lord Jesus Christ be with you all. Amen.

This salutation by John is extended to all people with the prayer that the grace of Jesus Christ be given to each person.

REFERENCES

Clarke's Commentary, Adam Clarke, LL.D., F.S.A., &c., Abingdon Press, Nashville, TN. ISBN 0-687-09121-7. Published United States 1824 by Abraham Paul for the New York branch of The Methodist Book Concern. References:

Revelation, chapter 4, verse 7, Ensign designations, Page 989

Revelation, chapter 6, verse 6, Roman Denarius, Page 994

Revelation, chapter 7, verse 14, Color scarlet definition from Isaiah 1:18, Page 23

Revelation, chapter 16, verse 16, Armageddon definition, Page 1035

Revelation, chapter 19, verse 16, Recognition by clothing and thigh. Page 1052

More Than Conquerors, William Hendriksen, Th. D., Baker Book House, Grand Rapids, Michigan, Copyright, 1939, 1967. ISBN 0-8010-4026-4. Photolithoprinted by Cushing-Malloy, Inc., Ann Arbor, Michigan, 1980 References:

Revelation, chapter 6, verse 4, Pages 121, 122, Machaira Sword history

Revelation, chapter 6, verse 8, Page 126, Rhomphaia Sword history

CPSIA information can be obtained at www.ICGtesting.com
Printed in the USA
LVOW111119090412

276790LV00001B/18/P